Everyone
on the side of truth
listens to me.

JESUS RESPONDING TO PILATE
(Jn 18:37)

D0111909

REVEALING
THE NEW AGE
JESUS

▶ Challenges to
Orthodox Views of Christ

DOUGLAS GROOTHUIS
Author of Unmasking the New Age

INTERVARSITY PRESS
DOWNERS GROVE, ILLINOIS 60515

© 1990 by Douglas Groothuis

All rights reserved. No part of this book may be reproduced in any form without written permission from InterVarsity Press, P.O. Box 1400, Downers Grove, Illinois 60515.

InterVarsity Press is the book-publishing division of InterVarsity Christian Fellowship, a student movement active on campus at hundreds of universities, colleges and schools of nursing in the United States of America, and a member movement of the International Fellowship of Evangelical Students. For information about local and regional activities, write Public Relations Dept., InterVarsity Christian Fellowship, 6400 Schroeder Rd., P.O. Box 7895, Madison, WI 53707-7895.

All Scripture quotations in this publication are from the Holy Bible, New International Version. Copyright © 1973, 1978, International Bible Society. Used by permission of Zondervan Bible Publishers.

Distributed in Canada through InterVarsity Press, 860 Denison St., Unit 3, Markham, Ontario L3R 4H1, Canada.

ISBN 0-8308-1298-9

Printed in the United States of America ∞

Library of Congress Cataloging-in-Publication Data

Groothuis, Douglas R., 1957-
    Revealing the New Age Jesus: challenges to orthodox views of
Christ/Douglas Groothuis.
        p.   cm.
    Includes bibliographical references.
    ISBN 0-8308-1298-9
    1. Jesus Christ—New Age movement interpretations—Controversial
literature. 2. Jesus Christ—History of doctrines—20th century.
3. New Age movement—Controversial literature. 4. Jesus Christ—
Person and offices. I. Title.
BT304.93.G76   1990
232—dc20   90-38165
                                                          CIP

---

13   12   11   10   9   8   7   6   5   4   3   2   1
99   98   97   96   95   94   93   92   91   90

*Dedicated
to the memory of my grandmother
Annice Kaiser Groothuis (1898-1989)*

Acknowledgments

Many more deserve acknowledgment for their contributions to this work than can be mentioned. Craig Blomberg, James Sire and Gordon Lewis read and made helpful suggestions on the manuscript and insured that the final product is better than it would have been otherwise—although I will take credit for any imperfections that remain. Lillian Groothuis and Paul and Jean Merrill provided moral and loving support. Roy Osborn kindly donated the computer with which the book was written.

Most of all, I acknowledge the spiritual, intellectual, moral and practical support of Rebecca Merrill Groothuis, my wife. Her editorial sagacity, theological insights and self-sacrifice were indispensable—again!

Chapter 1
Who Do You Say That I Am?

*J*esus of Nazareth. *No other name has inspired greater* devotion, evoked greater reverence, or ignited greater controversy.

In August of 1988 amidst an avalanche of criticism, Universal Studios released a film version of Nikos Kazantzakis's novel *The Last Temptation of Christ*. Material leaked from the script by disgruntled insiders sent conservative Christians—and not a few Jews and Muslims—into various degrees of outrage. One major Christian figure offered Universal ten million dollars to confiscate this offending interpretation of Jesus.

Noted filmmaker Martin Scorsese had produced a Christ of less than biblical stature. His Jesus is tormented over the ambiguities of his divine calling; he admits to personal sin, saying, "I am a liar, I am a hypocrite, I am afraid of everything . . . Lucifer is inside of me";[1] and barely resists his "last temptation" to leave the cross and his calling in pursuit of sexual satisfactions.

Jesus' theology in the film often slips out of the orthodox orbit, as when he pantheistically proclaims that "everything's part of God," a remark that caused one reviewer to speak of this Jesus as "a recent graduate of the Shirley MacLaine School of Theology."[2] After handling some dirt and stones Jesus announces, "This is my body too," thus deifying the cosmos in New Age fashion.[3]

In Kazantzakis's other writings, he displays similar mystical leanings. In the novel *The Last Temptation of Christ* he states, "Lizard, butterflies, ants . . . all were God."[4] In *Report to Greco* he says, "This world is not his vestment, as I once believed; it is God himself."[5] And, "There is no other way to reach God but this. Following Christ's bloody tracks, we must fight to transubstantiate the man inside of us into spirit, so that we may merge with God."[6]

At the beginning of the film, a personal disclaimer by Scorsese stated, "This film is not based on the Gospels but is a fictional exploration of the eternal spiritual conflict." But this did not dissuade many Christians from staging demonstrations, denouncing it as blasphemy and promising to boycott the film and everything else associated with Universal Studios.

Others defended the film's right of artistic exploration and decried the religious intolerance of fussy, fulminating fundamentalists. A review in a New Age-oriented journal called *Gnosis* attacked the fundamentalist "fetish of monotheism—the belief that there is only one true image of God."[7] The reviewer applauded the film's recasting of the traditional Jesus and surmised that those who held orthodox views may have "been dupes of a two thousand year old cover-up."[8] For him Jesus was a Gnostic, "like all the great explorers and discoverers of the spirit."[9]

In a cover story entitled "Who Was Jesus?" *Time* observed that "if the furor surrounding Scorsese's *Last Temptation of Christ* proves one thing, it is that in any era, seismic emotions are involved when people probe the nature of the man who is worshiped as God by well over a billion souls."[10]

Seismic shocks are seldom absent when deity is debated, and Jesus, whom John's Gospel calls God in the flesh (Jn 1:14), has triggered more intellectual, emotional and social earthquakes than any other historical figure. The evidence of his influence is everywhere, as esteemed historian Jaroslav Pelikan has observed:

> Jesus of Nazareth has been the dominant figure in the history of Western culture for almost twenty centuries. If it were possible, with some sort of supermagnet, to pull up out of that history every scrap of metal bearing at least a trace of his name, how much would be left? It is from his birth that most of the human race dates its calendars, it is by his name that millions curse and in his name that millions pray.[11]

Yet the crucial question remains, "Who was Jesus?" In his book on the Sermon on the Mount the popular New Age teacher Emmet Fox notes that whatever you make of him, "Jesus Christ is easily the most important figure that has ever appeared in the history of mankind."[12] Fox continues, "There can hardly, therefore, be a more important understanding than to inquire into the question of what Jesus really did stand for."[13]

Jesus himself, according to the canonical Gospels, displayed considerable skill in eliciting the opinion of others toward him.

> When Jesus came to the region of Caesarea Philippi, he asked his disciples: "Who do people say the Son of Man is?"
>
> They replied, "Some say John the Baptist; others say Elijah; and still others, Jeremiah or one of the prophets."
>
> "But what about you?" he asked. "Who do you say I am?"
>
> Simon Peter answered, "You are the Christ, the Son of the living God." (Mt 16:13-16)

Notice how Jesus deftly moved from the general to the personal, beckoning Peter from the opinion poll to the confessional. After one of his frequent "hard sayings" many half-hearted disciples deserted Jesus. He then asked the Twelve, "You do not want to leave too, do you?" And Peter responded, "Lord, to whom shall we go? You have the words of eternal life. We believe and know that you are the Holy One of God" (Jn 6:67-69).

Another time Jesus journeyed to Bethany in order to raise his friend
Lazarus from the dead. Prior to the grand miracle Jesus comforted
Lazarus's mourning sister Martha and spoke to her about the resur-
rection.

"He who believes in me will live, even though he dies; and whoever
lives and believes in me will never die. Do you believe this?"

"Yes, Lord," she told him. "I believe that you are the Christ, the
Son of God, who was to come into the world." (Jn 11: 25-27)

Yet many, of course, did not believe he was the Christ, the Son of God,
the Holy One of God, or the giver of the words of eternal life. The
Gospel of John records an event in Jerusalem during a great Jewish
feast when Jesus proclaimed:

If anyone thirst, let him come to me and drink. Whoever believes
in me, as the Scripture has said, "Out of his heart shall rivers flow
of living water." (Jn 7:37-38)

Not all within earshot ran to Jesus to slake their thirsty souls. Debate
raged over his identity. John then concludes the account by noting,
"Thus the people were divided because of Jesus" (Jn 7:43).

Jesus himself declared that deep divisions over him would cut like
the sharpest sword even within families:

"Do not suppose that I have come to bring peace to the earth. I
did not come to bring peace, but a sword. For I have come to turn
'a man against his father, a daughter against her mother, a daugh-
ter-in-law against her mother-in-law—a man's enemies will be the
members of his own household.' " (Mt 10:34-36)

So severe did the divisions eventually become that only the blood of
a crucifixion would satisfy the opposition.

Recent Gallup polls reveal that the large majority of the American
public highly esteems Jesus in one way or another, and few, New Age
or otherwise, actively oppose him. Although Bertrand Russell spurned
the character of Jesus by saying, "I do not grant either the superlative
wisdom or the superlative goodness of Christ as depicted in the Gospels,"[14] and Friedrich Nietzsche vigorously denounced him,[15] few today would be so militant. Gallup remarks, "Research indicates that

our image of Christ—while a bit murky in spots—is overwhelmingly favorable."[16]

When asked if Jesus was God or just another religious leader like Mohammed or Buddha, seventy per cent affirmed that he was God. When asked, "In your own life, how important is the belief that Christ was fully God and fully human," eighty-one per cent responded that this belief was either "very important" (fifty-eight per cent) or "fairly important" (twenty-three per cent).[17] Some ninety-one per cent believe that Jesus existed as an historical figure.[18]

After reviewing an impressive array of statistics regarding Americans' evaluation of Jesus, Gallup concludes that "virtually all Americans are, in some measure, drawn to the person of Christ."[19]

The actual nature of the magnet, however, seems a bit fuzzy in many minds, and so the resulting religiosity is amorphous at best. This ties in with Gallup's further observation of widespread biblical illiteracy: Only forty-two per cent of respondents knew that Jesus preached the Sermon on the Mount; only forty-six per cent could name the first four books in the New Testament; and only seventy per cent knew that Jesus was born in Bethlehem.[20]

The lack of knowledge also betrays a lack of commitment. Gallup says that despite our religiosity as Americans, "probing more deeply through surveys indicates that even if religion is an important force in our lives it is not the center of our lives. It does not have primacy. Interest may be high, but commitment is often low."[21]

The Jesus of the New Testament is the avowed enemy of all vague religiosity and superficial spirituality. He called for decision, claiming for himself spiritual primacy and ultimacy—like someone who had reality down pat and wasn't afraid to say so. Before commissioning his twelve disciples he instructed them, "Whoever acknowledges me before men, I will also acknowledge before my Father in heaven. But whoever disowns me before men, I will disown him before my Father in heaven" (Mt 10:32-33). In the Sermon on the Mount Jesus proclaimed, "Blessed are you when people insult you, persecute you and falsely say all kinds of evil against you because of me" (Mt 5:11). For

Jesus discipleship is not a psychological hobby or an interesting social activity, but a radical commitment to serve and obey him—even to the knife-point of persecution. Neither is self-denial optional for Jesus' followers: "If anyone would come after me, he must deny himself and take up his cross daily and follow me" (Lk 9:23).

In light of the Gospel record Jesus *should* be an issue of debate, dialog and discussion. He himself was a controversialist, but not in the sense of stirring controversy for controversy's sake. Rather, Jesus engaged in controversy for the sake of truth. As John Stott points out:

He was not "broad minded" in the popular sense that He was prepared to countenance any views on any subject. On the contrary . . . He engaged in continuous debate with the religious leaders of His day. . . . He said that He was the truth (Jn 14:6), that He had come to bear witness to the truth (Jn 18:37), and that the truth would set His followers free (Jn 8:31-32). As a result of His loyalty to the truth, He was not afraid to dissent publicly from official doctrines (if he knew them to be wrong), to expose error, and to warn His disciples of false teachers (Mt 7:15-20; Mk 13:5-6, 21-23; Lk 12:1). He was also extremely outspoken in his language, calling them "blind guides" (Mt 15:14; 23:16, 19, 24, 26), "wolves in sheep's clothing" (Mt 7:15), "whitewashed tombs" (Mt 23:27; Lk 11:44) and even a "brood of vipers" (Mt 12:23; 23:33).[22]

If these records are correct and Jesus is who he said he was, religious neutrality is impossible. Jesus said, "He who is not with me is against me, and he who does not gather with me scatters" (Mt 12:30). We must choose sides. "Who do you say that I am?" remains the question of the hour.

But even outside of orthodox Christianity, Jesus is hailed as a decisive figure in world history, though the man described bears little resemblance to the traditional image. A new image of Jesus is hailed by many who believe it to be authentic and inspiring for a New Age of spiritual discovery and transformation. Who does the New Age movement say Jesus is?

Jesus: Harbinger of a New Age?

In assorted New Age circles Jesus is often praised as a harbinger of the New Age. This "New Age" of self-realization, love and world peace will break forth when humans reclaim a lost divinity and manifest their latent potential for the healing of our beleaguered planet. Social and planetary transformation will be triggered through inner transformation and the release of evolutionary energies bubbling below the surface of ordinary consciousness. A few choice beings have blazed the path to this New Age. And Jesus is invariably proclaimed as one of these trailblazers.

In an article capturing the essence of the New Age Jesus, New Age writer John White presents Jesus as the West's most familiar example of "Cosmic Consciousness," a state of awareness attuned to oneness of being and universal energy, which releases vibrant evolutionary forces. White says, "Jesus' unique place in history is based upon his unprecedented realization of the higher intelligence, the divinity, the Ground of Being incarnated in him."[23]

White is but one voice in a growing chorus of New Age writers, teachers and prophets who insist that the Jesus of biblical orthodoxy is the product of misunderstanding and spiritual immaturity. White strives to free Jesus from the shackles of orthodoxy and to rediscover his true teachings and identity.

According to White, Jesus taught that sin is not the transgression of God's moral law for which we deserve punishment. It is simply "missing the mark" by not hitting the bull's eye of the God within us. The antidote to this error is not found in seeking forgiveness from God but in changing one's consciousness. "God does not condemn us for our sins," White insists. "Rather, we condemn ourselves *by* our sins. And thus forgiveness by God is not necessary; it is there always as unconditional love, the instant we turn in our hearts and minds to God."[24] This, in essence, means turning our minds back to our own identity as God.

When Jesus called people to "repent," White avers, this had nothing to do with sorrow over sin, but everything to do with going "beyond or higher than the ordinary mental state." This "means transcending self-centered ego and becoming God-centered, God-realized."[25] To go beyond these self-imposed limitations is "to become experientially aware" that "all is God and there is only God." This change of mind gives us the mind of Jesus when he said, "I and the Father are one."[26]

Jesus is lauded as the great illuminator, the archetype of higher awareness, an inspiring example of self-discovery. But the historical man, Jesus of Nazareth, is distinguished from "the Christ." "Christ, the Christos, the Messiah, is an eternal transpersonal condition of being to which *we must all someday come*. Jesus did not say that this higher state of consciousness realized in him was his alone for all time."[27] Moreover, according to White, Jesus does not bid us to worship him but to follow him on the path of enlightenment *"as if we were Jesus himself."*[28]

For White "the significance of the incarnation and resurrection is not that Jesus was human like us but rather that *we are gods like him*—or at least have the potential to be."[29] He believes it is more accurate to say "Christ was Jesus" than "Jesus was the Christ," because that "allows for *other* Christs—you and me."[30] Jesus is not "the sole path to cosmic consciousness" but one of many "evolutionary forerunners of a new Earth and a new Humanity" including Buddha, Krishna, Lao Tze, Moses and Mohammed. All taught that *"thou shalt evolve to a higher state of being and ultimately return to the godhead which is your very self."*[31]

White's affirmations resist orthodoxy at every point and his portrait of Jesus is echoed by many others in the New Age fold, whether their roots be in Gnosticism, Essenism, the Theosophical movement, the Mind Sciences, Eastern religions, Western occultism, channeling or elsewhere. Jesus is not the unique, unrepeatable and unsurpassable incarnation of a personal God, but rather a manifestation of a universal state of consciousness that anyone can attain through proper techniques. Jesus came into the world as an example of God-realization, not for the purpose of reconciling sinful humanity with a holy God through his vicarious suffering on the cross. According to White, Jesus does not deliver anyone from a literal hell, because hell is simply a state of mind that denies one's transcendent identity as God. Conversely, heaven is conscious union with God, a state of consciousness rather than a location.[32] We should never fling ourselves at Jesus' nail-pierced feet in worshipful abandon, but rather stand tall and salute one who has attained what we too shall one day possess as Christed beings, much as an aspiring and gifted commissioned officer salutes a five-star general.

The real Jesus would, many claim, stand against present "orthodox" perversions of his message as narrow-minded, dogmatic and exclusivistic. New Age author Michael Grosso relates that John White wrote him a note concerning Christians' outrage over *The Last Temptation of Christ* that read, "It's a lot of noise by immature/juvenile Christians who want to keep Jesus on a pedestal rather than grow up and relate to him as an elder brother."[33]

The New Age Jesus
It is not possible to present *the* New Age view of Jesus because there are a diversity of views. It might be better, though, to refer to the diversity as a *family* of related views, all sharing the same bloodline despite certain genetic idiosyncrasies. We can spot some essential unity even amidst the diversity.

1. Jesus is revered or respected as a highly spiritually evolved being who serves as an example for further evolution. Jesus may be called a Master, Guru, Yogi, Adept, Avatar, Shaman, Way-show-er or other terms of metaphysical endearment. Jesus' miracles are often accepted as manifestations of his mastery of divine energy or his tapping into the Christ power.

2. The individual, personal, historical Jesus is separated from the universal, impersonal, eternal Christ or Christ Consciousness, which he embodied but did not monopolize. Jesus is regarded as *a* Christ who didn't corner the market on the copious Christ Consciousness. So David Spangler can say that "the Christ is not the province of a single individual," although Jesus "focused the universal life/growth quality

we call the Christ."[34]

3. The orthodox understanding of Jesus as the supreme and final revelation of God is dismissed as illegitimate. Jesus is not seen as the one and only Christ that ever was, is or will be. This is viewed as too limiting and provincial. God cannot be so reserved as to restrict incarnation to one revelator. According to Janet Bock in a book on the "lost years and unknown travels" of Jesus, "For many, the position that Jesus was the only 'Son of God' . . . is, in effect, a limiting of the power of God, a shackling of divinity to one physical form for all eternity."[35]

4. Jesus' death on the cross (if recognized at all) is not accepted as having any ethical significance for salvation. It is either denied as an historical event or reinterpreted to exclude the idea that Jesus suffered *as the Christ* to pay the just penalty for human sin.

5. Jesus' resurrection from the dead is not viewed as a physical fact demonstrating his victory over sin, death and Satan but is rather (if recognized at all) understood as a spiritual triumph not unique to Jesus. There are many other "Ascended Masters."

6. Jesus' "second coming" is not a literal, physical and visible return in the clouds at the end of the age but is rather a stage in the evolutionary advancement of the race when the Christic energies escape the confinements of ignorance. Soli, an "off-planet being" channeled through Neville Rowe, tells his clients that "You are God, You are, each and every one, part of the Second Coming."[36] Some New Age figures may claim to embody this energy more perfectly than others and so better personify the Second Coming.

7. Exotic, extra-biblical documents are regarded as sources for authentic material about the life of Jesus not available from the canonical Scriptures. Although the Bible may be selectively studied and paid due respect, it is routinely eclipsed by alien sources that reveal a Jesus foreign to the Bible yet quite at home in New Age quarters. The quest for this "lost Christianity" follows several routes which, nevertheless, converge at key points.

Historically based claims may appeal to ancient Gnostic texts recently discovered (1945) in Nag Hammadi, Egypt, as the original message of a Gnostic Jesus that became "heretical" only through a manipulative church hierarchy. Neo-gnostics of various stripes argue that the genuine Jesus came to stir us to discover and rekindle the divine spark within, not rescue us from our sins. Commenting on a text from the Gnostic Gospel of Thomas that has Jesus say "He who drinks from my mouth will become as I am, and I shall be he," noted scholar of world religions and mythology, Joseph Campbell, comments:

> Now, that is exactly Buddhism. We are all manifestations of Buddha consciousness, or Christ consciousness, only we don't know it. The word "Buddha" means "the one who waked up." We are all to do that—to wake up to the Christ or Buddha consciousness within us. That is blasphemy in the normal way of Christian thinking, but it is the very essence of Christian Gnosticism and of the Thomas Gospel.[37]

Another brand of historical revisionism spotlights a Tibetan document published at the turn of the century by a Russian journalist that purports to tell of "the lost years of Jesus" (between ages 13 and 29), which he spent studying, teaching and traveling in the mystic East. Elizabeth Clare Prophet, the leader of Church Universal and Triumphant, hails the discovery as "an historical breakthrough that will shake the foundations of modern Christendom."[38]

Claiming to base their interpretation on the Dead Sea Scrolls or additional documents, other revisionists uncover "an Essene Jesus" who drastically differs from the figure that dominates the Gospels. New Age celebrity evangelist Shirley MacLaine typifies this approach by saying, "Christ was a member of the Essene Brotherhood, which, among other things, believed in reincarnation."[39] She goes so far as to identify Jesus as a proto-New Ager by saying that "Jesus and the Essenes, with their teachings on love and light and cosmic laws along with the Golden Rule of karma, sound very much like metaphysical seekers in the New Age today."[40]

Other revelations of a non-historical sort emanate from assorted channelers who extract information about—or even ostensibly from—

Jesus through their entities, spirit guides and ascended masters, or
from less personal sources such as the Akashic Records or the Collective Unconscious. An increasingly popular three-volume work
called *A Course in Miracles* presents itself as nothing less than a
transcript of a postmortem message from Jesus himself.

8. Historic orthodox doctrine is rejected and replaced by an "esoteric
interpretation" of biblical texts that yields unorthodox results. "Esoteric" refers to the hidden, secret or arcane meaning. For instance John
White interprets being "born again" as "dying to the past and the old
sense of self through a change in consciousness,"[41] rather than receiving
forgiveness of sin and new life through faith in Jesus as Lord and Savior.

Historic orthodoxy is shunned as "exoteric" (or external) religion,
a mere ossified shell of formal religiosity unconnected to the inner or
"esoteric" core of spiritual reality. For Christianity to be salvaged and
rehabilitated for this New Age, it must be reinterpreted esoterically.
According to White *"Exoteric* Judeao-Christianity must reawaken to
the truth preserved in its *esoteric* tradition."[42]

The esoteric enthusiasts sometimes lament their casting esoteric
pearls before exoteric swine. John White complains that:

> The institutional church tells us that Jesus was the only Son of God,
> that he incarnated as a human in order to die on the cross as a
> penalty for our sins, and thereby save the world. But that is a sad
> caricature, a pale reflection of the true story.[43]

Although he does not use the term *esoteric,* Joseph Campbell esoterically recasts a classical Christian doctrine when he digs for the mythological core of the Ascension of Jesus. He says:

> If you read "Jesus ascended into heaven" in terms of its metaphoric
> connotation, you see that he has gone inward—not into outer space
> but into inner space, to the place from which all being comes, into
> the consciousness that is the source of all things, the kingdom of
> heaven within.[44]

In other words Jesus did not ascend to the "right hand of the Father"
in cosmic triumph, but rather has descended into the divine depths of
the collective soul.

With such a background of interpretation New Agers can selectively approve certain (reinterpreted) biblical texts in reference to Jesus, such as "the kingdom of God is within you" (Lk 17:21), "I and the Father are one" (Jn 10:30) (taken to refer to all enlightened beings as well as Jesus), and " 'I have said, you are gods' " (Jn 10:34).

In his search for a "lost Christianity" philosopher Jacob Needleman offers a sustained reflection on the possibility of an esoteric tradition within Christianity that "actually produces real change in human nature, real transformation."[45]

Many besides Needleman are looking beyond, or beneath, orthodox claims for something more, something desperately needed, and the road often leads to Jesus. But which Jesus is to be followed: the Christ-conscious Master or the only Son of God?

Competing Christs and Ultimate Issues

Despite the fact that everyone wants to claim Jesus as one's own, he is not a ventriloquist's dummy who gladly mouths whatever anyone likes. Religious opinions are legion; thoughtful convictions on ultimate matters are far fewer, and views on Jesus are no exception. Our aim is to discover the authentic Jesus behind the welter of conflicting images. We are after the objective truth about Jesus of Nazareth, because, as the Theosophical Society's motto puts it, "There is no religion higher than truth."

Therefore, in the following chapters we will concentrate on the controversy over Christ by comparing rival *truth claims* about his identity and teaching. We do well to remember Blaise Pascal's warning, which remains timely though written three centuries ago: "Truth is so obscure in these times, and falsehood so established, that, unless we love the truth, we cannot know it."[46] Or, as Jesus puts it in the Sermon on the Mount:

Ask and it will be given to you; seek and you will find; knock and the door will be opened to you. For everyone who asks receives; he who seeks finds; and to him who knocks, the door will be opened. (Mt 7:7-8)

First we will present the biblical picture of Jesus. Next will be an examination and critique of what is often seen as the first Christian heresy, Gnosticism, the spirit of which abides in a diversity of New Age groups. Then we will test the New Testament to determine if its picture of Jesus is historically credible. After that will be an inspection of the fascinating claims concerning the "lost years" of Jesus by scrutinizing evidence concerning his alleged sojourn to the East. The relationship of Jesus and the Essenes will follow as we consider whether Jesus was indebted to this mystical school. Then the various claims regarding Jesus made by channelers will be analyzed. Finally, having laid this groundwork, the last chapter will evaluate the biblical and New Age versions of the Cosmic Christ.

Although our study will marshal logical arguments and sift through historical evidence, it is not a merely academic exercise. What is at stake is of far greater consequence than scoring theological points or winning debates. If the Jesus of the New Testament is the true Jesus, several cutting conclusions irresistibly follow. First, to trust and obey this Jesus means eternal life beginning here and now and continuing forever. John records Jesus praying to the Father: "Now this is eternal life: that they may know you, the only true God, and Jesus Christ, whom you have sent" (Jn 17:3). Second, to reject him means missing Incarnate Life itself and forfeiting one's own life eternally. As Jesus told his opposition, "if you do not believe that I am the one I claim to be, you will indeed die in your sins" (Jn 8:24).

The Jesus of the Gospels warned his disciples that spiritual counterfeits would arise. Speaking of false prophets dressed as wolves in sheep's clothing he said:

Not everyone who says to me, "Lord, Lord," will enter the kingdom of heaven, but only he who does the will of my Father who is in heaven. Many will say to me on that day, "Lord, Lord, did we not prophesy in your name, and in your name drive out demons and perform many miracles?" Then I will tell them plainly, "I never knew you. Away from me, you evildoers!" (Mt 7:21-23)

On the other hand if some variation of the New Age Jesus is genuine, then to follow him is to discover a helpful example of divine potential. To ignore or avoid him is not to court eternal ruin but is simply a spiritual miscue correctable in an upcoming incarnation. Or you may rest easy that, while Jesus was an exceptional exhibit of Christ-consciousness, he has no real primacy or ultimacy. A host of other spiritual masters will suffice.[47]

Objective truth is certainly not a matter of personal prudence or preference. That which we find unpleasant may in fact be true; conversely, that which we find pleasant may in fact be false. As one philosopher put it, "logic stands independent of our whims."[48] Put another way, truth is no respecter of persons. Yet a recognition of what is at stake is appropriate in our endeavor. This awareness of the weightiness of the issue in and of itself does not tell us which Jesus is authentic, but it does underscore the importance of our conclusions. Simply put, anyone interested in Jesus should be willing to consider seriously the biblical record because of what there is to gain and because of what there is to lose.

Notes

[1]Cited in John Leo, "A Holy Furor," *Time*, August 15, 1988, p. 35.
[2]Ibid.
[3]Ibid., p. 36.
[4]Nikos Kazantzakis, *The Last Temptation of Christ* (New York: Touchstone/Simon and Schuster, 1960), p. 127; cited in John Ankerberg and John Weldon, *The Facts on the Last Temptation of Christ* (Eugene, Oreg.: Harvest House, 1988), p. 47.
[5]Nikos Kazantzakis, *Report to Greco* (New York: Simon and Schuster, 1965), p. 468; cited in Ankerberg and Weldon, p. 47.
[6]Kazantzakis, *Report*, p. 289; Ankerberg and Weldon, p. 47. Kazantzakis' real motivation for his novel is found in his commentary on it: "It isn't a simple 'life of Christ.' It is a laborious, sacred, creative endeavor to reincarnate the essence of Christ, setting aside the dross—falsehoods and pettiness which all the churches and all the cassocked representatives of Christianity have heaped upon his [Jesus'] figure, thereby distorting it." Helen Kazantzakis, *Nikos Kazantzakis—A Biography Based on His Letters* (New York: Simon and Schuster, 1968), p. 505; cited in Ankerberg and Weldon, p. 48.
[7]Michael Grosso, "Testing the Images of God," *Gnosis*, Winter 1989, p. 42.
[8]Ibid., p. 41.
[9]Ibid., p. 42.
[10]Richard Ostling, "Who Was Jesus?" *Time*, August 15, 1988, p. 37.
[11]Jaroslav Pelikan, *Jesus through the Centuries* (New York: Harper and Row, 1987),

p. 1.

[12]Emmet Fox, *The Sermon on the Mount* (New York: Harper and Brothers, 1938), p. 1.

[13]Ibid., p. 2.

[14]Bertrand Russell, *Why I Am Not a Christian* (New York: Simon and Schuster, 1957), pp. 15-16.

[15]Nietzsche even entitled one of his books *The Antichrist*.

[16]George Gallup, Jr., and George O'Connell, *Who Do Americans Say That I Am?* (Philadelphia: Westminster Press, 1986), p. 19.

[17]Ibid., p. 20.

[18]Ibid., p. 19.

[19]Ibid., p. 89.

[20]Ibid., p. 62.

[21]Ibid.,p. 64.

[22]John R. W. Stott, *Christ the Controversialist* (Downers Grove, Ill.: InterVarsity Press, 1972), p. 18. I have incorporated into the text Scripture references originally in footnotes.

[23]John White, "Jesus and the Idea of a New Age," *The Quest,* Summer 1989, p. 14.

[24]Ibid., p. 16.

[25]Ibid., p. 15.

[26]Ibid., p. 17.

[27]Ibid., p. 14, emphasis his.

[28]Ibid., emphasis his.

[29]Ibid., p. 17, emphasis his.

[30]Ibid., p. 18, emphasis his.

[31]Ibid., p. 22, emphasis his.

[32]Ibid., p. 18.

[33]Cited by Grosso, p. 43.

[34]David Spangler, *Reflections on the Christ* (Glasgow, Scotland: Findhorn Foundation, 1977), p. 103.

[35]Janet Bock, *The Jesus Mystery* (Los Angeles, Calif.: Aura Books, 1984), p. 112.

[36]Otto Friedrich, "New Age Harmonies," *Time,* December 7, 1987, p. 66.

[37]Joseph Campbell, *The Power of Myth* (New York: Doubleday, 1988), p. 57.

[38]Elizabeth Clare Prophet, *The Lost Years of Jesus* (Livingstone Mont.: Summit University Press, 1984), flyleaf.

[39]Shirley MacLaine, *Going Within* (New York: Bantam Books, 1989), p. 178.

[40]Ibid., p. 181.

[41]White, p. 18.

[42]Ibid., p. 19, emphasis his.

[43]White, p. 17.

[44]Campbell, p. 56.

[45]Jacob Needleman, *Lost Christianity* (New York: Bantam Books, 1982), p. 4.

[46]Blaise Pascal, *Pensées* (864), Great Books edition.

[47]Some New Agers, such as Rudolph Steiner and David Spangler, give a central role to Jesus for the evolution of the planet. Yet they do not make one's response to him in this life determinative of one's eternal destiny.

[48]Eric von Kuehnelt-Leddihn, *Leftism* (New Rochelle, N.Y.: Arlington House, 1974), p. 38.

Chapter 2
Christ and Christianity: Jesus' Life and Teaching

*C*aricature is an awful enemy of truth, and not a few misunderstandings of the Jesus of the New Testament stem from partial pictures, selective perceptions, out-of-focus impressions, casual hearsay and, in some cases, outright distortions. The same can be said of the founders of other religions. The Buddha, Mohammed, Confucius and others have been caricatured. Proponents of the world's religions may even slander their own avowed prophets, holy men and women, and revelators when intellectual sloppiness and religious ignorance replace an ache for accuracy and a thirst for clarity.

In light of this propensity for confusion a careful look at the central character of the New Testament is in order for those both within and without Christian circles. We should be bloodhounds after the fundamental facts and follow the scent until the prize is found. As G. K. Chesterton said:

We must protest against a habit of quoting and paraphrasing at the same time. When a man is discussing what Jesus meant, let him state first of all what He said, not what the man thinks He would have said if He had expressed Himself more clearly.[1]

Many say that the Gospels are not biographies because they lack the attention to details indispensable for modern biographers. It is true that Matthew, Mark, Luke and John (and the rest of the Bible for that matter) do not satisfy many modern curiosities such as Jesus' physical appearance, the complete story of his childhood, the introspective minutiae of his mental life,[2] the explicit dating of every event[3] or other factors essential to a successful publisher's booklists in the 1990s.

Nevertheless, each Gospel offers a distinctive portrait of Jesus, rich with hard historicity. We hear of rulers, cities, provinces, rivers, mountains, festivals and the like. Although not a detail is uttered about (let's say) Jesus' specific taste in food or his choice of sandals, all the Gospels enter into great detail regarding the last few days of his earthly life leading to his crucifixion (the passion). This is no biographical accident, because the cross is central to the story. Remove it or minimize it and all else crumbles. The Gospels could thus be called focused biographies or distilled reports. Their purpose is not to relate exhaustive detail but to offer essential events. Historical facts are never secondary to or removed from the theological message; rather, they fit as smoothly as a soft hand into a silk glove, as we will see.

The burden of our investigation in this chapter is to see something of Jesus as he is presented in the Gospels and the rest of the New Testament, being sensitive to interpretations often on the lips, in the minds and in the books of New Age enthusiasts. We will look at the circumstances of Jesus' early life and something of his teaching on God, humanity and ethics. In the next chapter we will highlight Jesus' claims and credentials as the Christ. In chapter five we will look at the case for the reliability of these texts as historical documents. But before plunging into historiography, let us consider the biography to see just who emerges.

The Virgin Birth

Historians tell us that Jesus entered a world of religious confusion and social unrest. The "promised land" of Palestine had become occupied territory, a satellite of the vast Roman Empire. Although the centralized power of Rome provided the *Pax Romana* (the Peace of Rome) over much of the known world, the Jews of the first century were less than satisfied citizens. They saw themselves as a Chosen People belonging to God alone; yet they were subjugated to Caesar. How could God allow it? they questioned. And how could he provide deliverance? God's deliverance would begin in a virgin's womb.

Matthew tells us that "Jesus was born in Bethlehem in Judea, during the time of King Herod" (Mt 2:1), setting him squarely in datable, space-time history. In appearance he looked no different than any other Jewish newborn boy, yet his origin is recorded as unique. Both Matthew (1:18-25) and Luke (1:26-38) tell us that Jesus was conceived without the intervention of a human father when the Holy Spirit overshadowed his mother, Mary. So it is proper to speak of both a virgin conception and a virgin birth. Some miss the significance of this; we are not speaking of a mere biological oddity in a race not known for asexual reproduction (parthenogenesis).

The virginal conception of Jesus brackets him off, as it were, from all other humans in terms of origin.[4] Although fully human, Jesus does not inherit a sinful human nature. His human genesis is not primarily natural but supernatural; not initiated by humanity, but by God. From conception Jesus is a one-of-a-kind gift from God. Mary becomes the vessel for divine service and cries out in praise, "My soul glorifies the Lord and my spirit rejoices in God my Savior, for he has been mindful of the humble state of his servant" (Lk 1:46-47).

Yet this supernatural conception is not an artificial invasion by an alien intruder bent on violating everything natural. While utterly unique, it is not "out of place," for earth is the ordained theater of redemption. The incarnation is, in this sense, "in character" for God. C. S. Lewis had insightful understanding of this coincidence of the natural and the supernatural when he observed that if God works

miraculously to inject a new element, "immediately all Nature dom-
iciles this new situation, makes it at home in her realm, adapts all other
events to it." The one of a kind becomes involved in all other kinds
in the creation: "If God creates a miraculous spermatozoan in the
body of a virgin, it does not proceed to break any laws. The laws at
once take over. Nature is ready. Pregnancy follows, according to all
the normal laws, and nine months later a child is born."[5]

Although only two of the four Gospel writers mention the virgin
conception, and it does not seem to be a part of the core of the early
apostles' preaching, it nevertheless signifies and contributes to the
uniqueness of Jesus and should not be confused with divine-human
propagation as found in other religions. One Rosicrucian writer,
H. Spencer Lewis, accepts the virgin birth not only of Jesus but of all
Avatars (special periodic manifestations of God), of which Jesus is
only one.[6] This is both totally foreign to the biblical account, which
views the event as uniquely significant,[7] and at odds with accounts in
other religious contexts. John Frame notes that:

> There is no clear parallel to the notion of a *virgin* birth in pagan
> literature, only of births resulting from intercourse between God
> and a woman (of which there is no suggestion in Matthew and
> Luke), resulting in a being half-divine, half-human (which is far
> different from biblical Christology).[8]

Frame further notes that none of the pagan stories fix the event in
specific history as do Matthew and Luke.[9]

Christhood in a Manger

The events surrounding Jesus' infancy also point toward his distinc-
tiveness, even in his very name.

Joseph is told in a dream by an angel not to be afraid to take Mary
as his wife because "what is conceived in her is from the Holy Spirit.
She will give birth to a son, and you are to give him the name Jesus,
because he will save his people from their sins" (Mt 1:20-21). "Jesus"
is a transliteration of the Hebrew *Joshua,* which means "Jehovah is
salvation" or "is Savior." The name recognized the saving power of

God alone to rescue his people and was common for a Jewish man at the time.[10] The son of Mary is called Jesus because he himself "will save his people from their sins." His name does not commemorate a work done by another but explains his own unique identity.

Another angelic messenger met shepherds tending their flocks near the birthplace of Jesus. As the glory of the Lord shone around the angel, they were terrified, but the angel replied, "Do not be afraid. I bring you good news of great joy that will be for all the people. *Today* in the town of David a Savior has been born to you; he is Christ the Lord" (Lk 2:10-11, emphasis mine; cf. Mt 1:18).

The word *Christ* here is not really a proper name, as is Jesus, but a title, although "Jesus Christ" later became a shortened way to say "Jesus, the Christ." The title *Christ* refers to being "anointed" by God and is used in the ancient Greek translation of the Old Testament (the Septuagint) to refer to God's favor on those especially equipped by God, such as the priest anointed with holy oil (particularly the High Priest), the Old Testament prophets and, on occasion, a king of Israel.[11] But Jesus does not become the Christ at a given point in his life; he is the Christ from birth. Not only that, "he is Christ *the Lord."* None of the priests, prophets or kings of the Old Testament are called "the Lord"; rather, they are servants of the Lord. Thus did the wise men (Magi) come from the East, not to instruct the Christ but to worship him "who has been *born king* of the Jews" (Mt 2:2, emphasis mine).

This understanding sets the Christ of the New Testament against various New Age views that see Jesus as a man who realized his Christhood later in life through initiation (baptism, meditative techniques, or other methods) just as we too can attain our Christhood. As the *Metaphysical Bible Dictionary* (used in Unity) puts it, "Each of us has within him the Christ, just as Jesus had, and we must look within to recognize and realize our sonship, our divine origin and birth, even as He did."[12] According to the New Testament, he alone is virgin born; he alone saves people from sin; he alone is *the* Christ.

But it is not enough simply to explain the significance of the words

Jesus and *Christ* as used for the baby born in Bethlehem. We need to examine his short but stunning life, because it is here most dramatically that we discover his character and power.

Jesus met opposition even before uttering his first word. King Herod, having heard of the Magi's quest for the Christ, was disturbed and sought to uncover the baby, pretending he too wanted to worship. In reality he wanted to kill any rival to the throne. Nevertheless, an angel warned Joseph of the impending assassination, and the family fled to Egypt. In the meantime Herod ordered the destruction of all male boys in the vicinity of Bethlehem who were two years old or younger. After the executions and the demise of Herod, Jesus' family returned to Palestine, settling in Nazareth (Mt 2:13-23). Even from his infancy, worldly powers were ill at ease with Jesus, and this unrest caused later encounters of a cosmic dimension.

The Gospels do not give us detailed descriptions of Jesus' childhood and early manhood, but from the context there is every reason to assume that he matured, as any Jewish boy would, by receiving religious instruction in the family, attending services and festivals and learning the trade of his father, namely, carpentry (see Mk 6:3). Luke summarizes the time between Jesus' circumcision (at eight days) and age twelve by saying, "And the child grew and became strong; he was filled with wisdom, and the grace of God was upon him" (Lk 2:40).

Jesus showed a precocious interest in theology. During the Feast of Passover the twelve-year-old Jesus spent a good deal of time in the temple courts talking with the religious leaders. When Jesus was confronted by his parents concerning his behavior, he responded, "Why were you searching for me? . . . Didn't you know I had to be in my Father's house?" (Lk 2:49). What the Gospel writers see as Jesus' special and unique relationship with the Father was conspicuous even in his childhood.

The Gospel of Luke then sums up the rest of Jesus' youth and early manhood with one sentence: "And Jesus grew in wisdom and in stature, and in favor with God and man" (Lk 2:52). That which would be worthy of elaboration would come later. (We will return to this issue in depth in chapter seven, concerning "the lost years.")

Jesus in the Public Eye

The lion's share of the Gospel accounts track Jesus' public ministry, crucifixion and resurrection. Despite the fact that any summary of the ministry of Jesus will be inadequate, we will accent several aspects of his character and teaching.

Before Jesus preached his first sermon or healed his first cripple, his cousin John the Baptist was electrifying the country around the Jordan, preaching a baptism of repentance for the forgiveness of sins (Mt 3:2). Not one to mince words, John was a strange, ascetic figure dressed in camel's hair and subsisting on a diet of locusts and wild honey. He preached repentance from all immorality and baptized the multitudes, warning them of the wrath to come on those who would not turn to God from the heart. But his call to repentance was not an abstract appeal to moral uplift; he was the forerunner of Jesus, of whom he said, "He is the one who comes after me, the thongs of whose sandals I am not worthy to untie" (Jn 1:27).

Some thought John the Baptist might be the Christ, but when they asked him who he was, John replied plainly, "I am not the Christ" (Jn 1:20). New Age theology to the contrary, John did not assert his own Christhood (either actual or potential), but deferred to Jesus as the Christ.

When Jesus came to be baptized, John demurred, saying, "I need to be baptized by you, and do you come to me?" To which Jesus replied, "Let it be so now; it is proper for us to do this to fulfill all righteousness" (Mt 3:14-15). As John had said, Jesus was "the Lamb of God, who takes away the sin of the world" (Jn 1:29) and had no need of repentance; but Jesus wanted to endorse John's ministry as his forerunner and to identify with the people. After Jesus was baptized, as he was praying, "heaven was opened and the Holy Spirit descended upon him in bodily form like a dove. And a voice came from heaven: 'You are my Son, whom I love; with you I am well pleased' " (Lk 3:21-22). Although his baptism identified Jesus with the people, it also isolated him from the rest because the Holy Spirit and God the Father ratified him as "the Son" with a special mission.

There is no indication that Jesus received, attained or discovered Christhood at this point. His baptism, rather, specially equipped him to begin his divine mission. Luke tells us that "Jesus himself was about thirty years old when he began his ministry" (Lk 3:23).

Just as Herod schemed to destroy the infant Jesus, so did the devil want a shot at the mature Jesus face-to-face. Being filled with the Holy Spirit, Jesus was led into the wilderness to be tempted by the devil. After Jesus fasted, the devil presented four temptations, each of which was wired to explode Jesus' trust in the Father and to derail his divine mission. Each time Jesus countered the devil's distortion of Scripture and logic with the true revelation of God in the Old Testament by quoting from the book of Deuteronomy. After the devil's fourth unsuccessful attempt Jesus dispatched him and returned from the wilderness to begin gathering disciples (see Mt 4:1-11; Lk 4:1-13).

It is clear from these passages that Jesus is presented as engaging in person-to-person spiritual combat. The devil is not depicted as merely the "dark side" or "shadow" of the human psyche (as with C.J. Jung) or a mythological personification of cosmic powers (as with Joseph Campbell). Rather, *he* is an existing, intelligent being, the enemy of Jesus who tempts by twisting the meaning of the Bible itself. Yet Jesus resists his wiles, thus proving himself impervious to corruption, even under the most intensely intimidating circumstances imaginable. He is a man of integrity and power. But the final showdown with the devil is yet to come.

Jesus and His Kingdom

The claims and credentials of Jesus cannot be adequately addressed apart from his teaching on the kingdom of God, which forms the structure and provides the dynamics for his entire ministry. When Jesus began to preach he proclaimed, "Repent, for the kingdom of heaven is near" (Mt 4:17).

Jesus sometimes used slightly different expressions to refer to the kingdom of God, such as "the kingdom of heaven" or simply "the kingdom," or "my kingdom." Jesus took elements of the traditional Jewish understanding of the kingdom of God and transformed them through his radical teaching and actions. He proclaimed the dynamic reign and rule of God as actively involved in his own life and work. He said, "If I drive out demons by the Spirit of God, then the kingdom of God has come upon you" (Mt 12:28). It would not be inaccurate to say that Jesus preached the advent of a new age wherein God breaks into human history in unprecedented ways. The kingdom is inaugurated in the person of the King himself, Jesus. As F. F. Bruce notes:

> In Origen's great word, Jesus was the *autobasileia,* the kingdom in person; for the principles of the kingdom of God could not have been more completely embodied than in him who said to his Father, "not my will, but thine be done," and accepted the cross in that spirit.[13]

Jesus came as the very expression of the kingdom, "teaching in their synagogues, preaching the good news of the kingdom, and healing every disease and sickness among the people" (Mt 4:23). As his ministry unfolds in the gospels, his claims and credentials become clear.

Jesus was hailed as a master teacher. After the Sermon on the Mount, Matthew records that "the crowds were amazed at his teaching, because he taught as one who had authority" (Mt 7:28-29). Although always on the theological hot seat, he was never burned by any questioner and often turned the tables on his interlocutors, exposing their dishonesty. But what exactly did Jesus teach? Is it in line with New Age understandings? We will briefly consult his teachings on God, humanity and ethics.

Jesus' View of God

Jesus taught his disciples to pray in this manner: "Our Father in heaven, hallowed be your name, your kingdom come, your will be done on earth as it is in heaven" (Mt 6:9-10). Jesus viewed God as a personal being, able to be personally addressed in prayer; the kingdom is administered by the King who *hears*. God, as a personal being, is fatherly. In teaching on prayer, Jesus said that the Father *sees* what one prays in secret and *knows* what we need even before we ask (Mt 6:6). God will *forgive* us if we forgive others (Mt 6:14) and *reward* those who fast in humility according to his will (Mt 6:16-18).

From just these few verses we find that God is properly referred to as Father, that he administers his kingdom, that he hears us, sees us, knows what we need, will forgive us and reward us. This kind of language cannot possibly refer to the impersonal energy, force or principle so often emphasized in New Age circles. Moreover, God is a "Thou" or an "Other" with whom we relate; he is not the marrow of the universe. Jesus speaks of the fellowship he had with God the Father "before the creation of the world" (Jn 17:24; cf. Mk 13:19). This indicates that Jesus' relationship was with a Person and that God is prior to and distinct from the created universe. All is not uniformly one (monism).

Jesus said to pray that God's name be "hallowed," or revered as holy. He addressed God in prayer as "Holy Father" (Jn 17:11). He likewise taught that the heavenly Father is "perfect" (Mt 5:48) and "God is spirit, and his worshipers must worship in spirit and in truth" (Jn 4:24). We discover that God is holy, not in an unqualified, nebulous sense of "the sacred," but as ultimate, moral perfection.

Any old conception of God will not do for Jesus. Nothing less than the truth is required, and fallible opinion must succumb to divine reality. God is not all over the metaphysical map; he has a describable, intelligible, knowable nature. Theological truth must be separated from theological falsehood. In this spirit Jesus warned of *false* prophets and *false* Christs who are to come "and perform great signs and miracles to deceive even the elect—if that were possible" (Mt 24:24). To avoid deception, God must be known for who he is.

Jesus' View of Humanity

Jesus knows humans to be God's creatures. In dealing with the issue of divorce, he affirmed that "at the beginning of creation God 'made them male and female' " (Mk 10:6). God is the maker; we are the made. Jesus exalts humans above the animal world, assuring his listeners that they are "more valuable" than the birds of the air (Mt 6:26). Furthermore, Jesus considers humans as spiritual beings with much to gain and much to lose in the spiritual realm: "What good will it be for a man if he gains the whole world, yet forfeits his soul? Or what can a man give in exchange for his soul?" (Mt 16:26).

But is the soul divine? Jean Houston, popular New Age seminar leader and author, claims that Jesus taught that "God indwells every person. . . . [and] that the indwelling God, expressed as God-Son, Logos, Christ, or Chalice of Life, is the unique expression within us of the universal parent-being."[14] But consider Jesus' words to some of the Jews of his day who thought their national heritage assured them of a right standing before God:

> If God were your Father, you would love me, for I came from God and now am here. I have not come on my own; but he sent me. Why is my language not clear to you? Because you are unable to hear what I say. You belong to your father, the devil, and you want to carry out your father's desire. (Jn 8:42-44)

The Jesus of the Gospels disagrees with Houston. Because of their opposition to Jesus' teaching, some people are, ethically speaking, offspring of God's enemy, the devil (although all are created by God). Despite Jesus' teaching on our privileged status as a species, he never intimates we are ultimately one with God. Nor does he appeal to the Hindu doctrine of maya, which accepts only the appearance of finite, creaturely existence and affirms the *only* reality is divine.

Yet several of Jesus' teachings are used by New Age interpreters to support the idea of the divinity of the soul.

First, Jesus' statement that "the kingdom of God is within you" (Lk 17:21) is often taken to teach that God is within each of us. But a glance at the context of Jesus' words brings this into question.

Jesus was addressing his religious opposition, the Pharisees, who had asked him when the kingdom of God would come. Notice that the nature of humanity was not at issue, but the timing of the kingdom.

The issue was chronology, not anthropology. Jesus said, "The kingdom of God does not come with your careful observation, nor will people say, 'Here it is,' or 'There it is,' because the kingdom of God is within you" (Lk 17:20-21). Jesus then turned to his disciples and discussed the events leading up to his Second Coming (vv. 22-37). Again, in his response, he is not addressing the nature of the soul.

It seems unlikely that Jesus would ignore the gist of the Pharisees' statement on the timing of the kingdom, shift the subject to the nature of the soul, then inform the Pharisees, his sworn enemies, that they were divine, only to shift the subject back to the timing of the kingdom when talking to his disciples.

If neither the context nor the comment dealt with the nature of the soul, what did Jesus mean? Many scholars argue that the Greek word sometimes translated "within" is better translated "among" or "in your midst."[15] The New International Version lists "among" as an alternative reading. The Jerusalem Bible uses "among." The Revised Standard Version says "in your midst," as does the New American Standard Bible. Understood in this light, Jesus was saying that the reign and rule of God is in the present; it is not something only to appear in the future. The kingdom was being expressed that very moment in Jesus' every thought, word and deed.

Even if the verse is best rendered as "the kingdom of God is *within* you" this is not identical with saying *"God* is within you." Just as there is a simple difference between an earthly king and his kingdom, so is there a clear distinction between the kingdom of God and the God who is the King.

Second, Jesus' question "Is it not written in your Law, 'I have said you are gods?' " (Jn 10:34) is often used to support the New Age belief in the divine essence of humanity. But is this what Jesus was talking about when he spoke these words?

If we peek at the world of Jesus' words we can better read his meaning. During the Jewish Feast of Dedication, Jesus was in the temple. Some Jews asked him, "How long will you keep us in suspense? If you are the Christ, tell us plainly" (Jn 10:24).

Jesus then asserted that he had already told them because his miracles speak for him. They do not believe because they are not his sheep. His own sheep follow him and are given eternal life. He then spoke of the greatness of the Father and affirmed, "I and the Father are one" (Jn 10:30).[16]

His audience then picked up stones to stone him and Jesus asked them (sarcastically) for which great miracle they wished to stone him. They then answered that their anger was "for blasphemy, because you, a mere man, claim to be God" (Jn 10:33).

Jesus then said:

Is it not written in your Law, "I have said you are gods"? If he called them "gods," to whom the word of God came—and the Scripture cannot be broken—what about the one whom the Father set apart as his very own and sent into the world? Why then do you accuse me of blasphemy because I said, "I am God's Son"? Do not believe me unless I do what my Father does. But if I do it, even though you do not believe me, believe the miracles, that you may know and understand that the Father is in me, and I in the Father. (Jn 10:34-38)

The issue at hand in this passage was Jesus' claim "I and the Father are one," not a common claim in Jesus' day. His statement addressed the fact of his own uniqueness, not the essential divinity of all people. Our focus, though, will be primarily on Jesus' meaning of the phrase "you are gods."

New Age author John White asserts this:

The Christian tradition, rightly understood, seeks to have us all become Jesuses, one in Christ. . . . Jesus himself pointed out that this is what the Judaic tradition, which he fulfilled, is all about when he said, "Is it not written in your Law, 'I said you are gods'?" (Jn 10:34).[17]

Many New Age apologists interpret Jesus' remarks to mean something like this: "Look, don't get angry with me for claiming to be God. Deity is not my exclusive possession. Everyone is a god, even as your sacred Book says. So calm down!" Was this Jesus' argumentative strategy?

First of all, Jesus quoted from Psalm 82, which begins, "God presides in the great assembly; he gives judgment among the 'gods' " (v.
1). God then upbraids these "gods" for not defending the cause of "the
weak and fatherless" and not maintaining "the rights of the poor and
oppressed" (v. 3). These "gods" know "nothing, they understand nothing. They walk about in darkness" (v. 5). Verse six says (God speaking), "I said, 'You are "gods," you are all sons of the Most High.' "
Yet verse seven announces, "But you will die like mere men; you will
fall like every other *ruler"* (emphasis mine).

From the context of the passage Jesus quoted it is clear that the
"gods" are not participants in the ultimate reality of the universe. The
Hebrew word used for "gods" is *elohim,* which is sometimes used to
refer to *humans* who, in certain limited respects, function in a divine
capacity.[18] In this case the "gods" are "rulers" (v. 6) who have a God-
given jurisdiction to govern justly, a jurisdiction they have failed to
exercise; therefore, they "will die like mere men" (v. 7). The word for
"gods" *(elohim)* is not *Yahweh,* which is the personal name uniquely
used for God.

When Jesus adds that "the Scripture cannot be broken" (Jn 10:35),
he endorses the abiding truth of the Old Testament as a whole and
Psalm 82 in particular.[19] Jesus certainly recognized that the passage
does not teach the divinity of all people. For one thing, the text does
not say that all people are "gods," but only the rulers in question.
Secondly, the one true God judges these rulers ("gods") because of
their injustice. They held the high, God-given *office* of rulership (as
"gods") but did not possess the *essence* of gods as divine in their own
right. No, they offended the Ruler of the universe. Jesus also indicated
that he was not referring to the rulers as divine in their own right when
he said, "If he called them 'gods' *to whom the word of God came* . . ."
(v. 35; emphasis mine). These "gods" received and rejected the word
of God. They certainly were not God.

Jesus, then, was arguing from the lesser to the greater *(a fortiori):*
If these inferior rulers can rightly be called "gods," how much more
can Jesus, a truly righteous ruler sent from God, legitimately claim to

be "one with the Father." He told them to check the evidence. Jesus does the Father's will (Jn 10:36-37). The miracles confirm his integrity (Jn 10:37-38). Jesus concluded his argument by restating his claim to be one with the Father: "the Father is in me, and I in the Father" (Jn 10:38). He has not reduced himself to being one member in a pantheon of many gods. He is, rather, a righteous ruler: a true king. As he said to his accusers before the crucifixion, "You are right in saying I am a king. In fact, for this reason I was born, and for this I came into the world, to testify to the truth. Everyone on the side of truth listens to me" (Jn 18:37).

The text in John 10 observes that when Jesus finished speaking the crowd again tried to seize him. Apparently they understood him to have only amplified his earlier statement. Now they were all the more belligerent to halt the "blasphemy." The theological interchange did not switch to a discussion over the divinity of all people as would be expected if Jesus had just defended that proposition.[20]

Next, it is common in New Age environs to hear that Jesus taught that we are divine because he said that we would do "greater works" than he himself did. That is, we have the same access to supernatural power as he did. Commenting on this verse, John White says, "That is the human potential—the potential for growth into godhood."[21]

The context for this statement is a discourse given to the disciples before Jesus' crucifixion. When asked concerning "the way," Jesus explained, "I am the way and the truth and the life. No one comes to the Father except through me" (Jn 14:6). When asked about the Father, he said that "I am in the Father" and that "the Father is in me" (Jn 14:10). He then said that "anyone who has faith in me will do what I have been doing. He will do even greater things than these, because I am going to the Father. And I will do whatever you ask in my name, so that the Son may bring glory to the Father" (Jn 14:12-13). What does all this mean?

Whatever "things" Jesus had in mind—and we need not determine that here—they come, not from one's Divine Self, but from Jesus himself who alone is "the way and the truth and the life" (Jn 14:6).

The works are derived from God and are to bring glory to the Father through the Son, not to the self. Jesus gives ultimate priority to *"the* Father" and *"the* Son," not *the* self. Nothing in this text speaks of innate divinity as the energy required to do the works of faith of which Jesus speaks. That meaning cannot be extracted from the passage; it can only be injected illegitimately in the same way that red dye makes water look, but not taste, like wine.

Jesus' View of Sin

The soul, for Jesus, is not divine. It is a perilous possession that can be forfeited because the heart is evil. Jesus presupposes this idea in the Sermon on the Mount and uses it for a premise of his *a fortiori* argument: "If you, then, though *you* are evil, know how to give good gifts to your children, how much more will your Father in heaven give good gifts to those who ask him!" (Mt 7:11; emphasis mine). In a long and painful passage, Jesus zeroes in on the inner engines of uncleanness:

> What comes out of a man is what makes him "unclean." For from within, out of men's hearts, come evil thoughts, sexual immorality, theft, murder, adultery, greed, malice, deceit, lewdness, envy, slander, arrogance and folly. All these evils come from inside and make a man "unclean." (Mk 7:20-23)

Jesus lists no fewer than thirteen items of infamy residing in the human heart; and for the Jewish mind, the heart was the core and center of one's being and stood for a person's "entire mental and moral activity, both the rational and the emotional elements. In other words the heart was used figuratively for the hidden springs of the personal life."[22] No deeper could one go to ferret out a submerged divine essence.

Jean Houston refers to sin as "unskilled behavior" that can be transcended through sacred rituals that enact the Christ within us all.[23] Many other New Age writers speak of this "unskilled behavior" as simply ignorance of the greatness within. But the biblical Jesus moves in another moral world. It is psychologically taxing, to say the least, to imagine him calling theft, murder, adultery, greed and so on "unskilled behavior" tantamount to a beginner's disappointing first round on the golf course. Many people, in fact, become quite skilled at these behaviors.

For Jesus the issue of sin has eternal consequences. While "unskilled behavior" is nothing more than mere ignorance correctable through knowledge and practice, "evil" is something else entirely and a subject often on Jesus' lips. When Jesus was accused of casting out demons by demonic power, he responded:

The good man brings good things out of the good stored up in him, and the evil man brings evil things out of the evil stored up in him. But I tell you that men will have to give account on the day of judgment for every careless word they have spoken. For by your words you will be acquitted, and by your words you will be condemned. (Mt 12:35-37; cf. Jn 5:28-29)

For Jesus sin is not simply episodic, but dispositional;[24] a condition of the heart, not an occasional flare-up of the will. He said, "I tell you the truth, everyone who sins is a slave to sin" (Jn. 8:34). Jesus informed the most scrupulously religious leaders of his time, "Yet none of you keeps the [moral] law" (Jn 7:19).

The Ethics of Jesus

A discussion of Jesus' views on humanity and sin leads naturally into his view of ethics, because, in Jesus' mind, sin is the violation of God's principles for life. When asked what was the "greatest commandment in the law," Jesus replied:

"Love the Lord your God with all your heart and with all your soul and with all your mind." This is the first and greatest commandment. And the second is like it: "Love your neighbor as yourself." All the Law and the Prophets hang on these two commandments. (Mt 22:37-40)

When we see what specifics Jesus hung on the greatest commandment we find that Jesus' ethical teachings are uncompromisingly elevated. Cutting through the religious formalism and hypocrisy of his day,

Jesus went to the root of God's commands, revealing their deepest meaning.

Not only should we not externally murder, we should not internally assassinate another through anger and defamation. Jesus warned, "Anyone who says, 'You fool!' will be in danger of the fire of hell" (Mt 5:22). Not only should we not externally commit adultery, but "anyone who looks at a woman lustfully has already committed adultery with her in his heart" (Mt 5:28). So serious are these ethical concerns that Jesus admonished:

If your right eye causes you to sin, gouge it out and throw it away. It is better for you to lose one part of your body than for your whole body to be thrown into hell. And if your right hand causes you to sin, cut it off and throw it away. It is better for you to lose one part of your body than for your whole body to go into hell. (Mt 5:29-30)

These words put Jesus at variance with the Jesus of Joseph Campbell. Campbell interprets Jesus' teaching "Do not judge, or you too will be judged" (Mt 7:1) to mean that you should "put yourself back in the position of Paradise before you thought in terms of good and evil."[25] Campbell fails to notice that Jesus was not prohibiting all ethical discrimination, as if such dualities dissipate when one is enlightened. Far from jettisoning good and evil as required moral categories, Jesus was warning of hypocrisy. He went on to say of those who don't consider their own sin before looking at another's, "You hypocrite, first take the plank out of your own eye, and *then you will see clearly to remove the speck from your brother's eye"* (Mt 7:5, emphasis mine). Specks and logs need to be removed, not ignored, in a world spoiled by sin (see also Jn 7:24).

Campbell, believing he is agreeing with Jesus, continues, "One of the great challenges of life is to say 'yea' to that person or act or that condition which in your mind is the most abominable."[26] Jesus flatly rejected such amoralism; it has nothing to do with his message.

Marriage is to be held in the highest honor with divorce as a last resort on only one condition. One should not need an oath in order to speak the truth habitually. "Simply let your 'Yes' be 'Yes,' and your 'No,' 'No'; anything beyond this comes from the evil one" (Mt 5:37). Vengeance in interpersonal affairs must be left to God: "Love your enemies and pray for those who persecute you" (Mt 5:44). Piety—concerning giving, prayer and fasting— must never be motivated by a desire for recognition but by a desire to be rewarded by God alone: "your Father, who sees what is done in secret, will reward you" (Mt 6:18). Our treasures are ultimately spiritual, and we must shun materialism: "But store up for yourselves treasures in heaven, where moth and rust do not destroy, and where theives do not break in and steal. For where your treasure is, there your heart will be also" (Mt 6:20-21).

These few sentences sum up Jesus' ethical directives as presented in the fifth and sixth chapters of Matthew. While they barely scrape the ethical surface of Jesus' teaching, the Sermon on the Mount does provide a partial look at his uncompromising standards of holiness.

But if Jesus had believed that people had the moral strength to achieve perfect obedience to these standards, he never would have said, "For I have not come to call the righteous, but sinners" (Mt 9:13) or "For the Son of man came to seek and to save what was lost" (Lk 19:10). When Jesus was pressed by a large crowd "he had compassion on them, because they were like sheep without a shepherd. So he began teaching them many things" (Mk 6:34). The lost need a leader. Sinners need a Savior. Jesus believed he was that man. So strongly did he affirm this that he proclaimed that to disbelieve in him was sinful and disastrous.

In his farewell address to his disciples before the crucifixion, Jesus said that the Holy Spirit would come after he had returned to the Father and that the Spirit would "convict the world of guilt . . . because men do not believe in me" (Jn 16:8-9). So distressed was Jesus over the sin of his own people who would not accept him, he cried out, "O Jerusalem, Jerusalem, you who kill the prophets and stone those sent to you, how often I have longed to gather your children together, as a hen gathers her chicks under her wings, but you were not willing" (Mt 23:37).

In this chapter we have seen something of Jesus' early life and his teachings on God, humanity and ethics. Thus far, he does not fit the New Age mold, for he taught that God is personal, not impersonal; humans are creatures and not divine; sin is a reality; and that he, not the self, is the true focus of salvation. What remains to be seen is Jesus' unique claims in relation to his credentials.

Just why would Jesus expect anyone to see him as the one and only Christ that ever was, is or will be? Can he back up his statement, "I am the way and the truth and the life" (Jn 14:6)? If Jesus inaugurated the kingdom of God, what does this involve, and what are his qualifications to be its harbinger? To this we now turn.

Notes

[1]G. K. Chesterton, *Varied Types* (New York: Dodd, Mead and Co., 1908), p. 141, quoted in *The Quotable Chesterton,* ed. George J. Marlin, Richard P. Rabatin and John L. Sean (Garden City, N.Y.: Doubleday and Company, Inc., 1987), p. 171.

[2]One of the drawing points of the movie *The Last Temptation of Christ* was its unorthodox exploration of Jesus' psychological life.

[3]We will speak of the dating of the New Testament documents themselves in chapter six. The dates of the events recorded can be reasonably inferred through various means.

[4]Similarly, the resurrection brackets him off from all others relating to his destiny. This idea is developed by Karl Barth and is discussed in Bernard Ramm, *An Evangelical Christology: Ecumenic and Historic* (Nashville, Tenn.: Thomas Nelson, 1985), p. 69.

[5]C. S. Lewis, *Miracles* (New York: Macmillan, 1978), p. 59.

[6]H. Spencer Lewis, *The Mystical Life of Jesus* (San Jose, Calif.: The Supreme Grand Lodge of AMORC, 1974), pp. 74-75.

[7]Which Lewis himself grants, p. 74.

[8]John Frame, "The Virgin Birth," in *Evangelical Dictionary of Theology,* ed. Walter A. Elwell (Grand Rapids, Mich.: Baker, 1984), p. 1145, emphasis his.

[9]Ibid. On the uniqueness of the biblical view of the virgin birth, see Norman Anderson, *Jesus Christ: The Witness of History* (Downers Grove, Ill.: InterVarsity Press, 1985), pp. 74-75.

[10]A. E. Vine, *Vine's Expository Dictionary of Old and New Testament Words* (Old Tappan, N.J.: Fleming H. Revell Company, 1981), 2:274.

[11]Ibid., 1:190.

[12]"Christ," *Metaphysical Bible Dictionary* (Unity Village, Mo.: Unity School of Christianity, 1931), p. 150.

[13]F. F. Bruce, *New Testament History* (Garden City, N.Y.: Doubleday, 1972), p. 173, emphasis his.

[14]Jean Houston, *Godseed* (Amity, N.Y.: Amity House, 1988), p. 54.

[15]Bruce, *New Testament History,* p. 172.

[16]The Greek neuter case here indicates that Jesus is affirming that he is of one *essence* with the Father, not one *person*. We thus find something of the Trinity entailed—both Jesus and the Father are equally divine.

[17]John White, "Jesus and the Idea of a New Age," *Quest*, Summer 1989, pp. 17-18.

[18]See Gleason Archer, *Encyclopedia of Biblical Difficulties* (Grand Rapids, Mich.: Zondervan, 1982), p. 374.

[19]On Jesus' view of Scripture, see John W. Wenham, *Christ and the Bible* (Grand Rapids, Mich.: Baker Book House, 1984).

[20]For a helpful discussion of these verses in John, see Gary DeMar and Peter Leithart, *The Reduction of Christianity* (Ft. Worth, Tex.: Dominion Press, 1987), pp. 77-83.

[21]White, p. 17.

[22]Vine, 2:207.

[23]Houston, p. 21.

[24]I owe this phraseology to Keith Yandell.

[25]Joseph Campbell, *The Power of Myth* (New York: Doubleday, 1988), p. 66.

[26]Ibid.

Chapter 3
Claims and Credentials
of Christ

*B*y opening the Gospel accounts of Jesus' life and teaching, we have found a stirring and stunning figure. What the Gospels disclose about Jesus puts him some distance from what is claimed for him in New Age discussions. He is *Jesus,* the one who saves others from sin. He is *the Christ* from birth, the uniquely anointed one of God; and he is appointed for a special mission "to seek and to save what was lost" (Lk 19:10). He spoke of the kingdom of God, or a New Age, beginning with himself as King. He taught with authority, and his teachings do not harmonize with the basics of New Age theology.

The Gospels tell us that Jesus' claims and actions set off shock waves two thousand years ago, and the Richter scale is still registering the responses. New Age author John White joins Ralph Waldo Emerson in lamenting that the religion *of* Jesus has become a religion *about* Jesus: "The religion *about* Jesus puts him on a pedestal, regards him as a parental Big Daddy in the Sky and childishly petitions him to be responsible for us."[1] The religion *of* Jesus "calls every human being to [attain] the same state of cosmic unity and wholeness which Jesus himself demonstrated."[2]

Da Free John, a Western guru who claims to be on the same spiritual level as Jesus,[3] says that "the Teaching and Way of Jesus are not *unique*—they are simply *true.*"[4] He further says that "Jesus, Gautama [Buddha], Krishna, and other great Masters did not claim exclusive identity or oneness with God—as if each of them alone were Divine." Da Free John insists that they each taught that everyone was divine.[5]

A careful look at the primary documents of Christianity is required in order to address adequately the controversy over Jesus' question: "Who do you say I am?" (Mt 16:15). Although we will take up the historical reliability of the New Testament in chapter six, our working assumption is that the Gospels should be received as historical documents worthy of close attention. They clearly claim to recount the life of Jesus. In light of this must we choose a "religion of Jesus" and reject a "religion about Jesus"? The answer hinges on Jesus' claims and credentials.

We have already noted that Jesus never taught the divinity of humanity. We are creatures distinct from our Creator, and we are subject to sin, a condition much more serious than ignorance of our divine potential. If Jesus taught "the humanity of humanity," what do we find in the Gospels about him as a human being?

The Gospels plainly present a thoroughly human Jesus. He was no ghostly figure of pure spirit who only appeared to be in flesh-and-blood form. Jesus spoke of his own body (Mk 14:8), head (Lk 7:44-46), hands, feet, flesh and bones (Lk 24:39) and blood (Mt 26:28). He also displayed distinctively human feelings and qualities: he was moved by pity (Mk 1:41) and compassion (Mk 8:2; Lk 7:36), he was distressed (Mk 7:34; Lk 22:15; 8:12), angry (Mk 3:5), annoyed (Mk 10:14), surprised (Mk 6:6), disappointed (Mk 8:17; 9:19), hungry (Mk 11:12), and he asked questions revealing his ignorance of some things (Mk 6:38; 8:29; 9:21; 10:18). We find Jesus subject to his parents (Lk 2:51), regularly attending synagogue (Lk 4:16), praying (Lk 6:12), being tempted (Mt 4:1-11) and joyful (Lk 10:21).[6]

Although born of a virgin and of supernatural origin, Jesus partook of our humanity. Yet after seeing Jesus calm a savage storm by simply "rebuking the winds and the waves," his disciples "marveled, saying 'What kind of man is this?' " (Mt 8:27). This remains the operative question.

Jesus: Man of Miracles

Jesus was hailed not only as a great teacher but as a worker of miracles, a man of power. His miracles single him out as a master of his circumstances and accredit him with a unique authority. These miracles were always centered on establishing his teaching, demonstrating his compassion and declaring the kingdom of God. Before Jesus calmed the storm he said to the disciples, "You of little faith, why are you so afraid?" (Mt 8:26), thus challenging them to grow in their faith in him. Having calmed the storm, he demonstrated that he was a proper object of their faith. None of Jesus' miracles were reckless or ostentatious demonstrations of cosmic clout. He even refused to perform miracles on command for those demanding a sign (Lk 11:16-28; Mt 12:38-45).

Scholar A. E. Harvey commented on the propriety of Jesus' miracles in relation to other ancient literature:

> In general, one can say that the miracle stories in the gospels are unlike anything else in ancient literature. . . . They do not exaggerate the miracle or add sensational details. . . . To a degree that is rare in the writings of antiquity, we can say, to use a modern phrase, that they tell the story straight.[7]

Nevertheless, Gospel accounts of Jesus' ministry explode with supernatural manifestations. Calming the waves was a "nature miracle" in which Jesus commanded the inanimate world to obey him. Another marine miracle occurred when the disciples spied Jesus walking on the water while they were out on the lake in a high wind. "They cried out, because they all saw him and were terrified. Immediately he spoke to them and said, 'Take courage! It is I. Don't be afraid.' Then he climbed into the boat with them, and the wind died down. They were completely amazed. . . ." (Mk 6:50-51). On two other occasions Jesus, not a fisherman by trade, directed the disciples to catch extraordinarily large amounts of fish (Lk 5:4-11; Jn 21:1-11).

Jesus demonstrated compassion materially in two cases by supernaturally multiplying loaves and fish in order to stay the hunger of the crowds (4,000 and 5,000 men respectively)[8] who had been occupied by his teaching (Mt 15:32-38; 14:15-21). Although he had said that " 'Man does not live on bread alone, but on every word that comes from the mouth of God' " (Mt 4:4), he responded to human physical hunger.

The first "miraculous sign" in the Gospel of John was another transformation of nature concerning food. When wine ran out at a wedding in Cana, Jesus told the servants to fill six large jars with water, then promptly turned it to wine. John comments that he "thus revealed his glory, and his disciples put their faith in him" (Jn 2:11).[9]

What kind of man is this who subjected nature to his will rather than being subjected to its whims? He is a man of power.

Jesus was also known as a healer. He had the power to heal. The Gospels overflow with case after case of Jesus healing diverse physical infirmities—leprosy, dropsy, paralysis, fever, blindness, deafness, muteness, issues of blood—and all manner of human ills. When Jesus was in Gennesaret, people flocked to him, carrying the sick on mats to receive his aid. Mark notes that they "begged him to let them touch even the edge of his cloak, and all who touched him were healed" (6:56).

Although some healing may be psychosomatically explained, Jesus healed not only functional problems (in which the organism is intact but dysfunctional) but deep organic maladies involving physical degeneration. For instance he said to a man with a shriveled hand, "Stretch out your hand." The man obeyed and his hand was completely restored (Mt 12:13-14).

Jesus' healing power struck even at a distance. He was once addressed by a Roman military officer who spoke of his servant paralyzed and suffering terribly. Jesus immediately offered to heal the servant. The officer responded that he did not deserve to have Jesus come under his roof, but if Jesus would just say the word his servant would be healed. Jesus, astonished at his great faith, said, " 'Go! It will be done just as you believed it would.' And his servant was healed at that very hour" (Mt 8:5-13). (It is important to notice that while Jesus complimented the man on his faith in him, he did not correct his remark about being unworthy, as would be expected if Jesus believed the man were intrinsically divine. Jesus instead accepts his humility and responds accordingly.)

In spite of the awesome greatness of Jesus' power to heal, those who refused to believe in him did not receive his healing touch. Jesus' ministry offended many in his hometown. " 'Only in his hometown, among his relatives and in his own house is a prophet without honor.' He could not do any miracles there, except lay his hands on a few sick people and heal them. And he was amazed at their lack of faith" (Mk 6:4-6). The man of power would not force his power on anyone.

The receiving of Jesus' miraculous potency was often related to a person's faith in him; and it was never a matter of making a withdrawal from the same impersonal cosmic bank account Jesus used. Jesus, in harmony with the Father and the Spirit, was the source of healing. His credentials in this were unrivaled.

Although Jesus' enemies granted his ability to heal, they explained the power as coming from the devil, not God. But the character of Jesus gave no indication of demonic possession. Instead he demonstrated his power by exorcising a host of demons in order to set captives free. He proclaimed that his whole mission would be one of deliverance:

> The Spirit of the Lord is on me,
>   because he has anointed me to preach good news to the poor.
> He has sent me to proclaim freedom for the prisoners
>   and recovery of sight for the blind,
> to release the oppressed,
>   to proclaim the year of the Lord's favor. (Lk 4:18-19)

In one extraordinary case Jesus encountered a demonized man who fell on his knees before him crying, "What do you want with me, Jesus, Son of the Most High God? Swear to God that you won't torture me!" When Jesus asked him his name, he replied, "My name is Legion, for we are many." Jesus then cast out the demons, and they entered a herd of pigs, causing them to drown. Even a legion of demons was no match for Jesus. The once-possessed man, who was "sitting there, dressed and in his right mind," then begged Jesus to let him go with him. But Jesus responded, "Go home to your family and tell them how much the Lord has done for you, and how much he had mercy on you" (Mk 5:1-19). Jesus' power is power over evil spirits; it is the power of the Lord; and it is released in mercy.

Jesus' most spectacular displays of authority involved reversing the universal decay that besets all of earthly existence. He raised the dead to life. The Gospels record three such cases, the most dramatic being the raising of Lazarus.

Lazarus and his sisters were close friends of Jesus. When Jesus heard of Lazarus's illness he said, "This sickness will not end in death. No, it is for God's glory so that God's Son may be glorified through it" (Jn 11:4). Jesus then mysteriously waited several days before reaching Lazarus. Upon arriving he found that Lazarus had expired four days earlier. After comforting his sisters Jesus asked them where Lazarus was buried. He was deeply moved and wept with them. We now pick up the text to experience its full force:

Jesus, once more deeply moved, came to the tomb. It was a cave with a stone laid across the entrance. "Take away the stone," he said.

"But, Lord," said Martha, the sister of the dead man, "by this time there is a bad odor, for he has been there four days."

Then Jesus said, "Did I not tell you that if you believed, you would see the glory of God?"

So they took away the stone. Then Jesus looked up and said, "Father, . . . I knew that you always hear me, but I said this for the benefit of the people standing here, that they may believe that you sent me."

When he had said this, Jesus called in a loud voice, "Lazarus, come out!" The dead man came out, his hands and feet wrapped with strips of linen, and a cloth around his face. (Jn 11:38-44) John then reports that many who had come to visit Mary, Lazarus' sister, "put their faith in him" (Jn 11:45). The mighty miracle did, indeed, validate Jesus' claim that he was sent from God (v. 42).

Jesus wept over the grim reality of death. He was "deeply moved" over human suffering, but sorrow doesn't exhaust the meaning of the Greek word used in verses 33 and 38. The word carries with it a sense of outrage, anger and disgust over a world full of death and decay, a landscape racked with the effects of sin.[10] Yet Jesus was not impotent in the full face of death. He did nothing less than raise the dead man to life, revealing the glory of God and confirming Martha's earlier confession that he was "the Christ, the Son of God, who was to come into the world" (Jn 11:27). The miracle provoked belief in him. But another even more miraculous resurrection lay ahead.

This wonder-working Jesus was never theatrical about his miracles. Although supernatural, they form a natural part of his characteristic ministry. They are potent signs of the kingdom of God being manifested in and through Jesus.

When John the Baptist sent word to Jesus asking about the authenticity of his ministry, Jesus replied:

Go back and report to John what you hear and see: The blind receive sight, the lame walk, those who have leprosy are cured, the deaf hear, the dead are raised, and the good news is preached to the poor. Blessed is the man who does not fall away on account of me. (Mt 11:4-6)

The sheer number, power and compassion of Jesus' miracles put him in a category by himself. What kind of a man is this? He is, for the Gospel writers, one of a kind. He has unique credentials as a miracle-worker.

The Gospels give no indication that Jesus was a guru who tapped into cosmic power through yogic technique or occult initiation. Jesus' relationship to God is portrayed as an interaction with his Father, a

Father he often consulted in prayer, even spending all night in personal communion with him (Lk 6:12).[11] His was not the spirituality of a Hindu sage who cultivates the divine through the arduous disciplines of yoga.

Neither were his miracles those of a shaman, the medicine man or witch doctor of tribal religions now experiencing something of a comeback in modern culture.[12] Anthropologist-cum-shaman Michael Harner describes a shaman as:

> a man or woman who enters an altered state of consciousness—at will—to contact and utilize an ordinarily hidden reality in order to acquire knowledge, power, and to help other persons. The shaman has at least one, and usually more, "spirits" in his personal service.[13]

Jesus did not depend on entering altered states of consciousness, nor did he use exotic shamanic ritual materials or spirits (he drove them out!) for his healing.[14] The manifestation of the miraculous flowed out of his perfect obedience to his Father, his enablement from the Holy Spirit and his own personal potency as the Son. He did not serve as a catalyst for the activation of divine energy in others. He was the personal fountainhead of miraculous power.

Jesus did much more than exercise authority over nature, heal the physically sick, cast out demons and raise the dead. He practiced his own preaching by loving his neighbor. He lived a life of openness to all who would listen. He found an especially attentive audience in the lowest class of his day, "the tax collectors and sinners," those who fell between the cracks of social and religious respectability. He was known as the friend of the downcast, and many of them believed in him. They knew Jesus as a true friend and recognized his credentials as a miracle-worker whose compassion brought deliverance to the captives.

Jesus: A Man of Authority

It should be obvious by now that Jesus yearned for people to *believe in him.* Contrary to John White, the evidence so far displays that the religion *of* Jesus was also a religion *about* Jesus. He is the object of faith for healing. He commands nature with a word. He raises the dead. He casts out demons by simply commanding them to leave. This authority is resident within him as God's "beloved Son" and through his relationship to the Father and the Spirit, as was seen at his baptism. When his disciples were commissioned to move in his power, they received it from Jesus, not themselves. The disciples cast out demons in Jesus' name, not their own (Lk 10:17).

Given the foregoing testimony, can it be further shown that Jesus claimed to be uniquely God in the flesh, appointed for an unrepeatable mission—a claim so disputed by the expansive pantheism of the New Age? We have so far seen something of Jesus' impressive credentials as a teacher, preacher and healer. We are now in a good position to learn more of his claims about himself.

In Capernaum some resourceful people lowered a paralytic through an opening they made in the roof above Jesus. When Jesus recognized their faith, he said to the paralytic, "Son, your sins are forgiven." Some of the religious teachers responded, "Why does this fellow talk like that? He's blaspheming. Who can forgive sins but God alone?" Jesus countered:

"Why are you thinking these things? Which is easier: to say to the paralytic, 'Your sins are forgiven,' or to say, 'Get up, take your mat and walk'? But that you may know that the Son of Man has authority on earth to forgive sins . . ." He said to the paralytic, "I tell you, get up, take your mat and go home." He got up, took his mat and walked out in full view of them all. (Mk 2:8-12)

In both word and deed Jesus was claiming the uniquely divine prerogative to forgive sins. It is one thing for me to forgive myself for something or to forgive you for offending me; it is quite another for me to forgive someone else for offending you! Imagine, then, someone claiming to forgive your *every* sin.

At a dinner at a Pharisee's house, a woman of ill repute came to Jesus and anointed his feet with perfume and her own tears. When the Pharisee objected to this behavior, Jesus told a parable to the effect that this woman loved Jesus much because she was forgiven much.

Then Jesus said to her, "Your sins are forgiven." Again, those present
were theologically scandalized and questioned, " 'Who is this who even
forgives sins?' Jesus then said to the woman, 'Your faith has saved you;
go in peace' " (Lk 7:48-50).

Jesus valued faith in him, not faith as an independent tool capable
of plugging into a universal energy current. Jesus honored and encouraged faith in himself, a faith that heals and saves, *a faith about Jesus.*

Jesus also provoked faith in many by the confidence with which he
spoke of himself and his role. As E. Stanley Jones put it, "He never
used such words as 'perhaps,' 'may be,' 'I think so.' Even his words
had a concrete feeling about them. They fell upon the soul with the
authority of certainty."[15]

This "authority of certainty" is manifest in the fact that he never had
to apologize or hesitate, whether in word or deed. He issued challenging moral absolutes such as "love your enemies" (Mt 5:44) without
reservation. He made grand promises without caution, such as
"Blessed are those who hunger and thirst for righteousness, for they
will be filled" (Mt 5:6) and "If you hold to my teaching, you are really
my disciples. Then you will know the truth, and the truth will set you
free" (Jn 8:31-32). He confidently asserted that "heaven and earth will
pass away, but my words will never pass away" (Mt 24:35). He warned
his hearers that their eternal destiny depended on their response to him
(Mk 8:38). He foretold the future in no uncertain terms, not for cu-
riosity's sake or date-setting, but because of its bearing on the present
(Mt 24).[16]

Jesus not only warned his hearers of the Judgment Day, he proclaimed himself the Judge of the world. In warning of false prophets
to come in his name, Jesus declared that he will say to them on the
Day of Judgment, "I never knew you. Away from me, you evildoers!"
(Mt 7:23). Jesus stated that "the Father judges no one, but has given
all judgment to the Son" (Jn 5:22) and "whoever hears my word and
believes him who sent me has eternal life and will not be condemned;
he has crossed over from death to life" (Jn 5:24).

Yet not all will respond to his word in saving faith. Speaking of his authority as the Son of Man to judge, Jesus continued:

Do not be amazed at this, for a time is coming when all who are in their graves will hear his voice and come out—those who have done good will rise to live, and those who have done evil will rise to be condemned. (Jn 5:28-29)

The Son of Man will divide humanity on that day.

When the Son of Man comes in his glory, and all the angels with him, he will sit on his throne in heavenly glory. All the nations will be gathered before him, and he will separate the people one from another as a shepherd separates the sheep from the goats. (Mt 25:31-33)[17]

He later added that the goats "will go away to eternal punishment, but the righteous to eternal life" (Mt 25:46), all on the basis of how they responded to Jesus during their one life on earth. Reincarnation is not in view.[18]

The Uniqueness of Jesus, the Christ

Jesus' confidence in his authority makes perfect sense if, as we noted in the last chapter, he and the Father "are one" (Jn 10:30). He knows the Father and the Father knows him in a unique way. Jesus said, "All things have been committed to me by my Father. No one knows the Son except the Father, and no one knows the Father except the Son and those to whom the Son chooses to reveal him" (Mt 11:27). Jesus placed his own knowledge of the Father on the same level as the Father's knowledge of the Son, thus asserting his unique equality with the Father.[19] William Craig comments that this verse

tells us that Jesus claimed to be the Son of God in an *exclusive* and *absolute* sense. Jesus says here that His relationship of sonship to God is unique. And He also claims to be the *only one* who can reveal the Father to men. In other words, Jesus claims to be the absolute revelation of God.[20]

When challenged about his activities on the Sabbath, Jesus responded, "My Father is always at his work to this very day and I, too, am working" (Jn 5:17). John notes, "For this reason the Jews tried all the harder to kill him; not only was he breaking the Sabbath, but he was even calling God his own Father, making himself equal with God" (Jn 5:18). Jesus healed on the Sabbath on several occasions and once used the opportunity to proclaim, "The Son of Man is Lord even of the Sabbath" (Mk 2:28). The Lord of the Sabbath can be no less than the Lord of creation who made the Sabbath (Gen. 2:2), God himself.

When Jesus' disputants said, "Who do you think you are?" (Jn 8:53), Jesus concluded his response by saying, "I tell you the truth, before Abraham was born, I am!" (v. 58). John notes: "At this, they picked up stones to stone him, but Jesus hid himself, slipping away from the temple grounds" (v. 59). Jesus affirmed his existence as God, the "I Am" (Ex 3:14), from before Abraham's day. Although some claim that this statement is a reference to *reincarnation* (Jesus previously existing as another human), it makes more sense to see it as a reference to Jesus' *pre-incarnation* identity as God himself. That is exactly how his audience interpreted it. To interpret it otherwise is to wrench the text entirely out of its context.

In a famous passage on God's love for the world, Jesus also expressed his uniqueness by saying, "For God so loved the world that he gave his one and only Son, that whoever believes in him should not perish but have eternal life" (Jn 3:16). Jesus affirmed that he alone is the agent of redemption as God's "only Son." He further underscored this when he claimed, "I am the way and the truth and the life. No one comes to the Father except through me" (Jn 14:6).

New Age commentators to the contrary, in these passages Jesus is asserting something about himself by using the personal, first person pronoun "I." He does not say, "The God already within you is the way, the truth and the life," or "We are the way, the truth and the life." These ideas are emphatically excluded.

Nevertheless in an article called "The Gospel as Yoga," Ravi Ravindra quotes Jesus' words from John 14:6 and comments:

Whether the Father had incarnated himself in the body of Jesus of Nazareth, or whether Jesus became one with the Father, is not necessary for us to resolve here. . . . However, it is important to guard against a lowering of the level of insight: the significant truth, which alone has the power to lead to eternal life, resides in the egoless supreme identity in which "the Father and I are one," and less in any exclusive identification of the Father with this specific person or that.[21]

In other words, we should not overly concern ourselves with any specific revelation of God but rather consider the impersonal "egoless supreme identity." Ravindra goes on to cite references from Indian tradition, particularly the *Upanishads,* asserting that the essence of any person is identical with Brahman, the Absolute, and is beyond any "limiting particularity."[22]

When reading the Gospel accounts, however, one is struck with the sense that Jesus singled himself out of the crowd by his words and deeds. The particulars of his life were his unique credentials that cannot be accredited to Divinity-in-General, an impersonal force that is everything in general and nothing in particular. His claims could be made by anyone; but they could only be substantiated by Jesus. For the Gospel writers, God is focused in Jesus of Nazareth.[23] As John puts it, Jesus, "who is at the Father's side, has made him known" (Jn 1:18).

Jesus knew the Father not as "egoless supreme identity," but as his "Abba" (Mk 14:36), an Aramaic term of tender endearment used of intimate knowledge and affection for one's father. The English word "papa" comes close to capturing the meaning. Throughout the Gospels we find Jesus in communion with the Father as he prays. He hears the Father's voice and does the Father's will. Jesus is involved in a relationship with a personal God. Jesus' oneness with the Father (Jn 10:30) does not entail the dissolution of Jesus or the Father as persons. They are one in essence and substance; yet this oneness is not a featureless uniformity of Being (impersonal monism) but a living relationship. This can be seen throughout John's account of Jesus' long prayer to the Father before his crucifixion. Jesus says that the Father glorifies the Son and the Son glorifies the Father (Jn 17:4-5). This is the language of reciprocal communion, not monistic union. An "egoless supreme identity" is for Jesus a contradiction in terms and a devastating diminution of deity.

The ring of exclusivity is also heard in Jesus' warning:

Enter through the narrow gate. For wide is the gate and broad is the road that leads to destruction, and many enter through it. But small is the gate and narrow the road that leads to life, and only a few find it. (Mt 7:13-14)

Jesus claimed that he himself was the door to life: "I tell you the truth, I am the gate for the sheep. All who ever came before me were thieves and robbers, but the sheep did not listen to them. I am the gate; whoever enters through me will be saved" (Jn 10:7-9).

The Gospel of John catalogs several other of Jesus' "I am" statements that accentuate his uniqueness: "I am the bread of life" (6:48) and "I am the living bread that came down from heaven. If anyone eats of this bread, he will live forever. This bread is my flesh, which I will give for the life of the world" (6:51). "I am the light of the world. Whoever follows me will never walk in darkness, but will have the light of life" (8:12). "I am the good shepherd. The good shepherd lays down his life for the sheep" (10:11). "I am the resurrection and the life. He who believes in me will live, even though he dies" (11:25).[24]

We could rightly say that Jesus' teaching is unequivocally self-centered but without being selfish; for "the good shepherd lays down his life for the sheep" (Jn 10:11). Although John White believes that "the proper attitude toward [Jesus] is reverence, not worship,"[25] Jesus' words and actions provoked others to worship him no less than nine times. Jesus never rebuked the worshipers by scolding them as unenlightened sycophants. Here is the response of his disciples after seeing Jesus walk on water: "Then those who were in the boat worshiped him, saying, 'Truly you are the Son of God' " (Mt 14:33).[26]

Jesus does not transcend his ego to merge with the "egoless supreme identity." Nor does he bid his followers to align themselves with Divinity-in-General. He accepts their worship. Yes, he declares a kingdom breaking forth in power, but he is the ultimate source of that kingdom's power. He is the Christ.

Jesus the Christ

In the last chapter we discussed the term *Christ* as a title given to Jesus at his birth, but it is crucial to witness how it functioned in his ministry.

Christ is the Greek equivalent of the Hebrew word *Messiah*. So whenever Jesus is called "the Christ" he is being referred to as the Messiah. He himself openly admitted this to the Samaritan woman who said to him, " 'I know that Messiah (called Christ) is coming. When he comes, he will explain everything to us.' Then Jesus declared, 'I who speak to you am he' " (Jn 4:25-26). Jesus likewise admitted to being the Christ when he said to his disciples, "I tell you the truth, anyone who gives you a cup of water in my name because you belong to Christ will certainly not lose his reward" (Mk 9:41). He also taught his disciples, "You have one Teacher, the Christ" (Mt 23:10). He referred to himself as "Jesus Christ" when praying to the Father (Jn 17:3).

Originally in the Old Testament *Messiah* could refer to various people specially "anointed" by God for specific tasks to be performed in his service. But through various prophecies the concept was narrowed down to the person of the Messiah, one uniquely equipped by God for a divine mission.

Several strands made up the messianic expectation of the Old Testament. One was political. The Messiah would rule on David's throne in righteousness. Another was apocalyptic: the Son of Man would come from heaven to judge evil. The last was that of the suffering servant who bears the sin of his people.[27]

Jesus of Nazareth fulfilled all three expectations, although in ways not expected by many. In so doing he fulfilled scores of prophecies concerning his life, teaching, death and resurrection, only a few of which we will touch on.[28] He did not set up an earthly political rule but, nevertheless, viewed himself as King. He did not bring apocalyptic judgment at his Incarnation but promised that it will come when he returns at the end of the age. As the suffering servant, the Christ must go to the cross.

The Death of Christ

When Jesus explained to the disciples that he must go to Jerusalem to suffer many things, be killed and be raised to life on the third day, Peter cried out, "Never, Lord! This shall never happen to you!" (Mt 16:22). The same Peter who had boldly affirmed only a few moments earlier that Jesus was "the Christ, the Son of the living God" (v. 16) could not accept that the Christ was going to his death. Jesus responded to Peter, "Get behind me, Satan! You are a stumbling block to me; you do not have in mind the things of God, but the things of men" (v. 23).

The same devil who in the wilderness tempted the Christ to desert his divine mission was again insinuating compromise. Everything was at stake. The devil had a vested interest in a detour around the cross.

We have seen that on several occasions crowds wanted to stone him, but Jesus narrowly escaped because the time had not yet come for his death. Opposition from the religious establishment was building and would soon reach a critical point. Jesus faced his crucifixion not as an accident or a mistake, but as an inexorable part of his voluntary mission. B. B. Warfield has aptly commented that:

> He came into the world to die, and every stage of the road that led to this issue was determined not for Him but by Him: He was never the victim but always the Master of circumstance, and pursued His pathway from the beginning to the end, not merely in full knowledge from the start of all its turns and twists up to its bitter conclusion, but in complete control of them and of it.[29]

Before the cross Jesus was transfigured before his disciples as a foretaste of his later glory (see Rev 1:12-18). Jesus took Peter, James and John to a high mountain where Jesus "was transfigured before them. His face shone like the sun, and his clothes became as white as the light" (Mt 17:2). Then Moses and Elijah appeared and spoke with Jesus. While an astonished Peter was trying to pull himself together "a bright cloud enveloped them, and a voice from the cloud said, 'This is my Son, whom I love; with him I am well pleased. Listen to him!' " (vv. 5).

Jesus comforted his frightened disciples saying, "Get up. Don't be afraid" (v. 7). When they looked up they saw only Jesus, who then asked them to be quiet about the event until "the Son of Man has been raised from the dead" (v. 9). Yet Jesus also explained that "the Son of man is going to suffer at their hands," the same hands of those who killed John the Baptist (vv. 12-13).

Again we face the uniqueness of Jesus. Only *he* is transfigured before them, not Moses or Elijah. The voice from heaven confers on him alone unique authority and bids the disciples to "listen to him," which is reminiscent of the endorsement at Jesus' baptism. Only Jesus remains when Moses and Elijah vanish.[30] Yet Jesus must suffer and die.

As the hour approached Jesus becomes more explicit:

We are going up to Jerusalem, and the Son of Man will be betrayed to the chief priests and the teachers of the law. They will condemn him to death and will turn him over to the Gentiles to be mocked and flogged and crucified. On the third day he will be raised to life! (Mt 20:18-19)

We will not give all the details of the last days of Jesus' life, although it is important to remember that the Gospel accounts devote a high percentage of the narrative to this period of time. Herbert Lockyer observed that "one-third of Matthew, one-third of Mark, one-fourth of Luke, and one-half of John are devoted to the last hours of Jesus. Thus about one-third of the material making up the four gospels relates to the last week of Jesus."[31] I commend the reader to the Gospels themselves to understand and feel the full force of the narratives. We will sample a few key events and statements to better understand the death of Jesus in light of New Age teachings about him.

The impending death of Jesus harmonizes with his sense of mission. We noted that he said, referring to himself, "The good shepherd lays down his life for the sheep" (Jn 10:11). When explaining that his disciples should not jockey for power and prestige, but rather serve their neighbors, Jesus used himself as the supreme example by saying "the Son of Man did not come to be served, but to serve, and to give his life as a ransom for many" (Mt 20:28). Jesus would give his life

for many. He also said, "For the Son of man came to seek and to save
what was lost" (Lk 19:10). He must die in order to save them.

Jesus understood this, and even while facing betrayal by Judas he
affirmed, "The Son of Man will go just as it is written about him" (Mk
14:21). During the Last Supper Jesus illustrated the meaning of his
death through the common meal, saying of the bread which he broke,
"Take and eat; this is my body" (Mt 26:26). He then took the cup, gave
thanks and gave it to his disciples, saying, "Drink from it, all of you.
This is my blood of the covenant, which is poured out for many for
the forgiveness of sins" (vv. 27-28).

Shortly before Jesus' betrayal, he was in great agony over his coming death and prayed, "Abba, Father, everything is possible for you.
Take this cup from me. Yet not what I will, but what you will" (Mk
14:36). Soon after this, when Jesus was arrested, someone tried to
protect him by the sword. Jesus responded by rebuking the deed and
saying, "Do you think I cannot call on my Father, and he will at once
put at my disposal more than twelve legions of angels? But how then
would the Scriptures be fulfilled that say it must happen in this way?"
(Mt 26:53-54).

Although he could have summoned angelic deliverance, he chose
the cross.

Later the Jewish religious leaders said, "Tell us if you are the Christ,
the Son of God." Jesus replied, "Yes, it is as you say. But I say to all
of you: In the future you will see the Son of Man sitting at the right
hand of the Mighty One and coming on the clouds of heaven" (Mt
26:63-64). At this the high priest ripped his clothes, evidencing his
response to the blasphemy of someone equating himself with God in
this way. Jesus was then beaten and handed over to the Roman political officials, who further beat him, taunted him, spit upon him . . .
and had him crucified.

Yet New Age teaching either denies that Jesus was crucified and
killed or denies that his death was for the forgiveness of sin. The
pulsating heart of the Gospel accounts is surgically removed by New
Age theology.

According to Mark L. and Elizabeth Clare Prophet, "The doctrine of vicarious atonement for sin through the crucifixion of Jesus Christ is simply not what Jesus taught." This and other such pronouncements make up what they call "the lost teachings of Jesus."[32] In another book they refer to the idea of a blood sacrifice of Jesus as "an erroneous doctrine" that is "a remnant of pagan rite long refuted by the Word of the Lord" and never taught by Jesus himself.[33]

Da Free John agrees and says that Jesus "did not represent himself as a mediator or substitute sacrifice, since he did not presume any inherent separation or obstruction between creatures . . . and the Spiritual Divine."[34]

In contrast, the Gospel stories are charged with the idea of sacrifice, as we have shown and as we will further demonstrate.

Although crucifixion was the most gruesome form of execution in the ancient world, the Gospel writers give us few details of the act. We find that Jesus was savagely scourged before being crucified, and he carried the cross part way to Golgotha before another man was constrained to shoulder it the rest of the way (Jn 19:17; Mk 15:21). Jesus was nailed between two common criminals.

In the midst of the suffering of the cross, Jesus cried, "Father, forgive them, for they do not know what they are doing" (Lk 23:34). Jesus loved his enemies, even to the end, but didn't deny their need for divine forgiveness.

Jesus' last words on the cross were, "My God, my God, why have you forsaken me?" (Mk 15:34). After this:

> With a loud cry, Jesus breathed his last. The curtain of the temple was torn in two from top to bottom. And when the centurion, who stood there in front of Jesus, heard his cry and saw how he died, he said, "Surely this man was the Son of God!" (vv. 37-39)

Jesus' last gasp compelled belief in him.

The crucifixion and its meaning was revealed hundreds of years before the fact. Jesus himself often quoted from Isaiah 53 which said of the Messiah: "he poured out his soul to death, and was numbered with the transgressors; yet he bore the sin of many, and made intercession for the transgressors" (Is 53:12). It was fulfilled to the letter.

Isaiah speaks of one "despised and rejected by men; a man of sorrows, and acquainted with grief" (v. 3). "Surely he has borne our griefs and carried our sorrows; yet we esteemed him stricken, smitten by God, and afflicted. But he was wounded for our transgressions, he was bruised for our iniquities; upon him was the chastisement that made us whole, and with his stripes we are healed" (vv. 4-5). Although "all we like sheep have gone astray, . . . the Lord has laid on him the iniquity of us all" (v. 6). He was "like a lamb" led to the slaughter (v. 7), for he was "stricken for the transgression of my people" (v. 8). And although "he had done no violence nor was any deceit in his mouth" (v. 9), the Lord "makes himself an offering for sin" (v. 10). Isaiah concludes the chapter by saying, "Yet he bore the sin of many, and made intercession for the transgressors" (v. 12).

It takes little imagination to see Jesus as the Christ who is the suffering servant. But the suffering servant is also the risen Lord.

The Resurrection of Jesus

After Jesus' death on the cross he was buried in a tomb donated by Joseph of Arimathea. His disciples were crushed and left desolate, despite the fact that Jesus had said he would rise from the dead on the third day.

Then two women followers of Jesus reported that the tomb was empty. Although first met with disbelief, this report was confirmed by several disciples. Jesus himself then appeared to the disciples several times over a forty-day period as the Lord of Life. On one occasion Jesus demonstrated the tangible reality of his resurrected body by saying, "Look at my hands and my feet. It is I myself! Touch me and see; a ghost does not have flesh and bones, as you see I have" (Lk 24:39).

The resurrected Jesus elicited the faith of his doubting disciple Thomas when he appeared and said, "Put your finger here; see my hands. Reach out your hand and put it into my side. Stop doubting and believe" (Jn 20:27). Thomas then exclaimed, "My Lord and my God!" (v. 28). Jesus was demonstrated to be God in the flesh, crucified as the Christ had to be, but now risen from the dead as Lord.

The resurrected Jesus said, "This is what is written: The Christ will suffer and rise from the dead on the third day, and repentance and forgiveness of sins will be preached in his name to all nations" (Lk 24:46-47). On this basis did Christianity permeate the ancient world.[35]

The Jesus of the Gospels and More

The Jesus of Christianity is the Jesus of the four Gospels. He is a man of wisdom, power and compassion. Yet he is more than a man. He is God in human form.

The prologue to John's Gospel declares:

In the beginning was the Word, and the Word was with God, and the Word was God. He was with God in the beginning.

Through him all things were made; without him nothing was made that has been made. In him was life, and that life was the light of men. The light shines in the darkness, but the darkness has not understood it. (Jn 1:1-5)

Later John states that the Word has invaded human history:

The Word became flesh and made his dwelling among us. We have seen his glory, the glory of the One and Only, who came from the Father, full of grace and truth. (v. 14)

The word John uses for "Word" is the Greek *Logos*. While the term has been used in Greek philosophy to mean the *impersonal* ordering principle of the universe, John uses it to refer to the *personal* God of the universe who has taken on human nature to dispel the darkness of sin. (We will address the significance of the *Logos* in more depth in chapter ten.)

This Jesus is not a man who attained an impersonal Christ consciousness but is the Christ to whom the Old Testament pointed with great expectation. He is the suffering servant who declares he will die so that others may live free from sin and guilt. He is the resurrected one who commissions his followers to proclaim the gospel in *his name*.

Jesus highlighted his uniqueness and supremacy when he affirmed that:

All authority in heaven and on earth has been given to me. Therefore go and make disciples of all nations, baptizing them in the
name of the Father and of the Son and of the Holy Spirit, and
teaching them to obey everything I have commanded you. And
surely I am with you always, to the very end of the age. (Mt 28:18-
20)

Jesus has all authority as the one and only Christ. He bids his disciples
to disciple all nations according to his Word. He is with them always.
He has no successors and no equals.

Besides a reference to Isaiah 53, this chapter has only referred to the
Gospels for testimony concerning Jesus. The rest of the New Testament abundantly confirms what is said in the Gospels and further
elaborates on the meaning of Jesus and his mission. Just a few references will suffice for now (although we will look at other biblical
references throughout the rest of the book).

After Jesus' ascension Peter became a great preacher and the "fisher
of men" that Jesus had promised he would be. When standing before
the rulers and elders of the Jews in Jerusalem, Peter proclaimed, "Salvation is found in no one else, for there is no other name under heaven
given to men by which we must be saved" (Acts 4:12). Peter covers
all the bases: Salvation is found only in Jesus; he is the only name in
all creation through whom anyone can be saved.

The apostle John in his letter to the early church writes, "That which
was from the beginning, which we have heard, which we have seen
with our eyes, which we have looked at and our hands have touched—
this we proclaim concerning the Word of life" (1 Jn 1:1). He later says,
"He is the atoning sacrifice for our sins, and not only for ours but also
for the sins of the whole world. We know that we have come to know
him if we obey his commands" (2:2-3). He states that Jesus "appeared
so that he might take away our sins. And in him is no sin" (3:5). John
also notes triumphantly, "The reason the Son of God appeared was
to destroy the devil's work" (3:8).

The apostle Paul, not one of the original disciples but one later
transformed by Jesus, also accentuates the uniqueness and supremacy

of Jesus. "For there is one God and one mediator between God and men, the man Christ Jesus, who gave himself as a ransom for all men" (1 Tim 2:5-6).

According to the New Testament, *the religion of Jesus* is also *the religion about Jesus*. Jesus encouraged belief in him when he said, "The work of God is this: to believe in the one he has sent" (Jn 6:29; cf. Jn 3:16). He is the center of redemption who makes exclusive claims and backs them up with his credentials as a teacher, wonder-worker, healer, man of compassion, suffering servant and risen Lord. For this reason the apostle John describes a heavenly worship service centered on the ascended Jesus in which "ten thousand times ten thousand" angels sing:

Worthy is the Lamb, who was slain,

to receive power and wealth and wisdom
and strength

and honor and glory and praise! (Rev 5:12)

Although New Age proponents may praise Jesus, they do not bow in worship. John White maintains that Jesus must not be put on a pedestal. Yet we find biblical warrant that he was not placed upon a pedestal by any human being. He is rightfully on the pedestal of the universe but only through lowering himself by becoming the servant of all, the lamb who was willing to be sacrificed on the cross to give life to those who come to him in faith.[36] The apostle Paul writes that Christ Jesus,

Who, being in very nature God,

did not consider equality with God
something to be grasped,

but made himself nothing, taking the very
nature of a servant,

being made in human likeness.

And being found in appearance as a man, he
humbled himself

and became obedient to death—
even death on a cross!

Therefore God exalted him to the highest place
and gave him the name that is above every name,
that at the name of Jesus every knee should bow,
in heaven and on earth and under the earth,
and every tongue confess that Jesus Christ is Lord,
to the glory of God the Father. (Phil 2:6-11; cf. Is 45:23)

As we conclude our investigation of the New Testament's presentation of Jesus, it is important to be open to what this material in fact claims. The best way to do this is simply to read the material from beginning to end without attempting to superimpose interpretations. Randall Baer, an ex-New Age expert in crystals, comments that "the more of the Bible I read, especially the Gospels, the more I saw the teachings of Jesus plainly were at variance with the New Age philosophy at many key points."[37] These points of variance include: the sinful nature of humanity (as opposed to the divinity of humanity), our need for redemption through Jesus Christ (as opposed to needing no redemption from outside ourselves), the final judgment (as opposed to being one's own judge and denying hell) and the personal and visible Second Coming (as opposed to other "Christs" or the "Christ-consciousness").[38] This revelation was the key to Baer exiting the New Age and embracing the Jesus of the New Testament.

In the next chapters we will find challenges to the orthodox Jesus issued from revisionist claims that the historical basis for our understanding of Jesus is defective. The first challenge to the religion about Jesus came from the Gnostics, who claimed to transcend *faith* in Christ by *knowing* themselves to be Christ. To them we now turn.

Notes

[1]John White, "Jesus and the Idea of a New Age," *Quest,* Summer 1989, p. 17, emphasis his.

[2]Ibid.

[3]Da Free John, *The Four Fundamental Questions* (Clearlake Highlands, Calif.: The Dawn Horse Press, 1980), p. 54. John has a penchant for changing his name. The last I saw he was going by Love Free Ananda or Heart Master Da.

[4]Da Free John, "Pharisaical Christianity and the Radically Universal Message of Jesus," *The Laughing Man* 3, no. 2, p. 63.

[5]Da Free John, *Four Fundamental,* p.54.

[6]See David Wells, *The Person of Christ* (Westchester, Ill.: Crossway Books, 1984), pp. 41-42.

[7]A. E. Harvey, *Jesus and the Constraints of History* (Philadelphia: Westminster, 1982), p. 110. For a defense of the miraculous as philosophically and historically credible, see Lewis, *Miracles,* and Norman Geisler, *Miracles and Modern Thought* (Grand Rapids, Mich.: Zondervan, 1982).

[8]This figure probably does not count women and children.

[9]For other nature miracles, see Matthew 17:24-27; 21:18-22; Mark 11:12-14, 20-25.

[10]See Os Guinness, *The Dust of Death* (Downers Grove, Ill.: InterVarsity Press, 1975), pp. 384-85.

[11]On Jesus' prayer life, see Margaret Magdalen, *Jesus: Man of Prayer* (Downers Grove, Ill: InterVarsity Press, 1987).

[12]This is shown by a journal of recent origin called *The Shaman's Drum: A Journal of Experiential Shamanism.*

[13]Michael Harner, *The Way of the Shaman* (New York: Bantam, 1982), pp. 25-26.

[14]The Gospels record a few cases where Jesus' healing involves spittle or mud. But the use of these elements is secondary to Jesus' personal power. They do not indicate ritual magic or ceremony. In recent years Morton Smith has written several controversial books arguing that Jesus should be viewed as a magician. For a critique of his claim that there was a "secret gospel of Mark" indicating Jesus as a magician, see F. F. Bruce, *The Canon of Scripture* (Downers Grove, Ill: InterVarsity Press), pp. 298-315, and Joseph A. Fitzmayer, "How to Exploit a Secret Gospel," *America,* June 23, 1973, pp. 570-72. Concerning Smith's other claims see Howard Clark Kee, *Miracle in the Early Christian World* (New Haven: Yale University Press, 1983), pp. 211-12.

[15]E. Stanley Jones, *The Christ of the Indian Road* (New York: Grosset and Dunlap, 1925), p. 191.

[16]See John Stott, *Basic Christianity* (Downers Grove, Ill.: InterVarsity Press, 1976), p. 31.

[17]For the theological significance of Jesus' title as "the Son of Man" and for his other titles, see Bernard Ramm, *An Evangelical Christology,* pp. 107-16, and David Wells, *The Person of Christ* (Westchester, Ill.: Crossway, 1984), pp. 67-81.

[18]Statements such as this slam the door shut on reincarnation, a teaching often attributed to Jesus by reincarnationists. Jesus spoke of one final Judgment, not of many incarnations, nor of any intervening lifetimes before the Last Day. This will be taken up in more detail in the last chapter.

[19]B. B. Warfield's comments from *The Lord of Glory* are illuminating on this: "Speaking in the most solemn manner, he not only presents himself as the Son, as the sole source of knowledge of God . . . but places himself in a position, not of equality merely, but of absolute reciprocity and interpenetration of knowledge of the Father, as if the being of the Son were so immense that only God could know it thoroughly, and knowledge of the Son so unlimited that he could know God to perfection." Quoted in Herbert Lockyer, *Everything Jesus Taught* (San Francisco, Calif.: Harper and Row, 1984), p. 20.

[20]William Lane Craig, *Apologetics: An Introduction* (Chicago: Moody Press, 1984), p. 162, emphasis his. See also Gordon Clark, *The Trinity* (Jefferson, Md.: The Trinity Foundation, 1985), p. 14.

[21]Ravi Ravindra, "The Gospel as Yoga," *Parabola,* May 1988, pp. 41-42.

[22]Ibid., p. 42.

[23]On the idea of Jesus as "God in focus," see J. B. Phillips, *Your God Is Too Small* (New York: Macmillan, 1979), pp. 63-66.

[24]It has been argued that Jesus' "I am" statements were spoken such that they were claims to deity as well. See Ethelbert Stauffer, *Jesus and His Story* (New York: Alfred A. Knopf, 1974), pp. 174-95.

[25]White, p. 18.

[26]The other references in the Gospels to worshiping Jesus are: Matthew 8:2; 9:18; 15:25; 20:20; 28:9, 17: Mark 5:6; John 9:38.

[27]See R. C. Sproul, *Who Is Jesus?* (Wheaton, Ill.: Tyndale House, 1988), pp. 23-32.

[28]For a careful, developed treatment of this, see John Ankerberg, John Weldon, Walter Kaiser, *The Case for Jesus the Messiah* (Chattanooga, Tenn.: The John Ankerberg Evangelistic Association, 1989).

[29]B. B. Warfield, *The Person and Work of Christ* (USA: Presbyterian and Reformed Publishing Company, 1950), p. 17.

[30]For a treatment of the significance of the Transfiguration, see Francis Schaeffer, *No Little People* (Downers Grove, Ill.: InterVarsity Press, 1977), pp. 193-209.

[31]Lockyer, p. 27.

[32]Mark L. Prophet and Elizabeth Clare Prophet, *The Lost Teachings of Jesus,* vol. 2 (Livingstone, Mont.: Summit University Press, 1986), p. 374.

[33]Mark Prophet and Elizabeth Clare Prophet, *Science of the Spoken Word* (Livingstone, Mont.: Summit University Press, 1984), pp. 86-87.

[34]Da Free John, "Pharisaical Christianity," p. 61.

[35]We will defend the historicity and explain the cosmic significance of the resurrection in chapter ten.

[36]For an excellent study of both the transcendence and condescension of Jesus Christ, see Jonathan Edwards, "The Excellency of Christ," in *The Puritan Sage* (New York: Library Publishers, 1953), pp. 326-32.

[37]Randall N. Baer, *Inside the New Age Nightmare* (Lafayette, La.: Huntington House, 1989), p. 61.

[38]Ibid.

Chapter 4
Jesus and Gnosis

*P*opular opinion often comes from obscure sources. Many conceptions about Jesus, now current and credible in New Age circles, are rooted in a movement of spiritual protest. Until recently, the Gnostic movement was the concern only of the specialized scholar or the occultist. Yet Gnosticism provides much of the form and color for the New Age portrait of Jesus as an illumined Illuminator who serves as a cosmic catalyst for others' awakening.

Many essentially Gnostic notions received wide attention through the sagacious persona of Joseph Campbell, in the television series and best-selling book *The Power of Myth*. For example, in discussing the idea that "God was in Christ," Campbell affirms that "the basic Gnostic and Buddhist idea is that it is true of you and me as well." Jesus was an enlightened example who "realized in himself that he and what he called the Father were one, and he lived out of that knowledge of the Christhood of his nature." According to Campbell, anyone can live out his or her Christ nature. Campbell noted that a priest who heard him make this point in a lecture called it "blasphemy."[1]

Gnosticism has come to mean just about anything. Calling someone a Gnostic can make the person either blush, beam or fume. Whether used as an epithet for heresy or spiritual snobbery, or as a compliment for spiritual knowledge and esotericism, Gnosticism remains a cornucopia of controversy.

This is doubly so when Gnosticism is brought into a discussion of Jesus of Nazareth. Begin to speak of "Christian Gnostics" and some will exclaim, "No way! That is a contradiction in terms. Heresy is not orthodoxy." Others will affirm, "No contradiction. Orthodoxy is the heresy. The Gnostics were edged out of mainstream Christianity for political purposes." Speak of the Gnostic Christ or the Gnostic Gospels, and an ancient debate is moved to the theological front burner.

Gnosticism as a philosophy refers to a related body of teachings stressing the acquisition of "Gnosis," or inner knowledge. The knowledge sought is not strictly intellectual, but mystical; not merely a detached knowledge of or about something, but a knowing by acquaintance or participation. This Gnosis is the inner and esoteric mystical knowledge of ultimate reality. It discloses the spark of divinity within, thought to be obscured by ignorance, convention and mere exoteric religiosity.

This knowledge is not considered to be the possession of the masses, but of the Gnostics, the Knowers, who are privy to its benefits. While the orthodox may exult in the exoteric religious trappings that stress dogmatic *belief* and prescribed behavior, the Gnostic few pierce through the surface to the esoteric spiritual *knowledge* of God. The Gnostics claim the orthodox mistake the shell for the core; the orthodox claim the Gnostics dive past the true core into a nonexistent one of their own esoteric invention.

To adjudicate this ancient acrimony requires that we examine Gnosticism's perennial allure, expose its philosophical foundations, size up its historical claims and square off the Gnostic Jesus with the figure who sustains the New Testament.

Gnosticism: Ancient and Modern

Gnosticism is experiencing something of a revival, despite its historical status within Christianity as a vanquished Christian heresy. The magazine *Gnosis*, which bills itself as a "journal of western inner traditions," began publication in 1985 with a circulation of 2,500. As of March 1990, it sported a circulation of 11,000. *Gnosis* regularly runs articles on Gnosticism and Gnostic themes, such as "Valentinus: A Gnostic for All Seasons." The editor, Jay Kinney, is reported to have dabbled in "Eastern mysticism, yoga and assorted gurus" before he returned to a Christianity "far more esoteric than the midwestern Methodist church in which he was raised."[2] Apparently for Mr. Kinney, a "Christian Gnostic" is no contradiction in terms.

Some have even created institutional forms of this ancient religion. In Palo Alto, priestess Bishop Rosamonde Miller officiates at the weekly gatherings of Ecclesia Gnostica Mysteriorum (Church of Gnostic Mysteries) as she has done for the last eleven years. The chapel holds forty to sixty participants each Sunday and includes Gnostic readings in its liturgy.[3] Miller says she knows of twelve organizationally unrelated Gnostic churches throughout the world.[4] Stephen Hoeller, a frequent contributor to *Gnosis*, who since 1967 has been a bishop of Ecclesia Gnostica in Los Angeles, notes that "gnostic churches . . . have sprung up in recent years in increasing numbers."[5] He refers to an established tradition of "wandering bishops" who retain allegiance to the symbolic and ritual form of orthodox Christianity while reinterpreting its essential content.[6]

Of course these exotic-sounding enclaves of the esoteric are minuscule when compared to historic Christian denominations. But the real challenge of Gnosticism is not so much organizational as intellectual. Gnosticism in its various forms has often appealed to the alienated intellectuals who yearn for spiritual experience outside the bounds of the ordinary. Historian Patrick Henry observes that "the appeal of

Gnosticism . . . is the appeal to a person's sense of superiority to the world. It is not I who am the victim of the Fall, of original sin, but the world itself. We come trailing clouds of glory—into a polluted environment."[7] The Swiss psychologist Carl Jung, a constant source of inspiration for the New Age, did much to introduce Gnosticism to the modern world by viewing it as kind of proto-depth psychology, a key to psychological interpretation. According to Stephen Hoeller, an interpreter of Jung and author of *The Gnostic Jung:*

> It was Jung's contention that Christianity and Western culture have suffered grievously because of the repression of the Gnostic approach to religion, and it was his hope that in time this approach would be reincorporated in our culture, our Western spirituality.[8]

In his *Psychological Types,* Jung praised "the intellectual content of Gnosis" as "vastly superior" to the orthodox church. He also affirmed that "in light of our present mental development [Gnosticism] has not lost but considerably gained in value."[9] In 1916, after experiencing some bizarre paranormal events, Jung wrote in three nights a mystical piece called *The Seven Sermons to the Dead,* which he ascribed to Basilides, a Gnostic teacher of the second century in Alexandria. In his autobiography Jung states:

> I can say that I have never lost touch with my initial experiences. All my works, all my creative activity, has come from those initial fantasies and dreams. . . . Everything that I accomplished in later life was already contained in them, although at first only in the form of emotions and images.[10]

A variety of esoterically oriented groups have roots in gnostic soil. Madame Helena P. Blavatsky, who founded Theosophy in 1875, viewed the Gnostics as precursors of modern occult movements and hailed them for preserving an inner teaching lost to orthodoxy.[11] Theosophy and its various and varying spin-offs, such as Rudolph Steiner's Anthroposophy, Alice Bailey's Arcane School, the I Am movement, and the Church Universal and Triumphant all draw water from this same well, as do various other esoteric groups like the Rosicrucians. These groups share an emphasis on esoteric teaching, the hidden divinity of humanity and contact with non-material higher beings called masters or adepts.

A four-part documentary called *The Gnostics* was released in mid-1989 and was shown in one-day screenings across the country. Presented as "the spiritual drama-documentary narrative of the Gnostic heresy," the ambitious series charted the history of Gnosticism through dramatizations and interviews with world-renowned scholars on Gnosticism, such as Gilles Quispel, Hans Jonas and Elaine Pagels. The third episode was revealingly entitled "The Divinity of Man."

A review of the series in a New-Age-oriented journal gets into the heart of the revived Gnostic-orthodox debate, claiming that the "Gnostic Gospels . . . were written around the same time as the gospels of the New Testament but . . . were purposely left out."[12] The review refers to one of the most sensational and significant archaeological finds of the twentieth century, a discovery seen by some as overthrowing the orthodox view of Jesus and Christianity forever.

Gold in the Jar

In December of 1945, while digging for soil to fertilize his crops, an Arab peasant named Muhammad 'Ali found a red earthenware jar near Nag Hammadi, a city in upper Egypt. His fear of uncorking an evil spirit was shortly overcome by the hope of finding gold within. What was found has been for hundreds of scholars far more precious than gold. Inside the jar were thirteen leather-bound papyrus books (codices), dating from approximately AD 350. Although several of the texts were burned or thrown out, fifty-two texts were eventually recovered through many years of intrigue involving illegal sales, violence, smuggling and academic rivalry.[13]

Some of the texts found near Nag Hammadi were first published singly or in small collections, but the complete collection was not made available in a popular format in English until 1977. It was released as *The Nag Hammadi Library* and was reissued in revised form in 1988.

These documents are thought by some to have been the property of a monastery that existed near the middle of the fourth century. The arid climate of Egypt preserved these long-lost texts from corruption. Their burial protected them from confiscation. The collection contains several kinds of documents, most of which are recognized as Gnostic. Although many of the documents had been referred to and denounced in the writings of early church theologians such as Justin Martyr and Irenaeus, most of the texts themselves had been thought to be extinct. So, as Elaine Pagels put it in her best-selling book *The Gnostic Gospels,* "Now for the first time, we have the opportunity to find out about the earliest Christian heresy; for the first time, the heretics can speak for themselves."[14]

Pagels's book, winner of the National Book Critics Circle Award, arguably did more than any other effort to ingratiate the Gnostics to modern Americans. She made them accessible and even likeable. Her scholarly expertise (she was one of the first to translate the Nag Hammadi texts from Coptic into English), coupled with her ability to relate an ancient religion to contemporary concerns, made for a compelling combination in the minds of many. Her central thesis was simple: Gnosticism should be considered at least as legitimate as orthodox Christianity because the "heresy" was simply a competing strain of early Christianity. Yet we find that the Nag Hammadi texts present a Jesus at extreme odds with the one found in the Gospels.

Although the scholarly world has jumped at the opportunity to inspect, critique and compare the Nag Hammadi texts, controversy has raged over their dating, proper interpretation and relationship to Christianity. Neither is there scholarly agreement on the origins of Gnosticism, called "the Gnostic problem."[15] Yet we need not settle these disputes in order to delve into the heart of the matter: the biblical versus the Gnostic view of Jesus. But before discussing this we need a short briefing on Gnosis.

The Gnostic Message
Gnosticism in general, and the material from Nag Hammadi in particular, presents a spectrum of beliefs, although a central philosophical

core is roughly discernible, a core scholar Kurt Rudolph calls "the central myth."[16] Gnosticism teaches that something is desperately wrong with the universe and then delineates the means to explain and rectify the situation.

The universe, as presently constituted, is not good. Nor was it created by an all-good God. Rather, a lesser god, or demiurge (as he is sometimes called), fashioned the world in ignorance. The *Gospel of Philip* says, "The world came about through a mistake. For he who created it wanted to create it imperishable and immortal. He fell short of attaining his desire."[17] The origin of the demiurge, or offending creator, is variously explained. But the upshot is that some pre-cosmic disruption in the chain of beings emanating from the unknowable Father God resulted in the "fallout" of a substandard deity with less than impeccable credentials. The result was a material cosmos soaked with ignorance, pain, decay and death—a botched job, to be sure. This deity, nevertheless, despotically demands worship and even pretentiously proclaims his supremacy as the one true God.

This creator god is not the ultimate reality but, rather, a degeneration of the unknown and unknowable fullness of Being (or pleroma). Yet human beings, or at least some of them, are in the position potentially to transcend their imposed limitations, even if the cosmic deck is stacked against them. Locked within the material shell of the human race is the spark of this highest spiritual reality, which the creator accidently infused into humanity at their creation—on the order of a drunken jeweler who accidently mixes gold dust into junk metal. Simply put, spirit is good and desirable; matter is evil and detestable.

If this spark is fanned into flame, it can liberate humans from the maddening matrix of matter and the demands of its obtuse originator. What has devolved from perfection can ultimately evolve back into perfection through a process of self-discovery. This escape of the divine spark from its incarceration in the material can even be understood as the salvation of the deity itself, who wrestles free from ignorance and the domination of dark forces to ascend back to the highest level.[18]

Into this basic structure enters the idea of Jesus as a redeemer of those ensconced in materiality. He comes as one descended from the spiritual realm with a message of self-redemption. The body of Gnostic literature, which is wider than the Nag Hammadi texts, presents various views of this Redeemer figure.[19] There are, in fact, differing schools of Gnosticism with differing Christologies. Nevertheless a basic image emerges.

The Christ comes from the higher levels of intermediary beings (called aeons) not as a sacrifice for sin but as a Revealer, an emissary from error-free environs. He is not the personal agent of the Father-Creator revealed in the Old Testament. (That metaphysically disheveled deity is what got the universe into such a royal mess in the first place.) Rather Christ has descended from a more exalted level to be a catalyst for igniting the Gnosis latent within the ignorant. He gives a metaphysical assist to underachieving deities (that is, humans) rather than granting ethical restoration to God's erring creatures through the crucifixion and resurrection.

Nag Hammadi Unveiled

By inspecting a few of the Nag Hammadi texts, we encounter Gnosticism in Christian guise: Jesus dispenses Gnosis in order to awaken those trapped in ignorance; the body is a prison, the spirit alone is good; and salvation comes by discovering the "kingdom of God" within the Self.

One of the first Nag Hammadi texts to be extricated out of Egypt and translated into Western tongues was the *Gospel According to Thomas,* which is comprised of one hundred and fourteen sayings of Jesus. Although scholars do not believe it was actually written by the apostle Thomas, it has received the lion's share of scholarly attention. The sayings of Jesus are given minimal narrative setting, are largely not thematically arranged[20] and have a cryptic, epigrammatic bite to them. Although Thomas does not articulate every aspect of a full-blown Gnostic system, some of the teachings attributed to Jesus fit the Gnostic pattern. (Other sayings closely parallel or duplicate material found in the synoptic Gospels.)

The text begins by saying, "These are the secret sayings which the living Jesus spoke and which Didymos Judas Thomas wrote down. And he said, 'Whoever finds the interpretation of these sayings will not experience death.' "[21] Already we find the emphasis on secret knowledge (Gnosis) as redemptive. A comparison with a similar sounding text in John's Gospel reveals Thomas's Gnostic difference. In John, Jesus says, "I tell you the truth, if anyone keeps my word, he will never see death" (Jn 8:51). F. F. Bruce points out that John's intention is "essentially ethical, whereas that in the *Gospel of Thomas* is mainly intellectual."[22]

Unlike the accounts in the canonical Gospels, Jesus' crucifixion and resurrection are not narrated, and neither do any of the hundred and fourteen sayings directly refer to these events. Thomas's Jesus is a dispenser of wisdom, not the crucified and resurrected Lord.

Jesus speaks of the kingdom:

The kingdom is inside of you, and it is outside of you. When you come to know yourselves, then you will become known, and you will realize that it is you who are the sons of the living father. But if you will not know yourselves, you dwell in poverty and it is you who are that poverty.[23]

We noticed in the last chapter that the reference in Luke to "the kingdom is within you" concerned the timing of the kingdom, not the nature of humanity. In this case the emphasis is on self-knowledge as the key to the kingdom (although it mentions that the kingdom is "outside of you" as well).[24] The focus is not on faith in Jesus as the King incarnate, but on a realization that one is already a son of the living father.

This emphasis on self-knowledge as redemptive is also seen when, in saying #70, Jesus says, "That which you have will save you if you bring it forth from yourselves. That which you do not have within you [will] kill you if you do not have it within you."[25]

Other Gnostic documents center on the same theme. In the *Book of Thomas the Contender* Jesus speaks "secret words" concerning self-knowledge, "For he who has not known himself has known nothing, but he who has known himself has at the same time already achieved knowledge of the depth of the all." The expression "the all" can also be translated "the entirety."[26] Jesus then commends Thomas for beholding "what is obscure to men, that is, what they ignorantly stumble against."[27]

Pagels notes that many of the Gnostics "shared certain affinities with contemporary methods of exploring the self through psychotherapeutic techniques."[28] This includes the premises that, first, many people are unconscious of their true condition; and, second, "that the psyche bears within itself the potential for liberation or destruction."[29]

Gilles Quispel notes that for Valentinus, a Gnostic teacher of the second century, Christ is "the Paraclete from the Unknown who reveals . . . the discovery of the Self—the divine spark within you."[30] Stephen Hoeller says that in the Valentinian system "there is no need whatsoever for guilt, for repentance from so-called sin, neither is there a need for a blind belief in vicarious salvation by way of the death of Jesus."[31] Rather Jesus is savior in the sense of being a "spiritual maker of wholeness" who cures us of our sickness of ignorance.[32]

The *Gospel of Truth* describes the condition of ignorance:

Ignorance of the Father brought about anguish and terror; and the anguish grew like a fog, so that no one was able to see. For this reason, error became powerful.[33]

The heart of the human problem for the Gnostics is ignorance, sometimes called "sleep," "intoxication" or "blindness." In commenting on the *Gospel of Mary,* another Gnostic text, Karen L. King states, "The Savior argues, in effect, that sin is not a moral category, but a cosmological one; it is due to the improper mixing of the material and the physical."[34] This cosmological mix-up results in ignorance, but this ignorance is not necessarily terminal.

In the *Gospel of Thomas,* Jesus seems to disparage the physical world but affirms the value of the spirit: "If the flesh came into being because of the spirit, it is a wonder. But if spirit came into being because of the body, it is a wonder of wonders. Indeed I am amazed at how this great wealth has made its home in this poverty."[35] On the same theme Jesus says, "Whoever has come to understand the world has found (only) a corpse, and whoever has found a corpse is superior to the world."[36] The material world is lifeless; but one who sees it as such has transcended it.

The *First Apocalypse of James* goes even further. Here Jesus tells James that he will gain wisdom when he throws away the "the bond of flesh which encircles" him. Jesus continues, "Then you will reach Him-who-is. And you will no longer be James; you are the One-who-is."[37] Likewise, the *Gospel of Philip* speaks of an enlightened one who "is no longer a Christian but a Christ."[38]

And who is Jesus? He says, "It is I who am the light which is above them all. It is I who am the all. From me did the all come forth, and unto me did the all extend. Split a piece of wood and I am there. Lift up stone and you will find me there."[39]

Gnosticism on Crucifixion and Resurrection

Those Gnostic texts that discuss Jesus' crucifixion and resurrection display a variety of views that, nevertheless, reveal some common themes.

In the *Apocalypse of Peter,* Peter has a vision of two Jesuses on the cross, one being impaled and one laughing. The text then reads,

He whom you saw on the tree, glad and laughing, this is the living Jesus. But this one into whose hands and feet they drive the nails is the fleshly part which is the substitute being put to shame, the one who came into being in his likeness.

Later Jesus derides those who only see the crucified figure, and he "laughs at their lack of perception, knowing that they are born blind."[40]

In the *First Apocalypse of James,* James is consoled by a Jesus who says, "Never have I suffered in any way, nor have I been distressed. And this people has done me no harm."[41]

In the *Second Treatise of the Great Seth* Jesus says, "I did not die in reality, but in appearance." Those "in error and blindness . . . saw me; they punished me. It was another, their father, who drank the gall and vinegar; it was not I. They struck me with the reed; it was another, Simon, who bore the cross on his shoulder. I was rejoicing in the height over all. . . . And I was laughing at their ignorance."[42]

John Dart has discerned that the Gnostic stories of Jesus mocking his executors reverse the accounts in Matthew, Mark and Luke where the soldiers (Mk 15:20) and chief priests (Mk 15:20) mock Jesus.[43] In the biblical Gospels Jesus does not deride or mock his tormentors; on the contrary *while suffering from the cross,* he asks the Father to forgive those who had nailed him there.

In the teaching of Valentinus and his followers, the death of Jesus is movingly recounted, yet without the New Testament significance. Although the *Gospel of Truth* says that "his death is life for many," it views this life-giving in terms of imparting the Gnosis, not removing sin:

He was nailed to a tree (and) he became a fruit of knowledge of the Father. It did not, however, cause destruction because it was eaten, but to those who ate it gave (cause) to become glad in the discovery, and he discovered them in himself, and they discovered him in themselves.[44]

Pagels comments on this somewhat obscure text by saying that rather than viewing Christ's death as a sacrificial offering to atone for guilt and sin, this text "sees the crucifixion as the occasion for discovering the divine self within."[45]

In commenting on the *Treatise on the Resurrection,* Bentley Layton notes that in the Valentinian Gnostic theology "Jesus' suffering, traditionally understood to mean his real death on the cross, would not refer to biological death but simply the suffering sojourn of his spirit or soul on earth within the illusory realm of matter."[46]

Similarly, Gnostic accounts of Jesus' resurrection differ significantly from the New Testament record. A resurrection is enthusiastically affirmed, as in the *Treatise on the Resurrection,* which states, "Do not think the resurrection is an illusion. It is no illusion, but it is truth! Indeed it is more fitting to say that the world is an illusion rather than the resurrection."[47] Yet the nature of the post-resurrection appear-

ances differs from those in the biblical accounts. Jesus is disclosed
through spiritual visions rather than physical circumstances. According to Pagels, the Gnostics insisted that the resurrection "was not a
unique event in the past: instead, it symbolized how Christ's presence
could be experienced in the present."[48]

Unlike the biblical Gospels, many of the Gnostic documents begin
with resurrection accounts during which the exalted, non-bodily Jesus
imparts some secret wisdom to select disciples. According to the *Gospel of Mary,* Mary Magdalene goes into a trance and receives a vision
of the resurrected Jesus not available to the disciples. She strengthens
the grieving disciples, saying, "What is hidden from you I will proclaim to you"; she then proceeds to describe the ascent of the soul.[49]

The resurrected Jesus for the Gnostics is the spiritual Revealer who
imparts secret wisdom to the selected few, usually through visionary
appearances. The tone and content of Luke's account of Jesus' resurrection appearances to the apostles is a great distance from Gnostic
accounts: "After his suffering, he showed himself to these men and
gave many convincing proofs that he was alive" (Acts 1:3).

By now it should be apparent that the Jesus we observed in chapters
two and three has little in common with the Gnostic Jesus. He is
viewed as a redeemer in both cases, yet his nature as a redeemer and
the way of redemption diverge at crucial points. A review of these
points is in order before we investigate evidence concerning the authenticity of the Gnostic Jesus in the next chapter.

Did Christ Really Suffer and Die?

As in much modern New Age teaching, the Gnostics tended to divide
Jesus from the Christ. For Valentinus, Christ descended on Jesus at
his baptism and left before his death on the cross. Much of the burden
of the treatise *Against Heresies,* written by the early Christian theologian Irenaeus, was to affirm that Jesus was, is and always will be
the Christ. He says:

> The Gospel . . . knew no other son of man but Him who was of
> Mary, who also suffered; and no Christ who flew away from Jesus

before the passion; but Him who was born it knew as Jesus Christ the Son of God, and that this same suffered and rose again.[50] Irenaeus goes on to quote the Gospel of John's statement that "Jesus is the Christ" (Jn 20:31) against the notion that Jesus and Christ were "formed of two different substances" as the Gnostics taught.[51]

In dealing with the idea that Christ did not suffer on the cross for sin, Irenaeus argues that Christ would have never exhorted his disciples to take up the cross if he in fact was not to suffer on it himself, but instead fly away from it.[52]

For Irenaeus (the disciple of Polycarp, who himself was the disciple of the apostle John) the suffering of Jesus, the Christ, was paramount. It was indispensable to the apostolic "rule of faith" that Jesus Christ suffered on the cross to bring salvation to his people. While the various Gnostic schools saw Jesus as an Illuminator, Irenaeus, claiming to follow the apostles, knew him as crucified Savior. In his mind there was no divine spark in the human heart to rekindle; self-knowledge was not equal to God-knowledge. Rather, humans were stuck in sin and required a radical rescue operation. Because "it was not possible that the man . . . who had been destroyed through disobedience, could reform himself," the Son brought salvation by "descending from the Father, becoming incarnate, stooping low, even to death, and consummating the arranged plan of our salvation."[53]

In that "plan of our salvation," Jesus "bound the strong man [that is, Satan, Mt 12:29], and set free the weak, and endowed his handiwork with salvation by destroying sin. For he is a most holy and merciful Lord, and loves the human race."[54]

This harmonizes with the words of Polycarp, who was Irenaeus's teacher and "was instructed by the apostles and conversed with many who had seen Christ":[55]

Let us then continually persevere in our hope and the earnest of our righteousness, which is Jesus Christ, "who bore our sins in His own body on the tree," [1 Pet 2:24] "who did no sin, neither was guile found in his mouth" [1 Pet 2:22], but endured all things for us, that we might live in Him.[56]

Polycarp's mentor, the apostle John, said, "This is how we know what love is: Jesus Christ laid down his life for us" (1 Jn 3:16). He expands this: "This is love: not that we loved God, but that he loved us and sent his Son as an atoning sacrifice for our sins" (4:10).

The Gnostic Jesus is predominantly a dispenser of cosmic wisdom who discourses on abstruse themes like the spirit's fall into matter. Jesus of Nazareth certainly taught theology, but he dealt with the problem of pain and suffering in a far different way. He suffered for us, rather than escaping the cross or lecturing on the vanity of the body. E. Stanley Jones highlights this:

> He did not prove how pain and sorrow in the universe could be compatible with the love of God—he took on himself at the cross everything that spoke against the love of God, and through that pain and tragedy and sin showed the very love of God.[57]

The Matter of the Resurrection

For Gnosticism the inherent problem of humanity derives from the misuse of power by the ignorant Creator and the resulting entrapment of souls in matter. The Gnostic Jesus alerts us to this and helps rekindle the divine spark within. In the biblical teaching the problem is ethical; humans have sinned against a good Creator and are guilty before the throne of the universe.

For Gnosticism the world is bad, but the soul—when freed from its entrapments—is good. For Christianity the world was created good (Gen 1), but humans have fallen from innocence and purity through disobedience (Gen 3; Rom 3). Yet the message of the gospel is that the one who can rightly prosecute his creatures as guilty and worthy of punishment has deigned to visit them in the person of his only Son— not just to write up a firsthand damage report, but to rectify the situation through the cross and the resurrection.

In light of these differences the significance of Jesus' literal and physical resurrection should be clear. For the Gnostic who abhors matter and seeks release from its grim grip, the physical resurrection of Jesus would be anti-climactic if not absurd. Liberation does not come in corporeal packages; a material resurrection would be counter-productive and only recapitulate the original problem.

Jesus displays a positive attitude toward the creation throughout the Gospels. In telling his followers not to worry he says, "Look at the birds of the air; they do not sow or reap or store away in barns, and yet your heavenly Father feeds them" (Mt 6:26). And "Are not two sparrows sold for a penny? Yet not one of them will fall to the ground apart from the will of your Father" (Mt 10:29). He also says, "See how the lilies of the field grow. They do not labor or spin. Yet I tell you that not even Solomon in all his splendor was dressed like one of these" (Mt 6:28-29). These and many other examples presuppose the goodness of the material world and declare care by a benevolent Crea-tor. Gnostic dualism is precluded. Jesus liberally illustrates his mes-sage with images from fishing, farming and family affairs without the slightest indication that these are inherently inferior.

If Jesus recommends fasting and physical self-denial on occasion, it is not because matter is unworthy of attention or an incorrigible roadblock to spiritual growth, but because moral and spiritual resolve may be strengthened through periodic abstinence (Mt 6:16-18; 9:14-15). Jesus fasts in the desert and feasts with his disciples. The created world is good; but the heart is corrupt and inclines to selfishly mis-using a good creation. Therefore, it is sometimes wise to deny what is good without in order to inspect and mortify what is bad within. As Chesterton said:

> The essential difference between Christian and Pagan asceticism lies in the fact that Paganism in renouncing pleasure gives up some-thing which it does not think desirable; whereas Christianity in giving up pleasure gives up something which it thinks very desirable indeed.[58]

If Jesus is the Christ who comes to restore God's creation he must come as one of its own, a *bona fide* man. Although Gnostic teachings show some diversity on this subject, they tend toward Docetism, the doctrine that the descent of the Christ was spiritual, not material, despite any appearance of materiality. From a biblical viewpoint materiality is not the problem. Disharmony with the Maker is the problem. Adam and Eve were both material and in harmony with their good Maker before they succumbed to the serpent's temptation. Yet in biblical reasoning, if Jesus is to conquer sin and death for humanity, he must rise from the dead in a physical body, albeit a transformed one. A mere spiritual apparition would mean an abdication of material responsibility. As Norman Geisler has noted, according to biblical thought:

> Humans sin and die in material bodies and they must be redeemed in the same physical bodies. Any other kind of deliverance would be an admission of defeat. . . . If redemption does not restore God's physical creation, including our material bodies, then God's original purpose in creating a material world would be frustrated.[59]

Robert Gundry, in his study of the body in biblical theology, says that "to dematerialize resurrection, by any means, is to emasculate the sovereignty of God in both creative purpose and redemptive grace."[60]

For this reason at Pentecost the apostle Peter preached Jesus of Nazareth as "a man accredited by God to you by miracles, wonders and signs" (Acts 2:22). Though put to death by being nailed to the cross, "God raised him from the dead, freeing him from the agony of death, because it was impossible for death to keep its hold on him" (v. 24). Peter then quotes Psalm 16:10, which speaks of God not letting his "Holy One see decay" (v. 27). Peter says of David, the psalm's author, "Seeing what was ahead, he spoke of the resurrection of the Christ, that he was not abandoned to the grave, nor did his body see decay. God has raised this Jesus to life, and we are all witnesses of the fact" (vv. 31-32).[61]

For Peter, God's gift comes in a bodily package, the resurrected Jesus Christ.

The Gospels tell us that Jesus' resurrected body was seen (Mt 28:17), heard (Jn 20:15-16) and even touched (Mt 28:9). The resurrected Jesus is also recorded as eating food on at least four occasions (Lk 24:30, 42-43; Jn 21:12-13; Acts 1:4). The apostle Paul confesses that if the resurrection of Jesus is not an historical fact, Christianity is a vanity of vanities (1 Cor 15:14-19). And while he speaks of Jesus' (and the believers') resurrected condition as a "spiritual body," this does not mean non-physical or ethereal; rather, it refers to a body totally free from the results of sin and the Fall. It is a spirit-driven body, untouched by any of the entropies of evil.[62] Because Jesus was resurrected bodily, those who know him as Lord can anticipate their own resurrected bodies.

Jesus, Judaism and Gnosis

The Gnostic Jesus is also divided from the Jesus of the Gospels over his relationship to Judaism. For Gnostics, the God of the Old Testament is somewhat of a cosmic clown neither ultimate, nor good. In fact, many Gnostic documents invert the meaning of Old Testament stories in order to ridicule him. For instance the serpent and Eve are heroic figures who oppose the dull deity in the *Hypostasis of the Archons* (the *Reality of the Rulers*) and in *On the Origin of the World*.[63]

In the *Apocryphon of John,* Jesus says he encouraged Adam and Eve to eat of the tree of the knowledge of good and evil,[64] thus putting Jesus diametrically at odds with the meaning of the Genesis account, where this action is seen as the essence of sin (Gen 3). The same anti-Jewish element is found in the Jesus of the *Gospel of Thomas,* where the disciples say to Jesus, "Twenty-four prophets spoke in Israel, and all of them spoke in you." To which Jesus replies, "You have omitted the one living in your presence and have spoken (only) of the dead."[65] Jesus thus dismisses all the prophets as merely "dead."

The Jesus found in the New Testament quotes the prophets, claims to fulfill their prophecies and consistently argues according to the Old Testament revelation, despite the fact that he exudes an authority equal to it. Jesus says, "Do not think that I have come to abolish the Law or the Prophets; I have not come to abolish them but to fulfill them" (Mt 5:17). He corrects the Sadducees' misunderstanding of the afterlife by saying, "Are you not in error because you do not know the Scriptures or the power of God?" (Mk 12:24). To other critics he again appeals to the Old Testament: "You diligently study the Scriptures because you think that by them you possess eternal life. These are the Scriptures that testify about me . . ." (Jn 5:39).

When Jesus appeared after his death and burial to two of his disciples on the road to Emmaus, he commented on their slowness of heart "to believe all that the prophets have spoken." He asked, "Did not the Christ have to suffer these things and then enter his glory?" Luke then records, "And beginning with Moses and all the prophets, he explained to them what was said in all the Scriptures concerning himself" (Lk 24:25-27).

For both Jesus and the Old Testament, the supreme Creator is the Father of all living. They are one and the same. In Gnosticism, there is a disjunction between an unknowable "Father God" and a metaphysically impoverished Creator. There is also a separation of the Creator from the Redeemer.

God: Unknowable or Knowable?

Many Gnostic treatises speak of the ultimate reality or godhead as beyond conceptual apprehension. Any hope of contacting this reality, a spark of which is lodged within the Gnostic, must be filtered through numerous intermediary beings of a lesser stature than the godhead itself.

In the *Gospel of the Egyptians* the ultimate reality is said to be the "unrevealable, unmarked, ageless, unproclaimable Father." Three powers are said to emanate from Him: "they are the Father, the Mother, (and) the Son, from the living silence."[66] The text speaks of giving praise to "the great invisible Spirit" who is "the silence of silent silence."[67] In the *Sophia of Jesus Christ* Jesus is asked by Matthew, "Lord . . . teach us the truth," to which Jesus says, "He Who is is ineffable." Although Jesus seems to indicate that he reveals the ineffable, he says concerning the ultimate, "He is unnameable . . . he is ever incomprehensible. He is imperishable and has no likeness (to anything)."[68]

The *Tripartite Tractate,* a Valentinian document, says of the ineffable Father, "Not one of the names which are conceived, or spoken, seen or grasped, not one of them applies to him, even though they are exceedingly glorious, magnifying and honored."[69]

At this point the divide between the New Testament and the Gnostic documents could not be deeper or wider. Although the biblical Jesus had the pedagogical tact not to utter indiscriminately, "I am God! I am God!" the entire contour of his ministry points to him as God in the flesh. He says, "Anyone who has seen me has seen the Father" (Jn 14:9). As discussed in chapter three, the prologue to John's Gospel says that "In the beginning was the Word [Logos]" and that "Word was with God, and the Word was God" (Jn 1:1). John did not say, "In the beginning was the silence of the silent silence" or "the ineffable."

Incarnation means intelligible and tangible revelation from God to humanity. The Creator's truth and life are communicated spiritually through the medium of matter. "The Word became flesh and made his dwelling among us. We have seen his glory, the glory of the One and Only, who came from the Father, full of grace and truth" (Jn 1:14). In John's first epistle he speaks of "that which was from the beginning," and says, "The life appeared; we have seen it and testify to it, and we proclaim to you the eternal life, which was with the Father and has appeared to us" (1 Jn 1:1-3).

One messianic prophecy in the book of Jeremiah foretells a day when God himself, not some intermediary being spun out of the unknown and unknowable Pleroma, will come to his people.

"The days are coming," declares the LORD,
    "when I will raise up to David a righteous Branch,
a King who will reign wisely
    and do what is just and right in the land.
In his days Judah will be saved
    and Israel will live in safety.
This is the name by which he will be called:
    The LORD Our Righteousness." (Jer 23:5-6)

Many Jewish rabbis considered this verse messianic as they did several other passages speaking of the Branch (Jer 33:15; Is 4:2; Zech 3:8; 6:12-13).[70] As we have seen, Jesus claimed to be uniquely God on earth, as the Messiah.[71] Jesus himself, by citing Psalm 110:1, teaches that "Christ" (that is, the Messiah) is King David's Lord (Mk 12:35-37). A classic messianic text affirms that God himself will arrive on the human scene:

> For to us a child is born,
>
>   to us a son is given,
>
>   and the government will be on his shoulders.
>
> And he will be called
>
>   Wonderful Counselor, Mighty God,
>
>   Everlasting Father, Prince of Peace. (Is 9:6)

The apostle John writes of these realities made flesh in Jesus and declares that he "has made him [the Father] *known*" (Jn 1:18; emphasis mine).[72]

Although Jesus revered God the Father as holy and as transcendent, he did not view God as unknown or unknowable. This counters the teaching of Joseph Campbell, who, in many ways, taught a Gnostic view of God. In his popular book and television series, *The Power of Myth,* he affirmed a "transtheological" notion of an "undefinable, inconceivable mystery, thought of as a power, that is the source and supporting ground of all life and being."[73] He also said, "God is beyond names and forms. . . . God, the ultimate, is beyond pairs of opposites, that is all there is to it."[74] So strong is Campbell's emphasis on transcendence that he affirms that God "transcends thingness."[75]

Irenaeus encountered these Gnostic invocations of the ineffable. He refers to a Valentinian Gnostic teacher who explained the "primary Tetrad" (fourfold emanation from ultimate reality): "There is a certain Proarch who existed before all things, surpassing all thought, speech, and nomenclature" whom he called "Monotes (unity)." Along with this power there is another power called Hentotes (oneness) who, along with Monotes, produced "an intelligent, unbegotten, and undivided being, which beginning language terms 'Monad.' " Another entity called Hen (One) rounds out the primal union.[76] Irenaeus satir-

ically responds with his own suggested Tetrad, which also proceeds
from "a certain Proarch":

> But along with it there exists a power which I term *Gourd;* and
> along with this Gourd there exists a power which again I term
> *Utter-Emptiness*. This Gourd and Emptiness, since they are one,
> produced . . . a fruit, everywhere visible, eatable, and delicious,
> which fruit-language calls a *Cucumber*. Along with this Cucumber
> exists a power of the same essence, which again I call a *Melon*.[77]

Irenaeus's point should be well taken. If spiritual realities surpass our
ability to name or even think about them, then any name under the
sun (or within the Tetrad) is just as appropriate, or inappropriate, as
any other, and we are free to affirm with Irenaeus that "these powers
of the Gourd, Utter Emptiness, the Cucumber, and the Melon,
brought forth the remaining multitude of the delirious melons of Valentinus."[78]

Whenever a Gnostic writer, ancient or modern, simultaneously asserts that a spiritual entity or principle is utterly unknown and unnameable and begins to give it names and ascribe to it characteristics,
we should hark back to Irenaeus. If something[79] is ineffable it is necessarily unthinkable and unreportable and unapproachable. The "silence of the silent silence" is as far as anyone can get, claims of Gnosis
to the contrary.[80] Let no one vainly attempt to utter the unutterable.

Gnosticism and Modern Thought

Modern-day Gnostics, neo-Gnostics or Gnostic sympathizers should
also be aware of some Gnostic elements which decidedly clash with
modern tastes. Although Elaine Pagels ingratiated the Gnostics to
millions with her book *The Gnostic Gospels,* several tenets of Gnosticism could be found hard to swallow.

First, although Pagels, like Jung, has shown the Gnostics in a positive psychological light, the Gnostic outlook is just as much theological and cosmological as it is psychological. Stephen Hoeller also
moves in the Jungian ambiance and speaks for many when he says,
"Gnosticism can be understood in psychological terms, so that the

religious mythogems treated by the Gnostics are taken to symbolize intra-psychic powers of the mind."[81]

But the Gnostic message is all of a piece, and the psychology should not be artificially divorced from the overall world view. In other words Gnosticism should not be reduced to psychology, as if we know better what a Basilides or a Valentinus *really* meant than they did.

The historic Gnostic world-view was exceedingly ripe with personified spiritual forces arranged in descending order from the unknowable godhead. The Gnostic documents do not present their system as a crypto-psychology (with various cosmic forces representing psychic functions), but as a religious and theological explanation of the origin and operation of the universe. Those who want to adopt consistently Gnostic attitudes and assumptions should keep in mind what the Gnostic texts, to which they appeal for authority and credibility, actually say.

Second, the Gnostic rejection of matter as illusory, evil, or, at most, second-best is at odds with many New Age sentiments regarding the value of nature and the need for an ecological awareness and ethic. Trying to find an ecological concern in the Gnostic corpus is on the order of harvesting wheat in Antarctica. For the Gnostics, as scholar Pheme Perkins puts it, "most of the cosmos that we know is a carefully constructed plot to keep humanity from returning to its true divine home."[82]

Third, Pagels and others to the contrary, the Gnostic attitude toward women was not proto-feminist. Gnostic groups did sometimes allow for women's participation in religious activities, and several of the emanational beings were seen as feminine. Nevertheless, even though *Ms.* magazine gave *The Gnostic Gospels* a glowing review,[83] women fare far worse in Gnosticism than many think.

Simply because Gnosticism uses feminine religious symbolism, that does not guarantee the exaltation of the feminine. Kathleen McVey's critique of Pagels deserves full quotation:

Pagels's citation of excerpts from gnostic writings without their requisite contexts obscures the overall relation of male and female divine powers. For example, when Ialdabaoth boasts (in clear parody of Yahweh) that he is the only God, his Mother reprimands him, "Do not lie, Ialdabaoth." Since nothing of the context is revealed by Pagels, one might imagine that the female divine principle is superior to the male. But the Mother here is herself the "abortion" of Sophia, who is, in turn the youngest of thirty aeons descended from the ineffable Father. Sophia's fall . . . is ultimately the cause of the existence of the material world, from which the gnostic must escape.[84]

The concluding saying from the *Gospel of Thomas* has less than a feminist ring.

Simon Peter said to them, "Let Mary leave us, for women are not worthy of life." Jesus said, "I myself shall lead her in order to make her male, so that she too may become a living spirit resembling you males. For every woman who will make herself male will enter the kingdom of heaven."[85]

The issue of the role of women in Gnostic theology and community cannot be adequately addressed here,[86] but it should be noted that the Jesus of the Gospels never spoke of making the female into the male, no doubt because Jesus did not perceive the female to be inferior to the male. Going against the social customs, he gathered women followers and revealed to an outcast Samaritan woman that he was the Messiah, which scandalized his own disciples (Jn 4:1-39). As we will see later, the Gospels record women as the first witnesses to Jesus' resurrection, and this in a society where women were not considered qualified to be legal witnesses.

Writing in *Parabola,* a journal of mythology, Ann Belford Ulanov perceptively says:

Nowhere in the texts of Scripture do we find Jesus treating women in degrading ways. Not once. Indeed, we find the opposite. To the Samaritan woman he announces that he is life giving water. To Martha, he is the coming resurrection. To the Magdalene, he is risen. He speaks theology with women. . . . He really knew women's lives, really spoke to them, called them to follow him.[87]

Fourth, despite an emphasis on reincarnation in some Gnostic writings, several Gnostic documents speak of the damnation of those who are incorrigibly non-Gnostic,[88] particularly apostates from Gnostic groups.[89] If one chafes at the Jesus of the Gospels warning of "eternal destruction," chafings are likewise readily available from Gnostic doomsayers.

Nag Hammadi and the Christian Canon

If the preceding discussion has thrown the contrast between the Gnostic Jesus and the biblical Jesus into clear relief, we still have not settled the issue of the historical reliability of the Gnostic and New Testament texts. Does Nag Hammadi reopen the Christian canon, as it were? Should these documents cause us to expand or revise our view of Jesus? What are the credentials of the New Testament books in relation to the status of the Gnostic texts?

Concerning the Gnostic-orthodox controversy, biblical scholar F. F. Bruce is so bold as to say that "there is no reason why the student of the conflict should shrink from making a value judgment: the gnostic schools lost because they deserved to lose."[90] The Gnostics lost once, but do they deserve to lose again? We will seek to answer this in the next chapter.

Notes

[1] Joseph Campbell, *The Power of Myth* (New York: Doubleday, 1988), p. 210.
[2] Don Lattin, "Rediscovery of Gnostic Christianity," *San Francisco Chronicle,* April 1, 1989, p. A-5.
[3] Ibid., p. A-4.
[4] Ibid., p. A-5.
[5] Stephen A. Hoeller, "Wandering Bishops," *Gnosis,* Summer 1989, p. 24.
[6] Ibid.
[7] Patrick Henry, *New Directions in New Testament Study* (Philadelphia: Westminster Press, 1979), p. 94.
[8] "The Gnostic Jung: An Interview with Stephen Hoeller," *The Quest,* Summer 1989, p. 85.
[9] C. G. Jung, *Psychological Types* (Princeton, N.J.: Princeton University Press, 1976), p. 11.
[10] C. G. Jung, *Memories, Dreams, and Reflections* (New York: Vintage Books, 1973), p. 192. The piece itself is reprinted on pp. 378-90.

[11]See Richard Smith, "The Modern Relevance of Gnosticism," in James M. Robinson, ed., *The Nag Hammadi Library* (San Francisco, Calif.: Harper and Row, 1988), pp. 532-49.

[12]"Gnosticism," *Critique,* June—September 1989, p. 66.

[13]For the full story of these events see John Dart, *The Jesus of History and Heresy* (San Francisco, Calif.: Harper and Row, 1988), pp. 1-49.

[14]Elaine Pagels, *The Gnostic Gospels* (New York: Random House, 1979), p. xxxv.

[15]For an able summary of this controversy see Ronald Nash, *Christianity in the Hellenistic World* (Grand Rapids, Mich.: Zondervan, 1984), pp. 203-61.

[16]Kurt Rudolph, *Gnosis: The Nature and History of Gnosticism* (San Francisco, Calif.: Harper and Row, 1987), pp. 57ff.

[17]Robinson, p. 154.

[18]In reviewing the movie *The Last Temptation of Christ,* Michael Grosso clearly affirms this idea when he rejects the perfect God of orthodoxy for an imperfect God who "would have to throw in his lot with us. Our fortunes would rise and fall together. The divine adventure would be the mirror image of the human adventure. *It would not only be that God is our Savior; we would ourselves become the Saviors of God*—it's the title of a book by Kazantzakis" (Michael Grosso, "Testing the Images of God," *Gnosis,* Winter 1989, p. 44, emphasis mine).

[19]Some of our information comes not from primary documents but from writings of the early Christian apologists (heresiologists) who sought to refute the so-called Gnostics ("those who claim to know").

[20]See Dart, pp. 162-92, for a plausible reconstruction of the original order of the sayings.

[21]Robinson, p. 126.

[22]F. F. Bruce, *Jesus and Christian Origins outside the New Testament* (Grand Rapids, Mich.: Eerdmans, 1974), pp. 112-13.

[23]Robinson, p. 126.

[24]Some argue that since this passage speaks of the kingdom as inside as well as outside, it is really a mixture of orthodox and gnostic elements.

[25]Robinson, p. 134.

[26]This is Bentley Layton's translation in *The Gnostic Scriptures* (Garden City, N.Y.: Doubleday and Company, Inc., 1987), p. 403. He says "in classic gnosticism the 'entirety' is the sum total of spiritual reality deriving from the first principle, by way of the Barbelo aeon [intermediary being]."

[27]Robinson, p. 201.

[28]Pagels, p. 124.

[29]Ibid., p. 126.

[30]Christopher Farmer, "An Interview with Gilles Quispel," *Gnosis,* Fall/Winter 1985, p. 28.

[31]Stephen A. Hoeller, "Valentinus: A Gnostic for All Seasons," *Gnosis,* Fall/Winter 1985, p. 24. On Valentinus's view of Christ's death, see below.

[32]Ibid., p. 25.

[33]Robinson, p. 40.

[34]Ibid., p. 523.

[35]Ibid., p. 130.

[36]Ibid., p. 132.

[37]Ibid., p. 263.

[38]Ibid., p. 150.
[39]Ibid., p. 135.
[40]Ibid., p. 377.
[41]Ibid., p. 265.
[42]Ibid., p. 365.
[43]Dart, p. 97.
[44]Robinson, p. 41.
[45]Pagels, p. 95. On Valentinus' view of Christ's role in redemption see Hans Jonas, *The Gnostic Religion* (Boston: Beacon Press, 1963), pp. 195-96.
[46]Layton, p. 317.
[47]Robinson, p. 56.
[48]Pagels, p. 11.
[49]Robinson, pp. 525-27.
[50]Irenaeus, *Against Heresies* 3.16.5.
[51]Ibid.
[52]Ibid., 3.18.5.
[53]Ibid., 3.18.2.
[54]Ibid., 3.18.6.
[55]Ibid., 3.3.4.
[56]*The Epistle of Polycarp,* ch. 8, in *The Apostolic Fathers,* ed. A. Cleveland Coxe (Grand Rapids, Mich.: Eerdmans, 1987), p. 35.
[57]E. Stanley Jones, *The Christ of the Indian Road* (New York: Grosset & Dunlap, 1925), p. 194.
[58]G. K. Chesterton, *G. F. Watts* ((London: Duckworth, 1975), p. 32; quoted in George J. Marlin, Richard P. Rabatin, John L. Swan, eds., *The Quotable Chesterton* (Garden City, N.Y.: Image Books, 1987), p. 32.
[59]Norman L. Geisler, "I Believe . . . in the Resurrection of the Flesh," *Christian Research Journal,* Summer 1989, pp. 21-22.
[60]Robert Gundry, *Soma in Biblical Theology* (Cambridge: Cambridge University Press, 1976), pp. 181-82, quoted in Geisler.
[61]For a discussion of how the apostle understood this psalm to predict the resurrection, see Walter C. Kaiser, *The Uses of the Old Testament in the New* (Chicago: Moody Press, 1985), pp. 25-41.
[62]For a detailed and convincing defense of this interpretation, see William Lane Craig, "The Bodily Resurrection of Jesus," *Gospel Perspectives,* vol. 1, ed. R. T. France and David Wenham (Sheffield: JSOT Press, 1980), pp. 47-74. Pagels wrongly believes that the apostle Paul taught a nonphysical view of resurrection (see p. 6).
[63]For a review of this phenomenon, see Dart, pp. 60-74.
[64]Robinson, p. 117.
[65]Ibid., p. 132.
[66]Ibid., p. 209.
[67]Ibid., p. 210.
[68]Ibid., pp. 224-25.
[69]Ibid., p. 62. In an article in *Gnosis,* David R. Fideler says that "every Valentinian account, without exception, refers to the *complete ineffability* of the Father who exists, 'before the Beginning' " (Fall/Winter 1985, p. 17, emphasis mine).
[70]See John Ankerberg, John Weldon, Walter Kaiser, *The Case for Jesus, the Messiah*

(Chattanooga, Tenn.: John Ankerberg Evangelistic Assoc., 1989), pp. 62-65.

[71]The apostle Paul explicitly refers to Jesus as righteousness in Romans 3:21-26.

[72]For more on the Messiah as divine, see Jon A. Buell and O. Quentin Hyder, *Jesus: God, Ghost, or Guru?* (Grand Rapids, Mich.: Zondervan, 1978), pp. 113-19.

[73]Campbell, p. 31.

[74]Ibid., p. 49.

[75]Ibid.

[76]Irenaeus, 1.11.3.

[77]Ibid., 1.11.4.

[78]Ibid.

[79]We might better call it x and not *something* because, for Campbell, the ultimate is even beyond *thingness*. *It* might even be beyond *x-ness*.

[80]For a further critique of the idea of experiencing the ineffable, see Keith E. Yandell, "On Windowless Experiences," *Christian Scholar's Review* 4, no. 4 (1975):311-18.

[81]Hoeller, p. 24.

[82]Pheme Perkins, "Popularizing the Past," *Commonweal* 9 (November 1979):634.

[83]Kenneth Pitchford, "The Good News About God," *Ms.*, April 1980, pp. 32-35.

[84]Kathleen McVey, "Gnosticism, Feminism and Elaine Pagels," *Theology Today*, January 1981, p. 500. For the primary sources, see *Against Heresies* 1.1.1-8 and the *Apocryphon of John* in Robinson, pp. 104-23. One may note that the male Creator is not directly accused of creating matter in this case, but this simply shows the diversity within the basic Gnostic orbit.

[85]Robinson, p. 138. Bruce Chilton notes that "Thomas is notoriously anti-sexual; within this Gospel, sexual polarities are part of the evil which it is the business of salvation to overcome" (Bruce Chilton, "The Gospel According to Thomas As a Source of Jesus' Teaching," *Gospel Perspectives*, vol. 5, ed. David Wenham [Sheffield: JSOT Press, 1985], p. 169).

[86]See the discussion by Elisabeth Schüssler Fiorenza, "Word, Spirit and Power: Women in Early Christian Communities," in Rosemary Radford Ruether and Eleanor McLaughlin, *Women of Spirit* (New York: Simon and Schuster, 1979), pp. 44-70.

[87]Ann Belford Ulanov, "The God You Touch," *Parabola*, August 1987, p. 24.

[88]See for instance, *The Book of Thomas, the Contender*, in Robinson, p. 205.

[89]See Layton, p. 17.

[90]F. F. Bruce, *The Canon of Scripture* (Downers Grove, Ill.: InterVarsity Press, 1988), p. 277.

Chapter 5

Jesus, Gnosis and Historical Reliability

*T*he last chapter outlined the stark contrasts between the Gnostic Jesus and "the Word made flesh." The respective views of Jesus are lodged within mutually exclusive world views concerning claims about God, the universe, humanity and salvation. But our next line of inquiry is to be historical. Do we have a clue as to what Jesus, the man from Nazareth, actually did and said as a player in space-time history? Should the Gnostic sayings of the *Gospel of Thomas* or the resurrection sermons of the immaterial Gnostic Jesus capture our attention as reliable reports of the mind of Jesus, or does the Son of Man of the biblical Gospels speak with the authentic voice? Or should we remain in utter agnosticism about the historical Jesus?

Unless we are content to chronicle a cacophony of conflicting views of Jesus based on pure speculation or passionate whimsy, historical investigation is non-negotiable. Christianity has always been an historical religion, and any serious challenge to its legitimacy must attend to that fact. Its central claims are rooted in events, not just ideas; in people, not just principles; in revelation, not just speculation; in incarnation, not just abstraction. Renowned historian Herbert Butterfield speaks of Christianity as a religion in which "certain historical events are held to be part of the religion itself" and are "considered to . . . represent the divine breaking into history."[1] He further explains the relationship of the historical to the theological:

> The Incarnation, the Crucifixion and the Resurrection are events which happen in time, but it is claimed that they have an extra dimension, so to speak, and they carry a fullness of meaning calculated almost to break the vessel that contains it. To the limit that is possible with finite things we regard them as capturing into time a portion of eternity.[2]

We discover this in the prologue to Luke's Gospel. Historical accuracy was no incidental item:

> Many have undertaken to draw up an account of the things that have been fulfilled among us, just as they were handed down to us by those who from the first were eyewitnesses and servants of the word. Therefore, since I myself have carefully investigated everything from the beginning, it seemed good also to me to write an orderly account for you, most excellent Theophilus, so that you may know the certainty of the things you have been taught. (Lk 1:1-4)

The text affirms that Luke was after nothing less than historical certainty, presented in orderly fashion and based on firsthand testimony.

If Christianity centers on Jesus, the Christ, the promised Messiah who inaugurates the kingdom of God with power, the objective facticity of this Jesus is pre-eminent. If Christians seek to pray "in Jesus' name" their view of Jesus must be correct in order not to fall into false worship or even idolatry. Likewise, if purportedly historical documents like those from Nag Hammadi challenge the biblical documents' portrait of Jesus, both the Gnostic and the New Testament Gospels must be brought before historical scrutiny.

This chapter inspects the historical standing of the Gnostic writings in terms of their historical integrity, authenticity and veracity. The evidence for the reliability of the New Testament will, in chapter six, provide background for the discussions of the "lost years of Jesus," the "Essene Jesus," the Jesus of the channelers and the "Cosmic Christ." Since Gnosticism was the first direct challenge to Christianity, it is appropriate to lock historical horns with it before going on to grapple with other challenges to orthodoxy.

Although much excitement has been generated by the Nag Hammadi discoveries, not a little misunderstanding has been mixed with enthusiasm. The overriding assumption of many is that the treatises unearthed in upper Egypt contained "lost books of the Bible" of historical stature equal to or greater than the New Testament books. Much of this has been fueled by the titles of some of the documents themselves, particularly the so-called Gnostic Gospels: the *Gospel of Thomas, Gospel of Philip, Gospel of Mary, Gospel of the Egyptians* and the *Gospel of Truth.* The connotation of a "Gospel" is that it presents the life of Jesus as a teacher, preacher and healer and is similar in style, if not content, to Matthew, Mark, Luke and John.

Yet a reading of these "Gospels" reveals an entirely different genre of material. For example, the introduction to the *Gospel of Truth* in *The Nag Hammadi Library* reads, "Despite its title, this work is not the sort found in the New Testament, since it does not offer a continuous narration of the deeds, teachings, passion, and resurrection of Jesus."[3] The introduction to the *Gospel of Philip* in the same volume says that although it has some similarities to a New Testament Gospel, "the Gospel of Philip is not a gospel like one of the New Testament gospels. . . . [The] few sayings and stories about Jesus . . . are not set in any kind of narrative framework like one of the New Testament gospels."[4] In introducing the *Gospel According to Philip* Bentley Layton notes that "the term 'gospel' does not here refer to the Christian literary genre called gospel (e.g. the Gospel of Mark)."[5] Biblical scholar Joseph A. Fitzmyer criticized the title of Pagels's *The Gnostic Gospels* because it insinuates that the heart of the book concerns lost Gospels that have come to light, when in fact the majority of Pagels's references are from early church fathers' sources or other non-Gospel material.[6]

The "superstar" of the Nag Hammadi collection in view of scholarly and popular attention is the *Gospel of Thomas*. Yet Thomas also falls outside of the genre of the New Testament Gospels—despite the fact that many of its 114 sayings are directly or indirectly related to Matthew, Mark and Luke. *Thomas* has almost no narration and its structure consists of discrete sayings. Unlike the canonical Gospels, which provide a social context and narrative for Jesus' words, *Thomas* is more like various beads almost haphazardly strung on a necklace. This, in itself, makes proper interpretation difficult. F. F. Bruce observes that

> the sayings of Jesus are best to be understood in the light of the historical circumstances in which they were spoken. Only when we have understood them thus can we safely endeavor to recognize the permanent truth which they convey. When they are detached from their original historical setting and arranged in an anthology, their interpretation is more precarious.[7]

Bruce contrasts the obscure genre of the *Gospel of Thomas* with the New Testament, which speaks not only of "what the sayings of Jesus meant in the situation of his ministry but also of how they were understood some decades later in the early church."[8]

Without undue appeal to the subjective it can be safely said that the Gnostic material on Jesus has a decidedly different "feel" than the biblical Gospels. There, Jesus' teaching emerges naturally from the overall contour of his life. In the Gnostic materials Jesus seems, in many cases, more of a lecturer on metaphysics than a Jewish prophet. In the *Letter of Peter to Philip* the apostles tell the resurrected Jesus, "Lord, we would like to know the deficiency of the aeons and of their pleroma."[9] Such philosophical abstractions were never on the lips of the disciples—the fishermen, tax collectors and Zealots of the biblical accounts. Jesus then discourses on the pre-cosmic fall of "the mother" who acted in opposition to "the Father" and so produced ailing aeons.[10]

Whatever is made of the historical "feel" of these documents, their actual status as historical records should be brought into closer scrutiny to assess their factual reliability.

The Reliability of the Gnostic Documents

Reliability deals with trustworthiness. If a document is historically reliable, it is trustworthy as objectively true; there is good reason to believe that what it affirms essentially fits what is the case. It is faithful to fact. Historical reliability can be divided into three basic categories: integrity, authenticity and veracity.[11]

Integrity concerns the preservation of the writing through history. Do we have reason to believe the text as it now reads is essentially the same as when it was first written? Or has substantial corruption taken place through distortion, additions or subtractions?

As we will see in the next chapter, the New Testament has been preserved in thousands of diverse and ancient manuscripts which enable us to reconstruct the original documents with a high degree of certainty. But what of Nag Hammadi?

Before the discovery at Nag Hammadi, Gnostic documents not inferred from references in the church fathers were few and far between. Since 1945, though, there are many primary documents. Scholars date the extant manuscripts from A.D. 350-400, which is quite old as documents relating to the origin of Christianity are concerned. The original writing of the various documents, of course, took place sometime before A.D. 350-400, but not, according to most scholars, before the second century.

The actual condition of the Nag Hammadi manuscripts varies considerably. James Robinson, the editor of *The Nag Hammadi Library*, notes that

> there is the physical deterioration of the books themselves, which began no doubt before they were buried around 400 C.E. [then] advanced steadily while they remained buried, and unfortunately was not completely halted in the period between their discovery in 1945 and their final conservation thirty years later.[12]

Reading through *The Nag Hammadi Library* one often finds notations such as ellipses, parentheses and brackets, indicating spotty marks in the texts. Often the translator has to venture tentative reconstructions of the writings because of textual damage. The *Zostrianos* and *Marsanes* writings, for example, are extremely fragmentary and difficult to reconstitute. The situation may be likened to putting together a jigsaw puzzle with numerous pieces missing: one is forced to recreate the pieces by using whatever context is available. Robinson adds, "When only a few letters are missing, they can often be filled in adequately, but larger holes must simply remain a blank."[13]

Concerning translation, Robinson relates that "the texts were translated one by one from Greek to Coptic, and not always by translators capable of grasping the profundity or sublimity of what they sought to translate."[14] Particularly is this the case of the translation of a portion of Plato's *Republic*. He notes, however, that most of the texts are more adequately translated, and that when there is more than one version of a particular text, the better translation is clearly discernible. Nevertheless, he is "led to wonder about the bulk of the texts that exist only in a single version,"[15] because these texts cannot be compared with other translations for accuracy.

Robinson comments further on the integrity of the texts:

There is the same kind of hazard in the transmission of the texts by a series of scribes who copied them, generation after generation, from increasingly corrupt copies, first in Greek and then in Coptic. The number of unintentional errors is hard to estimate, since such a thing as a clean control copy does not exist; *nor does one have, as in the case of the Bible, a quantity of manuscripts of the same text* that tend to correct each other when compared.[16]

Authenticity concerns the authorship of a given writing. Do we know who the author was? Or must we deal with an anonymous or pseudepigraphic one? A writing is considered authentic if it can be shown to have been written by its stated or implied author.[17] In the next chapter we argue that the Gospels are written by their namesakes: Matthew, Mark, Luke and John. But what of Nag Hammadi?

For example, the *Letter of Peter to Philip* is dated at the end of the second century or even into the third.[18] This certainly rules out a literal letter from the apostle to Philip. The genre of this text is known as pseudepigrapha, which refers to writings falsely ascribed to noteworthy individuals to lend credibility to the material. Although interesting in explaining the development of Gnostic thought and its relationship to biblical writings, the *Letter of Peter to Philip* should not be overtaxed as delivering reliable history of the events it purports to record.

There are few if any cases of known authorship with the Nag Hammadi and other Gnostic texts. Scholars speculate as to authorship but do not take pseudepigraphic literature as authentically apostolic. Even the *Gospel of Thomas*, probably the document closest to the New Testament events, is virtually never considered to be written by the apostle Thomas himself.[19] The marks of authenticity in this material are, then, spotty at best.

Veracity concerns the truthfulness of the author of the text. Was the author in a position to relate adequately what is reported, in terms of both chronological closeness to the events and observational savvy? Did he or she have sufficient credentials to relay historical truth?

Some in their enthusiasm over Nag Hammadi have lassoed texts into the historical corral that date several hundred years after the life of Jesus. For instance, in a review of the movie *The Last Temptation of Christ*, Michael Grosso speaks of hints of Jesus' sexual life "right at the start of the Christian tradition." He then quotes from the *Gospel of Philip* to the effect that Jesus often kissed Mary Magdalene on the mouth.[20] The problem is that the text is quite far from "the start of the Christian tradition," being written, according to one scholar, "perhaps as late as the second half of the third century."[21]

As we have already noted in regard to the *Letter of Peter to Philip*, several of the texts referring to Jesus were written quite late and would be better viewed as later commentaries on his life than as primary historical sources.

Craig Blomberg states that "most of the Nag Hammadi documents, predominantly Gnostic in nature, make no pretense of overlapping with the gospel traditions of Jesus' earthly life."[22] He observes that "a number claim to record conversations of the resurrected Jesus with various disciples, but this setting is usually little more than an artificial framework for imparting Gnostic doctrine."[23]

What, then, of the veracity of the documents? We do not know with any high probability who wrote most of them. Whatever the philosophical merits of the Nag Hammadi texts (and we found several defects in the last chapter), their historical veracity concerning Jesus seems slim. Yet some scholars advance a few candidates as providing historically reliable facts concerning Jesus.

In the case of the *Gospel of Truth* some scholars see Valentinus as the author[24] or at least as authoring an earlier version.[25] Yet Valentinus dates into the second century (d. A.D. 175) and was thus not a contemporary of Jesus. Harold Attridge and George MacRae date the document between A.D. 140 and 180.[26] Layton recognizes that "the work is a sermon and has nothing to do with the Christian genre properly called 'gospel.' "[27]

The text differs from many in Nag Hammadi because of its recurring references to New Testament passages and the Gospel tradition. Layton notes that "it paraphrases, and so interprets, some thirty to sixty scriptural passages almost all from the New Testament books."[28] He goes on to note that Valentinus shaped these allusions to fit his own Gnostic theology.[29] In discussing the use of the synoptic gospels (Matthew, Mark and Luke) in the *Gospel of Truth,* C. M. Tuckett concludes that "there is no evidence for the use of sources other than the canonical gospels for synoptic material."[30] This would mean that the *Gospel of Truth* gives no independent historical insight about Jesus but rather reinterprets previous material.

The *Gospel of Philip* is thick with Gnostic theology and contains several references to Jesus; however, it does not claim to be a revelation from Jesus but more of a Gnostic manual of theology.[31] According to C. M. Tuckett's analysis, all the references to Gospel material seem to stem from Matthew and not from any other canonical Gospel or other source independent of Matthew. Andrew Hembold has also pointed out that both the *Gospel of Truth* and the *Gospel of Philip* show signs of "mimicking" the New Testament; they both "know and recognize the greater part of the New Testament as authoritative."[32] This would make them derivative, not original, documents.[33]

Tuckett has also argued that the *Gospel of Mary* and the *Book of Thomas the Contender* (not to be confused with the *Gospel of Thomas*) are dependent on synoptic materials and that "there is virtually no evidence for the use of pre-synoptic sources by these writers. These texts are all 'post-synoptic,' not only with regard to their dates, but also with regard to the form of the synoptic tradition they presuppose."[34] In other words these writings are simply drawing on preexistent Gospel material and rearranging it to conform to their Gnostic world-view. They may embellish, delete, twist or revise Gospel information, but they do not contribute historically authentic, new material.

The *Apocryphon of James* claims to be a secret revelation of the risen Jesus to James his brother. It is less obviously Gnostic than some Nag Hammadi texts and contains some more orthodox-sounding phrases, such as "Verily I say unto you none will be saved unless they believe in my cross."[35] It also affirms the unorthodox, such as when Jesus says, "Become better than I; make yourselves like the son of the Holy Spirit."[36] While one scholar dates it sometime before A.D. 150,[37] Blomberg believes it gives indications of being "at least in part later than and dependent upon the canonical gospels."[38] Its esotericism certainly puts it at odds with the canonical Gospels, which, in the next chapter, we will find to be better attested historically.

Thomas on Trial

The Nag Hammadi text that has provoked the most historical scrutiny is the *Gospel of Thomas*. Because of its reputation as the lost "fifth Gospel" and its often esoteric and mystical cast, it is often quoted in New Age circles. A recently published book by Robert Winterhalter is entitled *The Fifth Gospel: A Verse-by-Verse New Age Commentary on the Gospel of Thomas.* He claims that Thomas knows "the Christ both as the Self, and the foundation of individual life."[39] Some of the sayings in the *Gospel of Thomas* do seem to teach this. But is this what the historical Jesus taught?

The scholarly literature on *Thomas* is vast and controversial; nevertheless, a few important considerations arise in assessing its veracity as history. Because it is more of an anthology of mostly unrelated sayings rather than an ongoing story about Jesus' words and deeds, *Thomas* is outside the genre of "Gospel" in the New Testament. Yet some of the 114 sayings closely parallel or roughly resemble statements in the synoptics,[40] either by adding to them, deleting from them, combining several references into one or by changing the sense of a saying entirely.[41]

The above explanation of Thomas uses the synoptic Gospels as a reference point for comparison. But is it likely that *Thomas* is independent of these sources and gives authentic, although "unorthodox," material about Jesus?

There certainly are sayings that harmonize with biblical material, and direct or indirect relationships can be found to all four canonical Gospels. In this sense *Thomas* contains both orthodox and unorthodox material, if we use "orthodox" to mean the material in the New Testament. For instance, the Trinity and unforgivable sin are referred to in the context of blasphemy:

> Jesus said, "Whoever blasphemes against the father will be forgiven, and whoever blasphemes against the son will be forgiven, but whoever blasphemes against the holy spirit will not be forgiven either on earth or in heaven." [44][42]

In the next saying Jesus speaks of the "evil man" who "brings forth evil things from his evil storehouse, which is in his heart, and says evil things" [45][43] (see Lk 6:43-46). This can be read to harmonize with the New Testament Gospels' emphasis on human sin, not just ignorance of the divine spark within.

Although it is not directly related to a canonical Gospel text, the following statement seems to state the biblical theme of the urgency of finding Jesus while one can: "Jesus said, 'Take heed of the living one while you are alive, lest you die and seek to see him and be unable to do so' " [59][44] (cf. Jn 7:34; 13:33).

At the same time, we find texts of a clearly Gnostic slant as noted earlier. How can we account for this?

The original writing of Thomas has been dated variously between A.D. 50 and 150 or even later, with many scholars opting for a second century date.[45] Of course an earlier date would lend more credibility to it, although its lack of narrative framework still makes it more difficult to understand than the canonical Gospels. While some argue that Thomas uses historical sources independent of those used by the New Testament, this is not a uniformly held view, and arguments are easily found which marshall evidence for Thomas' dependence (either partial or total) on the canonical Gospels.[46]

Blomberg claims that "where Thomas parallels the four gospels it is unlikely that any of the distinctive elements in Thomas predate the canonical versions."[47] When Thomas gives a parable found in the four Gospels and adds details not found there, "they can almost always be explained as conscious, Gnostic redaction [editorial adaptation]."[48]

James Dunn elaborates on this theme by comparing Thomas with what is believed to be an earlier and partial version of the document found in Oxyrhynchus, Egypt, near the turn of the century.[49] He notes that the Oxyrhynchus "papyri date from the end of the second or the first half of the third century, while the *Gospel of Thomas* found at Nag Hammadi was probably written no earlier than the fourth century."[50]

Dunn then compares similar statements from Matthew, the Oxyrhynchus Papyri and the Nag Hammadi text version of Thomas:

Matthew 7.7-8 and 11.28—". . . Seek, and you will find; . . . he who seeks finds. . . ." "Come to me . . . and I will give you rest."

Pap. Ox. 654.5-9—(Jesus says:) Let him who see(ks) not cease (seeking until) he finds; and when he find (he will) be astounded, and having (astoun)ded, he will reign; an(d reigning), he will (re)st. (Clement of Alexandria also knows the saying in this form.)

Gospel of Thomas 2—"Jesus said: He who seeks should not stop seeking until he finds; and when he finds, he will be bewildered (beside himself); and when he is bewildered he will marvel, and will reign over the All.[51]

Dunn notes that the term "the All" (added to the earlier document) is "a regular Gnostic concept" (see chapter four on this also) and that, "as the above comparisons suggest, the most obvious explanation is that it was one of the last elements to be added to the saying."[52] Dunn further adds that the Nag Hammadi version of Thomas shows a definite "gnostic colouring" and gives no evidence for the thesis that a form of Gnostic Christianity already existed in the first century. He continues:

Rather it confirms the counter thesis that the Gnostic element in Gnostic Christianity is a second century syncretistic outgrowth on the stock of the earlier Christianity. What we can see clearly in the case of this one saying is probably representative of the lengthy process of development and elaboration which resulted in the form of the *Gospel of Thomas* found at Nag Hammadi.[53]

Other authorities substantiate the notion that whatever authentic material *Thomas* may convey concerning Jesus, the text from Nag Hammadi shows signs of Gnostic tampering. Marvin W. Meyer judges that *Thomas* "shows the hand of a gnosticizing editor."[54] Winterhalter, who reveres *Thomas* enough to write a devotional guide on it, nevertheless says of the Nag Hammadi *Thomas* that "some sayings are spurious or greatly altered, but this is the work of a later Egyptian editor."[55] (He thinks, though, that the wheat can be successfully separated from the chaff.)[56] Robert M. Grant has noted that:

The religious realities which the Church proclaimed were ultimately perverted by the Gospel of Thomas. For this reason Thomas, along with other documents which purported to contain secret sayings of Jesus, was rejected by the Church.[57]

Here we find ourselves agreeing with the writings of the early Christian defenders of the faith who maintained that Gnosticism in the church was a corruption of original truth and not an independently legitimate source of information on Jesus or the rest of reality. Fitzmyer drives this home in criticizing Pagels's view that the Gnostics have an equal claim on Christian authenticity. He says that her way of handling the Nag Hammadi material

> throughout the book gives the unwary reader the impression that the difference between "orthodox Christians" and "gnostic Christians" was one related to the "origins of Christianity." Time and time again she is blind to the fact that she is ignoring a good century of Christian existence in which those "gnostic Christians" were simply not around.[58]

In this connection it is also telling that ouside of the *Gospel of Thomas,* which does not overtly mention the resurrection, other Gnostic documents claiming to impart new information about Jesus do so through spiritual, post-resurrection dialogs, often in the form of visions (see chapter four) that are not subject to the same historical rigor as claims made about the earthly life of Jesus. This leads Dunn to comment that:

> Christian Gnosticism usually attributed its secret [and unorthodox] teaching of Jesus to discourses delivered by him, so they maintained, in a lengthy ministry after his resurrection (as in *Thomas the Contender* and *Pistis Sophia*). *The Gospel of Thomas* is unusual therefore in attempting to use the Jesus-tradition as the vehicle for its teaching. . . . Perhaps Gnosticism abandoned the *Gospel of Thomas* format because it was to some extent subject to check and rebuttal from Jesus-tradition preserved elsewhere.[59]

Dunn thinks that the more thoroughly the Gnostics challenged the already established orthodox accounts of Jesus' earthly life, the less credible they became; but with post-resurrection accounts, no checks were forthcoming. They were claiming additional information vouchsafed only to the elite. He concludes that Gnosticism

> was able to present its message in a sustained way as the teaching of Jesus only by separating the risen Christ from the earthly Jesus and by abandoning the attempts to show a continuity between the Jesus of the Jesus-tradition and the heavenly Christ of their faith.[60]

What is seen by some as a Gnostic challenge to historic, orthodox views of the life, teaching and work of Jesus was actually in many cases a retreat from historical considerations entirely. Only by doing so could the Gnostics attempt to establish the credibility of the Gnostic documents.

Gnostic Underdogs?

Although Pagels and others have provoked sympathy, if not enthusiasm, for the Gnostics as the underdogs who just happened to lose out to orthodoxy, the Gnostics' historical credentials concerning Jesus are less than compelling. While it is romantic to "root for the underdog," the Gnostic underdogs show every sign of being heretical hangers-on who tried to harness Christian language for conceptions antithetical to early Christian teaching.

Many sympathetic with Gnosticism make much of the notion that the Gnostic writings were suppressed by the early Christian church. But this assertion does not, in itself, provide support one way or the other for the truth or falsity of Gnostic doctrine. If truth is not a matter of *majority* vote, neither is it a matter of *minority* dissent. It may be true, as Pagels says, that "the winners write history," but that doesn't necessarily make them bad or dishonest historians. If so, we should hunt down Nazi historians to give us the real picture of Hitler's Germany and relegate all opposing views to that of dogmatic apologists who just happened be on the winning side.

In *Against Heresies,* Irenaeus went to great lengths to present the theologies of the various Gnostic schools in order to refute them biblically and logically. If suppression had been his concern, the book never would have been written as it was. Further, to argue cogently against the Gnostics, Irenaeus and the other anti-Gnostic apologists would presumably have had to be diligent to correctly represent their foes in order to avoid ridicule for misunderstanding them. Patrick Henry highlights this in reference to Nag Hammadi:

While the Nag Hammadi materials have made some corrections to the portrayal of Gnosticism in the anti-Gnostic writings of the church fathers, it is increasingly evident that the fathers did not fabricate their opponents' views; what distortion there is comes from selection, not from invention. It is still legitimate to use materials from the writings of the fathers to characterize Gnosticism.[61] It is highly improbable that all of the Gnostic materials could have been systematically confiscated or destroyed by the early church. James Dunn finds it unlikely that the reason we have no unambiguously first-century documents from Christian Gnostics is because the early church eradicated them. He believes it more likely that we have none because there were none.[62] But by archaeological virtue of Nag Hammadi, we now do have many primary source Gnostic documents available for detailed inspection. Yet they do not receive superior marks as historical documents about Jesus. In a review of *The Gnostic Gospels,* noted biblical scholar Raymond Brown affirmed that from the Nag Hammadi "works we learn not a single verifiable new fact about Jesus' ministry, and only a few new sayings that might plausibly have been his."[63]

Another factor foreign to the interests of Gnostic apologists is the proposition that Gnosticism expired largely because it lacked life from the beginning. F. F. Bruce notes that "Gnosticism was too much bound up with a popular but passing phase of thought to have the survival power of apostolic Christianity."[64]

Exactly why did apostolic Christianity survive and thrive? Robert Speer pulls no theological punches when he proclaims that "Christianity lived because it was true to the truth. Through all the centuries it has never been able to live otherwise. It can not live otherwise today."[65] To test this bold claim, we must consider the New Testament documents, particularly the Gospels, to see if their picture of Jesus is historically reliable.

Notes

[1]Herbert Butterfield, *Christianity and History* (New York: Charles Scribners and Sons, 1950), p. 119.
[2]Ibid., p. 12.

[3]Harold W. Attridge and George W. MacRae, "Introduction: The Gospel of Truth" in James M. Robinson, ed., *The Nag Hammadi Library* (San Francisco: Harper and Row, 1988), p. 38.

[4]Wesley W. Isenberg, "Introduction: The Gospel of Philip," in Robinson, p. 139.

[5]Bentley Layton, *The Gnostic Scriptures* (Garden City, N.Y.: Doubleday and Company, Inc., 1987), p. 325.

[6]Joseph Fitzmyer, "The Gnostic Gospels According to Pagels," *America,* February 16, 1980, p. 123.

[7]F. F. Bruce, *Jesus and Christian Origins outside the New Testament* (Grand Rapids, Mich.: Eerdmans, 1982), p. 154.

[8]Ibid., p. 155.

[9]Robinson, p. 434.

[10]Ibid., p. 435. See the discussion of supposed "Gnostic feminism" in the previous chapter for more on this theme.

[11]This follows the breakdown of Cornelius Hagerty, *The Authenticity of the Sacred Scriptures* (Houston, Tex.: Lumen Christi Press, 1969), pp. 225-26, who uses it only in discussing the New Testament documents. We will again invoke these categories in the next chapter.

[12]Robinson, p. 2.

[13]Ibid.

[14]Ibid.

[15]Ibid.

[16]Ibid., emphasis mine.

[17]Certainly it is granted that some of the canonical books or portions of books in the Old Testament do not readily tell us their author. This need not necessarily disqualify a document from being historically reliable, but it is one factor to be considered along with the two others to be mentioned.

[18]Marvin W. Meyer, "Introduction: The Letter of Peter to Philip," in *Nag Hammadi,* p. 433.

[19]See Ray Summers, *The Secret Sayings of the Living Jesus* (Waco, Tex.: Word Books, 1968), p. 14, and Craig Blomberg, *The Historial Reliability of the Gospels* (Downers Grove, Ill.: InterVarsity Press, 1987), p. 209.

[20]Michael Grosso, "Testing the Images of God," *Gnosis,* Winter 1989, p. 43.

[21]Wesley W. Isenberg, "Introduction: The Gospel of Philip," Robinson, p. 141. Although Bentley Layton doesn't hazard a guess as to the date of composition, he refers to Philip as an instance of "Valentinian pseudepigraphy" (Layton, p. 326).

[22]Craig Blomberg, *The Historical Reliability of the Gospels* (Downers Grove, Ill.: InterVarsity Press, 1987), p. 208.

[23]Ibid.

[24]Such as Gilles Quispel, "An Interview," *Gnosis,* Fall/Winter 1985, p. 28; and Bentley Layton, p. 251.

[25]Such as Stephen Hoeller, "Valentinus: A Gnostic for All Seasons," *Gnosis,* Fall/Winter, p. 25.

[26]Robinson, p. 38.

[27]Layton, p. 251.

[28]Ibid.

[29]Ibid.

[30]C. M. Tuckett, "Synoptic Tradition in the Gospel of Truth and the Testimony of Truth," *Journal of Theological Studies,* n.s. 35 (1984):145.

[31]Blomberg, pp. 213-14.

[32]Andrew K. Hembold, *The Nag Hammadi Texts and the Bible* (Grand Rapids, Mich.: Baker Book House, 1967), p. 89.

[33]We will further comment on this fact in chapter six.

[34]Christopher Tuckett, "Synoptic Tradition in Some Nag Hammadi and Related Texts," *Vigiliae Christiane* 36, no. 2 (1982): 184.

[35]Robinson, p. 32.

[36]Ibid.

[37]Francis E. Williams, "Introduction: The Apocryphon of James," in *Nag Hammadi,* p. 30.

[38]Blomberg, p. 213.

[39]Robert Winterhalter, *The Fifth Gospel* (San Francisco, Calif.: Harper and Row, 1988), p. 13.

[40]Although scholars differ on this, in my own reading of Thomas I noted that parts or all of 48 of the 114 sayings significantly resemble New Testament references. Saying 17 is very similar to Paul's statement in 2 Corinthians 2:9. Layton, pp. 380-99, lists possible cross-references in his translation/annotation.

[41]Summers, pp. 24-32.

[42]Robinson, p. 131. See Bruce, *Jesus and Christian,* p. 130-31 on the relation of this to the canonical Gospels. Compare this saying with Luke 12:10.

[43]Ibid.

[44]Ibid., p. 132.

[45]Layton, p. 377.

[46]For technical treatments that see Thomas as dependent on the canonical Gospels, see Craig L. Blomberg, "Tradition and Reaction in the Parables of the Gospel of Thomas," *Gospel Perspectives,* vol. 5, pp. 177-205; and Christopher Tuckett, "Thomas and the Synoptics," *Novum Testamentum* 30, no. 2 (1988): 132-57.

[47]Blomberg, *Historical Reliability,* p. 211.

[48]Ibid., p. 212.

[49]For a scholarly defense of the well-established position that the Oxyrhynchus fragments are earlier portions of Thomas, see Joseph A. Fitzmyer, "The Oxyrhynchus Logoie of Jesus and the Coptic Gospel According to Thomas," in Joseph Fitzmyer, *Essays on the Semitic Background of the New Testament* (Missoula, Mont.: Scholars Press, 1974), pp. 355-433.

[50]James D. G. Dunn, *The Evidence for Jesus* (Philadelphia: Westminster Press, 1985), p. 101.

[51]Ibid.

[52]Ibid., p. 102.

[53]Ibid. See also pp. 96-98 for a more general discussion of the implausibility of a bona fide "Christian Gnosticism" in the first century.

[54]Marvin W. Meyer, "Jesus in the Nag Hammadi Library," *Reformed Journal,* June 1979, p. 15.

[55]Winterhalter, p. 4.

[56]Interestingly, Winterhalter on p. 14 notes that the Oxyrhynchus version of saying 2, mentioned by Dunn above, is more authentic than the Nag Hammadi version, but he

does not speak of the later Gnostic influence. He affirms Thomas' overall authenticity as an historical record of Jesus' words.

[57]Robert M. Grant in collaboration with David Noel Freedman, *The Secret Sayings of Jesus* (Garden City, N.Y.: Doubleday and Company, Inc., 1960), p. 115.

[58]Fitzmyer, "The Gnostic Gospels According to Pagels," p. 123. Fitzmyer grants the existence of "protognostic tendencies at the end of the first century" but not the full-fledged Gnosticism of the Nag Hammadi documents (ibid.). On the issue of Gnostics as late-comers see also Patrick Henry, *New Directions* (Philadelphia: Westminster Press, 1979), pp. 116-19.

[59]James D. G. Dunn, *Unity and Diversity in the New Testament* (Philadelphia: Westminster Press, 1977), pp. 287-88.

[60]Ibid., p. 288; emphasis his. See also Blomberg, *Historical Reliability,* p. 219.

[61]Patrick Henry, p. 282.

[62]Dunn, *Evidence,* pp. 97-98.

[63]Raymond E. Brown, "The Gnostic Gospels," *The New York Times Book Review,* January 20, 1980, p. 3.

[64]F. F. Bruce, *The Canon,* p. 278. See also Henry, pp. 93-119.

[65]Robert E. Speer, *The Finality of Jesus Christ* (Westwood, N.J.: Fleming H. Revell Company, 1933), p. 108.

Chapter 6
The New Testament
Witness to Jesus

*I*f the Gnostic challenge failed to establish a Gnostic Jesus because of insufficient historical evidence, what do the New Testament books contribute to our understanding of Jesus of Nazareth? Has the orthodox Jesus simply rested on a blind faith in the biblical record— "the Bible says it, I believe it, that settles it"—or are there solid reasons to believe these documents are factually and verifiably true?

Although some Christians have disdained reason as opposed to faith, the New Testament itself repeatedly appeals to historical evidence to substantiate its claims. The biblical writers call for faith, but it is a faith based on knowable fact. When the apostle Paul defended Christianity before King Agrippa and Festus, he exclaimed, "What I am saying is true and reasonable." Paul went on to say that the events of Jesus' life that he described were historical facts: "The king is familiar with these things, and I can speak freely to him. I am convinced that none of this has escaped his notice, *because it was not done in a corner"* (Acts 26:26, emphasis mine).

Christianity is an inseparable mixture of timeless truths and temporal events. Without the Jesus of the New Testament historic Christianity shatters into a thousand pieces. In chapters two and three we looked at the Jesus shown us in the Gospels. Now it is time to look at the nature of the New Testament itself, to see if the Jesus it presents can be trusted as the Jesus who actually is.

In evaluating the Gnostic texts we spoke of historical reliability in terms of *integrity* (has the modern text been accurately preserved?), *veracity* (is the message given true to fact?) and *authenticity* (did the purported writer of the document actually write it?). In assessing the New Testament we will begin by inspecting its integrity. Can these ancient documents be trusted today?

The interest in the Nag Hammadi literature in New Age circles should prove that thoroughly modern spiritual seekers are not afraid to dive deep into antiquity in search of revelation. Yet, as we have observed, these texts are often in fairly poor condition, and in most every case cannot be compared with other manuscripts of the same book to insure accuracy. Not a little guesswork went into these translations. Nevertheless many seekers seem more drawn to these documents than to the New Testament. But in terms of manuscript evidence, sometimes called the bibliographic test of historicity, the New Testament completely eclipses Nag Hammadi or any other ancient documents of its time period.

The Integrity of the New Testament

The integrity of the documents concerns the accuracy of the *transmission* of the texts through history, the journey from then to now. It can be broken down into the number, type and age of the extant manuscripts of the New Testament. The greater the number of manuscripts and the closer their age to the date of the original writing, the greater will be the integrity of the document.

Since 1976, the scholarly world has had at its disposal at least 5,366 handwritten manuscripts in the Greek language alone.[1] The number has steadily increased during the last few decades as archaeologists uncover more records of the world's most copied and collected books. The manuscripts range from small fragments to complete New Testaments. They can be divided into four types.

First, papyrus fragments are small portions of ancient papyrus scrolls. The oldest of 88 known fragments[2] contains portions of John and dates from approximately A.D. 125.[3] The Chester Beatty Papyri are much larger, containing much of our New Testament and dating from about A.D. 200.[4] Second, the important uncial, so-called because of the formal Greek script in which the manuscripts are written, number 274 (usually not entire New Testaments).[5] These date from the fourth to the tenth centuries A.D.[6] Codex Vaticanus (B) is dated from approximately A.D. 350 and contains most of the Bible and other documents.[7] Third, 2,795 manuscripts[8] from the ninth to the fifteenth centuries are written in a less formal Greek script called minuscules.[9] Fourth, lectionaries are manuscripts of church service books, the majority of which consist of only passages from the Gospels. Some contain other New Testament books. These date from the ninth century and number 2,209.[10]

Besides these ancient Greek manuscripts, there are 8,000 copies of the Latin Vulgate translation, originally done by Jerome (382-405), and other manuscripts of varying dates in Syriac, Coptic and other languages.[11]

We have dipped into the rather arcane well of ancient documents to make this arresting point: The New Testament is better attested by ancient manuscripts than any other piece of ancient literature. Positive evidence for its integrity consists of the number, quality and age of the manuscripts. There exists no original document (autograph) for any ancient work; therefore scholars seek to compare manuscripts to determine the original text. This is known as textual criticism (or analysis).

With the relatively early dates of the New Testament manuscripts, their plentiful number and frequently high quality, scholars believe they can restore the original texts with a very high degree of accuracy. Scholars readily trust the integrity of many ancient documents that have fewer manuscripts and a much greater time gap between the earliest extant manuscripts and the original writing than the New Testament. For instance, Caesar's *The Gallic Wars* dates from 100-44 B.C. The earliest copy is from A.D. 900, with a time gap of 1,000 years. Further, there are only ten copies.[12] In discussing the identity of Jesus, a cover story in *Time* granted that "existing copies of the New Testament are far older and more numerous than those of any other ancient body of literature."[13]

John Warwick Montgomery notes that "if one compares the New Testament documents with universally accepted writings of antiquity, the New Testament is more than vindicated."[14] He also mentions a debate he had with philosopher Avrum Stroll in which Montgomery challenged Stroll that he must discard all of ancient literature if he discarded the Bible. Stroll declared, "All right, I'll throw out my knowledge of the ancient world." To this the chairman of the classics department cried, "Good Lord, Avrum, not *that!*"[15] If we conserve the classics with their comparatively slim historical integrity, the New Testament must all the more be retained.

Because of the large number of New Testament texts, certain variations are found between texts. This is evidenced in English translations of the Bible, where an alternative reading is listed in the margin or at the bottom of the page. But it should be remembered that these variants are few and far between and usually do not affect the meaning of any given sentence. Modern English Bible translations list the most significant of these variants in footnotes, so they are easy to consult. It can thus be seen that no variant reading calls any important Christian doctrine into question.

Cornelius Hagerty helps explain this:

The more manuscripts discovered the more error, but most of them are such things as omissions of lines, changes in spelling, and transpositions of words, due to carelessness of copyists. They do not affect the meaning of the text. Copyists do not make the same mistakes, and their errors may be corrected by comparing manuscripts.[16]

The very existence of variants in early manuscripts witnesses to the fact that the respective documents were not products of an artificial homogenization; that is, they were not intentionally and illegitimately standardized. This underscores the reliability of the manuscripts, as John Wenham states:

It is clear that there was already a wide diversity of variants in the late second century, which tells us one important thing. It means that there had been no systematic editing of the documents to make them conform to some standard version.[17]

He further argues that there is good reason to believe that the variants themselves predate the second-century manuscripts and can be traced to the first century. Because of this, "the very existence of variants is itself powerful evidence against the systematic, tendentious alteration of the manuscripts in the very early stages of the history of the text."[18] The existence of early variants argues against any contrived tampering with the material. Small, inconsequential deviations in copying are evidence of human error, not deception.

Stephen Neill and Tom Wright comment that the paucity of significant textual variants is "astonishing." They conclude:

Anyone who reads the New Testament in any one of half a dozen recent Greek editions, or in any modern translation, can feel confident that, though there may be uncertainties in detail, in almost everything of importance he is close indeed to the text of the New Testament books as they were originally written.[19]

It is instructive to remember James Robinson's admission that the Nag Hammadi texts are not subject to the same checking procedure as are the biblical texts. Most stand alone and many are quite fragmentary. In their case translators can use only internal tests to fill in the gaps, whereas New Testament textual scholars and translators have numerous manuscripts available from which to piece together the original. If something is unclear or missing in one manuscript, it can be checked against others.

If one chucks the New Testament because of its antiquity, how much more does Nag Hammadi deserve the circular file? But if one is willing to take seriously Nag Hammadi, how much more should the New Testament be respected?

If we have given sufficient reason to trust the basic integrity of the New Testament concerning its textual attestation and accuracy of transmission, we still need to consider the authenticity and veracity of the material lest our texts be nothing more than faithfully preserved falsehoods.[20]

The Veracity of the Gospels and Acts

The New Testament receives high marks for the relatively short time-gap between the dates of the earliest extant manuscripts and the dates of the original writing of the manuscripts. But another time gap must be considered: that between the events and the recording of those events. Of course, generally speaking, the smaller the time gap the better for insuring historical accuracy. Rather than discussing every New Testament book, we will center on the Gospels, Acts and several of the apostle Paul's letters.[21] The issue is this: when were these documents written, and was the time gap so long as to disqualify them as reliable historical reports?

One sure way to fix the outer limit of the age of the Gospels is to cite post-apostolic church fathers who quote from or refer to these sources. Since we know when the church fathers wrote, we can be assured that the Gospels predate them. This is called external documentary evidence.

As mentioned in chapter four, Polycarp, mentor to Irenaeus and disciple of the apostle John, cites several New Testament passages in a short section of his letter to the Philippians, written about A.D. 110. The entire letter goes on to quote from or refer to all four Gospels, the book of Acts and thirteen other New Testament books. We can be sure that these books were in circulation by A.D. 110.[22]

Ignatius wrote seven short letters in approximately A.D. 108, in which he quotes or refers to every Gospel, Acts and the nineteen other New Testament books.[23]

Matthew, Mark and Luke are mentioned by Clement, writing from Rome in about A.D. 96. He also refers to eight other books of the New Testament.[24]

By virtue of these three ancient documents, we can conclude that at least twenty-five of the twenty-seven books of the New Testament were in circulation by about the year 100.[25] This method of dating very conservatively fixes an outer limit: the books cannot be dated after about A.D. 100. But they are very likely to be dated considerably earlier, as we will soon see.[26]

Most modern scholars believe that Mark was written before Matthew and Luke, because it seems the latter two quite often refer to material in Mark, using it as one of their primary sources.[27] We also know that Luke was written some time before Acts because the author of Acts speaks of his "former book," in which he wrote about "all that Jesus began to do and to teach" (Acts 1:1). This "former book" is, in all likelihood, Luke's Gospel. Therefore, if we can date Acts, we can date Luke sometime before it. We can also infer that Mark and Matthew precede Luke, because it appears that Luke relies on Mark and Matthew as sources of information (see Lk 1:1-4, where he mentions previously existing documents about Jesus).[28]

At this point in the argument, we need not even assume Luke is the actual author of the Gospel of Luke or Acts (this properly concerns the authenticity issue). All we need presuppose is that the same author wrote both books, which is very likely the case on stylistic grounds alone. We are here concerned only with proximity in time.

Acts is a history of the early apostolic church in action. As such it is loaded with historical detail. In light of this, four separate considerations argue for an early date for Acts.[29]

First, although much of Acts concerns activities around Jerusalem, it does not record the fall of Jerusalem in A.D. 70, when Roman armies obliterated it. (This event is assuredly dated by the Jewish historian Josephus.) This was a profoundly important event in the ancient world and signified the end of a distinct Jewish state. If the author of Acts wrote after A.D. 70, it seems improbable that he would have omitted this great catastrophe.

Furthermore, the Gospels depict Jesus as repeatedly predicting the fall of Jerusalem because of its rejection of the Messiah (Lk 13:22-35, etc.). Would the author of the Gospel of Luke, if writing after A.D. 70, not mention *this* fulfillment of prophecy, especially when the Gospel of Luke itself records Jesus' life as a fulfillment of various prophecies?

Second, Acts does not mention Nero's intense persecution of Christians in the mid-60s. In fact Acts' general attitude toward Rome is favorable. Other persecutions are recorded, such as Stephen's martyrdom (Acts 7) and the subsequent persecution of the church in Jerusalem (Acts 8), so it would seem odd for the writer to leave Nero unscathed if the document were composed after these persecutions. This seems about as likely as an African Christian historian writing in 1990 on the history of the church in Uganda without mentioning the savage persecution by Idi Amin in the 1970s.

Third, the martyrdoms of James (61) and Peter (65) are not referred to in Acts. It would be highly unusual for these deaths to be left out if the book were written after this time because James and Peter are key players in the book of Acts.

Fourth, the writer does not give us the outcome of Paul's trial (28:30). This is probably because it was still not known at the time Acts was written. If Paul were martyred in A.D. 64, as is commonly held, this would argue for Acts being written before that.[30]

Given these four factors, we can make a reasonable case that the original composition of Acts was in the early sixties A.D. This would make Luke, Mark and Matthew even earlier, perhaps as early as the mid-forties or mid-fifties, just one or two decades after the death of Jesus.[31]

Our argument does not necessarily commit the logical fallacy of the argument from silence; it is, rather, an argument appealing to what appears to be conspicuous absence. We have said that *if* Acts were older than A.D. 70, *then* we would expect to see several important factors that are, in fact, absent. This *conspicuous absence* argues for an earlier date.[32] More positively, the material we find *present* in Acts fits very well with it being written in the early sixties A.D.

The dating of Acts and the Gospels is hotly contested and absolute certainty is unavailable. William F. Albright, the distinguished archaeologist and biblical scholar, affirmed that "every book of the New Testament was written by a baptized Jew between the forties and the eighties of the first century A.D. (very probably sometime between about A.D. 50 and 75)."[33]

Yet, even if we argue that all of the Gospels are somewhat older, the time gap need not discourage those seeking accurate information on Jesus. F. F. Bruce, who dates "Mark at around A.D. 64 or 65, Luke shortly before 70, and Matthew shortly after 70,"[34] has noted that "the time elapsing between the evangelistic events and the writing of most of the New Testament books [including the Gospels] was, from the standpoint of historical research, satisfactorily short."[35]

It is often assumed that the synoptic Gospels depended, to some degree, on previously written (and now unavailable) material about the life of Jesus. Luke seems to state this openly when he speaks of the many others who "have undertaken to draw up an account of the things that have been fulfilled among us" (Lk 1:1). This can also be inferred with Mark and Matthew.[36]

Bruce also notes that these "written sources of our Synoptic Gospels are not later than c. A.D. 60." He believes that some of these sources may even be rooted in notes taken as Jesus himself was speaking.[37] This concept is important in dealing with the common objection that the Gospel writers made up false stories about Jesus. Bruce continues:

> It can have been by no means so easy as some writers seem to think to invent words and deeds of Jesus in those early years, when so many of His disciples were about, who could remember what had and had not happened.[38]

Bruce also notes that the earlier Christians were careful to distinguish the words of Jesus and their own conclusions or judgments, as did Paul (see 1 Cor 7).[39] Furthermore, since Christianity began amidst hostility and controversy, "the disciples could not afford to risk inaccuracies (not to speak of willful manipulations of the facts), which would at once be exposed by those who would be only too glad to do so."[40]

Paul Barnett observes that "it is instructive to compare the literary evidence for Jesus with that of other famous men of antiquity."[41] Tiberius, the Roman emperor during whose lifetime Jesus died, was born in 42 B.C. and reigned from A.D. 14-37. One account of his earlier military exploits dates at A.D. 30, but the major accounts are much later, with Tacitus writing about A.D. 110, Suetonius about A.D. 120 and Dio Cassius about A.D. 220.[42]

Barnett also notes that "the major outlines of Alexander [the Great's] career are not doubted despite a period exceeding four hundred years separating the man and the chief source of information on him."[43] If we date the Gospels very circumspectly at no earlier than A.D. 90 (and they are probably much earlier), we have a time span of fewer than sixty years.

Since John's Gospel seems independent of Matthew, Mark and Luke, the dating of Acts does not bear on its date of composition in the manner explained above. It is often dated last of the four Gospels at sometime near A.D. 90 because of several reasons, one being a reference by Clement of Alexandria (recorded by Eusebius) that John wrote to supplement the writings of the other Gospels.[44] Irenaeus also comments that John wrote after the first three Gospels.[45] Many have argued that John's developed theology is an indication of a later date because such theological sophistication takes time to develop and because he uses language and concepts not available to earlier writers.

The latter argument loses its punch, though, when we consider that Paul's letter to the Romans is dated in the A.D. 50s and is every bit as theologically "developed" as John.[46] Robust theology may appear quickly, especially if one is taught by Jesus himself. The Dead Sea Scrolls, which are dated no later than A.D. 70, use some terminology similar to John, so this kind of language was functioning in Palestine earlier than was once thought. Moreover, the words by Clement and Irenaeus that John was written last need not necessarily mean it was written in the 90s, especially if the synoptic Gospels were written as early as we have just argued. Therefore, John could be dated earlier, although it is granted that this is a minority viewpoint. Even if we date John at around A.D. 90, this is fewer than sixty years removed from the events themselves, a time gap much shorter than that of most classical literature. Many scholars date John in the nineties, while trusting its historical accuracy because of apostolic authorship and corroboration with ancient history.

Yet, some readers may still be troubled by the time period, however long it may have been, separating the life of Jesus and the first written records we now possess. Was there sufficient time for historical distortions? In an age of instant news via magazine, newspaper and television, the idea of a time gap of several decades between the life of Jesus and the dating of our Gospels may be disturbing. Yet, besides the veracity of available written sources used by the Gospel writers, this ignores another key fact: the importance of oral tradition in the ancient Near East. Although the Jews were "people of the book," written resources were far less available than they are today. Consequently, memorization of religious teaching was fundamental to instruction. If people could not easily write it down or tape it, they had to memorize it. The idea of oral tradition goes beyond "hearsay." It was an integral part of the historical memory of the people.

The Jesus of the Gospels is certainly an unforgettable figure. The events of his ministry were indelibly etched on his disciples' minds as the records relate, and it is highly likely that his disciples memorized large amounts of his teachings. Memorization was widespread and impressive in ancient rabbinic circles (with many rabbis memorizing the entire Old Testament!).[47] As Blomberg has noted, "the gospels depict Jesus as . . . a teacher of wisdom and phrase over 90% of his sayings in forms which would have been easy to remember, using figures and styles of speech much like that found in Hebrew poetry."[48] If we add to this that Jesus spoke the Word of God with a prophet's authority, presented himself as the Savior and impelled his disciples to learn and teach his message, there appears a strong dynamic for faithfully remembering his words and deeds.[49]

So even if we date all the Gospels quite late (which I find no good reason for doing) and thus weaken our case for their traditional authenticity, the gap does not increase so measurably as to render their testimony unreliable. Historians have indeed noted that longer time gaps are required for legendary material to take firm hold.

The noted historian of Roman times A. N. Sherwin-White observes that the sources for Roman and Greek history are often at least one or two generations removed from the events they relate; yet this does not prevent historians from confidently consulting the material. White argues that the works of the Greek historian Herodotus equip us to test the rate of legendary accumulation. They show that even two generations is not enough of a time span to allow legendary tendencies to destroy primary facts. When White consults the Gospels, he finds that if the Gospel stories were to contain legends, the rate of legendary development would have to have been "unbelievable" in its rapidity. The Gospels were written too soon after the events to allow for this process of distortion.[50]

In responding to radical Gospel critics in the mid-nineteenth century, Julius Mueller comments that "legendary fiction . . . prefers the mysterious gloom of grey antiquity." It "is wont to seek a remoteness of age, along with that of space, and to remove its boldest and more rare and wonderful creations into a very remote and unknown land."[51] The New Testament is not this kind of legendary fiction. In all likelihood the Gospels were circulated when some of Jesus' contemporaries were still living (or at least many of the second generation would have heard about him from eyewitnesses). In this kind of situation legendary frosting is difficult to apply. The memory of the events would be too close at hand for sugary embellishments.

J. B. Phillips, the celebrated modern translator of the Bible, finds the Gospels and mythological tales to be entirely different:

> I have read, in Greek and Latin, scores of myths, but I did not find the slightest flavour of myth here. There is no hysteria, no careful working for effect, and no attempt at collusion. These are not em-

broidered tales. The material is cut to the bone.[52]
He further speaks of the "almost childlike candour and simplicity" of
the accounts and affirms that "no man could ever have invented such
a character as Jesus." A "real Event" must lie behind the Gospels.[53]

External Confirmation of Veracity

The veracity or truthfulness of documents can also be checked by
looking for confirmation of their historical content from external
sources. This is often called the external test of reliability. This is such
a vast subject that we can only touch on it, noting that the New
Testament documents have been substantially confirmed by archaeology and other ancient writings. (We should also remember that the
New Testament is better attested than any other piece of ancient literature, so we might better speak of the New Testament confirming
other accounts.)

Various archaeological discoveries harmonize with historical details
found in the Gospels. For instance, the discovery of the bones of
Yohan Ben Ha'galgol shed light on the method of crucifixion recorded
in the Gospels. In 1968 an ancient Jewish burial site was accidentally
unearthed. In it were fifteen stone ossuaries holding the bones of
thirty-five Jews who were killed in the fall of Jerusalem in A.D. 70.
One ossuary identified its victim as Yohan, whose feet were pierced
by a long nail still attached to some wood. Nails had also pierced his
wrist and the puncture showed that he had moved up and down on
the cross while struggling for breath. His legs had also been broken.
After describing the above in much more detail, Gary Habermas concludes, "In this case the crucifixion process recorded in the Gospels
has been largely corroborated by this new discovery."[54] Archaeological findings have also corroborated the pool of Bethesda (cf. Jn 5:2),
discovered in 1888;[55] the existence of Pontius Pilate, mentioned on a
fragment of a Latin plaque;[56] the greatness of the Temple during Jesus'
time;[57] the kind of tomb Jesus was buried in, many of which have been
unearthed in Palestine;[58] and many other items. These findings do not
in themselves prove that everything the Gospels say is true, but they

harmonize well with the Gospel accounts.

Luke's writings were scrupulously scrutinized by the renowned archaeologist Sir William Ramsay, who began his investigation assuming that Acts was a basically unreliable document written in the middle
of the second century. His studied conclusion was far different: "Luke
is a historian of the first rank. . . . In short this author should be
placed along with the very greatest of historians."[59] Archaeology also
gives us material on censuses that fits in some detail with Luke's
mention of a Roman census.[60]

John's Gospel, once thought to be too theological to be of much
historical worth, has more recently received respect as precise history.
After discussing John's knowledge of the buildings and landscapes of
ancient Palestine, Barnett comments that "the archaeological evidence
is that the author had minute local knowledge which, however, he
discloses in quite inconspicuous ways."[61]

Added to the external archaeological evidence are significant references to Jesus found in the writings of Jewish and Roman historians,
early church fathers and others. Habermas collected 110 separate facts
about Jesus from these sources that agree with the New Testament
accounts.[62]

The Authorship of the Gospels

We now move from a consideration of the veracity or truthfulness of
the events recorded in the Gospels and Acts (in light of their date of
composition) to the question of *authenticity:* the identity and qualifications of the persons who recorded the events.

Determining the authorship of any document involves both internal
and external criteria. We look at the document itself to ascertain its
author, and we look to outside attestation of the authorship. For
instance it is not impossible to determine who wrote an unsigned
editorial in the local newspaper. We can look at the writing style of
the document itself (internal evidence), and we can gather external
evidence (by calling the newspaper, comparing the writing to signed
editorials and so on).

Concerning external criteria of authenticity, the unanimous tradition of Christianity has been that Matthew wrote Matthew, Mark wrote Mark, Luke wrote Luke and John wrote John. Although tradition can certainly be wrong, the burden of proof seems to be on those who would dispute this claim. Hagerty explains this in legal terms:

Prescription is a process by which a right is acquired through long use. It is important for a lawyer to show a court on which side of a case lies the burden of proof. Now it is an undisputed fact that Matthew, Mark, Luke and John have been credited with being the authors of the Gospels since the last quarter of the second century. . . . The burden of proof is definitely on any modern scholar who contradicts this ancient tradition.[63]

During the first quarter of the fourth century, the church historian Eusebius in his *Ecclesiastical History*[64] quotes from the writings of the Bishop Papias of Hierapolis (c. A.D. 70-140) who wrote a treatise in five books on the sayings of the apostles and other contemporaries of Christ. The quotation mentions that Mark, the interpreter of Peter, wrote a record of Christ. It also mentions that Matthew recorded the sayings of Jesus.[65]

Irenaeus explicitly names the authors of all four Gospels, explains the occasion for their being written and quotes from them (and almost all the books of the New Testament) extensively.[66] In *Against Heresies* (A.D. 180), he speaks of these writings that are "the ground and pillar of our faith," saying that:

Matthew . . . issued a Gospel among the Hebrews. . . . Mark, the disciple and interpreter of Peter, did also hand down to us in writing what had been preached by Peter. Luke also, the companion of Paul, recorded in a book the Gospel preached by him. Afterward, John, the disciple of the Lord, who had leaned on His breast, did himself publish a Gospel during his residence at Ephesus in Asia.[67]

Even before Irenaeus, Justin Martyr (A.D. 100-165), in his *First Apology*, speaks this way concerning the Lord's Supper:

For the Apostles *in their memoirs composed by them which are called gospels,* have delivered unto us what was enjoined upon them: that Jesus took bread, and when He had given thanks said "This do ye in remembrance of me."[68]

Justin Martyr also speaks of "the memoirs of the apostles" when recounting Jesus' baptism and subsequent temptation by the devil.[69]

An ancient Latin manuscript called the Muratorian Fragment, dating from about A.D. 190, also mentions "the third book of the gospel: according to Luke" which was written by a "physician whom Paul had taken along with him as a legal expert." The document also states that Luke wrote "in accordance with [Paul's] opinion."[70] The text also mentions "the fourth gospel" which "is by John, one of the disciples."[71]

The testimony of other writers such as Origen (A.D. 185-254), Clement of Alexandria (A.D. 150-215) and Tertullian (A.D. 155-220) agrees with the attributions given by Irenaeus.[72] These scholars did not take the Gospels' authorship lightly, especially given their situation as apologists. Hagerty also notes "that it cannot be too strongly emphasized that the scholars of the early centuries had access to sources of information that later scholars and critics did not."[73] In other words they were in a good position to know the truth and had a vested interest as defenders of the faith to do so.

If external criteria point toward traditional authorship, what of internal matters? Do the Gospels themselves betray their authorship?

The Gospels do not openly reveal their authors, but various factors fit well with the external evidence. We have already argued in general for early dates for the Gospels. The dating of Matthew, Mark and Luke as pre-A.D. 70 certainly leaves open the possibility of them being penned by these men. (Even if they were written closer to A.D. 90 by persons other than the traditional authors, contrary to strong external evidence, the time gap need not disqualify them from being reliable history.)

Certain features of the Gospel of Matthew fit with the predilections of a diligent tax collector, especially an attention to detail that matches "the methodical arrangement of this Gospel."[74] Although Mark and

Luke record the dispute over paying taxes, Matthew uses a more precise Greek term for a state coin, something a tax collector would notice.[75] Also noticeable is his frequent reference to money, an interest in large amounts (18:24; 25:15), and a general interest in statistics (e.g., 1:17).[76]

Only Matthew records the call of the tax collector to be a disciple. Mark and Luke refer to him as Levi but in the lists of apostles call him Matthew. The Gospel of Matthew consistently refers to him as Matthew, which could indicate that "the name Matthew came to have greater significance than the name Levi from the time of his dramatic call to follow Jesus."[77]

The internal evidence for Matthew's authorship is not, in itself, overwhelming; but nothing in the Gospel excludes it[78] and much external evidence encourages it.

Again, with the Gospel of Mark we find no explicit reference to authorship, but neither do we find anything in the Gospel which is incompatible with Mark, "the disciple and interpreter of Peter," as Irenaeus put it, being the author. The Gospel's dramatic style mirrors the rather flamboyant and dramatic character of Peter himself as evidenced in all four Gospels. New Testament scholar C. H. Dodd also noted the similarity between the outlines of the life of Christ given in Peter's sermons in Acts (10:34-43) and the chronology of the Gospel of Mark, thus giving more evidence to a connection to the apostle Peter.[79] Mark is the only Gospel that refers to a rather strange detail of the passion story: a young man wearing nothing but a linen cloth who escaped being captured when he ran away naked, leaving his garment behind (Mk 14:51-52). Many have taken this to be a veiled (or unveiled, actually) reference to Mark himself.[80] There is also good reason to identify Mark with the John Mark referred to in several other New Testament texts.[81]

The writer of Luke speaks in the first person as does the writer of Acts, which is written as a continuation of Luke. Both books are addressed to Theophilus, have common concerns and similar style. The author of Luke does not directly identify himself, but he was a companion of Paul as several "we" passages in Acts reveal (16:10-17; 20:5-15; 21:1-18; 27:1—28:16). Paul mentions his "dear friend Luke, the doctor" (Col 4:14) and Luke his "fellow worker" (Philem 24), so Luke is the likeliest candidate, which fits well with the strong external evidence.

The Gospel of John claims to be written by a disciple of Jesus. After describing the death of Jesus, the text reads, "The man who saw it has given testimony, and his testimony is true. He knows that he tells the truth, and he testifies so that you also may believe" (19:35). It also says, "This is the disciple who testifies to these things and who wrote them down. We know that his testimony is true" (21:24). The "we" here very likely refers not to a group of authors but to the disciples whom John often refers to as "we" (see 1:14; 2:11).[82] Though the disciple does not explicitly identify himself, his references to "the disciple whom Jesus loved," taken together with several other references, identifies him as John.[83] (The three Letters of John show such a strong stylistic resemblance to the Gospel of John that they, too, can be considered penned by the apostle.)

Our survey finds good external and internal reasons to view the Gospels as written by their traditional authors. The significance of this is that each author was in a position to flesh out the historical facts about Jesus. Matthew and John were disciples themselves, so their testimony has the ring of eyewitnesses. Luke very likely was not an eyewitness but inspected the records carefully (Lk 1:1-4) and has traditionally been viewed as the companion of Paul who, although also not an eyewitness to the earthly Jesus, is, as we will see, a reliable source of information as well. Mark may or may not have been an eyewitness, but it is very likely that his Gospel bears the stamp of the apostle Peter himself.[84] Although we cannot range over the vast amount of historical claims made in the Gospels, it must be noted that they bear the marks of historicity. They are plentiful in references to politics, geography, specific individuals and the minutiae of history. The fact that they contain a theological message is not a sufficient reason to jettison their historical reliability. The New Testament can be "full of faith and full of fact."[85] As David Wells has noted:

> It is consistent with the practice of historical research in other fields
> to assume the New Testament record is innocent in respect to the
> accuracy of its portrayal of Jesus until proven guilty. . . . It is true
> that the Gospels were written in the context of faith, but that does
> not mean that they are thereby distorted.[86]

R. T. France asks, "How much worthwhile biography has ever been
written by authors who did not have a deep personal motivation for
writing?"[87] Yet this motivation need not exclude historical integrity.

This is all the more compelling when we realize that the writers of
the Gospels had no ulterior motives for dishonesty: this was no "get
rich quick" scheme, and Christian discipleship often meant persecution by unresponsive Jews and threatened political forces.

We just noted John's declaration that he preserved the truth about
Jesus in order that his readers would believe that truth. Even the
skeptical Will Durant in his multi-volume series, *The Story of Civilization,* says that

> despite the prejudices and theological preconceptions of the evan-
> gelists, they record many incidents that mere inventors would have
> concealed—the competition of the apostles for high places in the
> Kingdom, their flight after Jesus' arrest, Peter's denial, the failure
> of Christ to work miracles in Galilee, the references of some aud-
> itors to his possible insanity, his early uncertainty as to his mission,
> his confessions of ignorance as to the future, his moments of bit-
> terness, his despairing cry on the cross; no one reading these scenes
> can doubt the reality of the figure behind them.[88]

These comments should not lead one to think that the Gospels present Jesus as sinning. They rather show him in the fullness of his
humanity.

Durant, who was himself not a Christian, believed it would be a
"miracle far more incredible than any recorded in the Gospels" if "a
few simple men should in one generation have invented so powerful
and appealing a personality, so lofty an ethic and so inspiring a vision
of human brotherhood."[89]

Do the Gospels Contradict Each Other?

Our case for the trustworthiness of the Gospels has been steadily building, but some will object that the four different accounts of Jesus contradict each other, thus vitiating their force as historical. So Joseph Campbell says, "We just don't know much about Jesus. All we know are four contradictory texts that purport to tell us what he said and did."[90]

We do, in fact, know much about Jesus, even if the Gospels are not biographies *in the modern sense* (see chapter two) and, as we will see below, there is good historical evidence from Paul about Jesus. Furthermore the basic outline of the life, person and work of Jesus is presented by all four Gospel writers without contradiction or ambiguity. His essential claims and credentials are heralded by all the writers. But are the Gospels contradictory in any sense?

To answer this would involve a careful look at the relationships between four separate and substantial texts. Yet a few general remarks help soften Campbell's and other New Agers' objections. The very fact that we have four distinct accounts actually strengthens the evidence for Jesus. We are not dependent on merely one witness: neither do the accounts evidence a contrived uniformity.

Each Gospel was written by a different author, at a different time, with a different style and with a different audience in mind. Each, of course, had to be selective in his choice of material. Many supposed contradictions evaporate quite quickly by keeping this in mind. Two newspapers, for instance, may write up the last game of the World Series somewhat differently without contradicting each other. If John records a miracle not mentioned by Matthew, Mark and Luke, this is no contradiction, but rather an addition. If Matthew omits something in Mark, it is no contradiction but a deletion. One account may also paraphrase an event somewhat differently without actually contradicting another account. In most cases a little historical snooping can resolve apparent contradictions. A good "harmony of the gospels" gives a composite picture of all four accounts. Simply consulting the notes of The New International Version Study Bible is very helpful in working with apparent contradictions, as is the book *The Historical Reliability of the Gospels* by Craig Blomberg.[91]

We have come this far in our scrutiny of the Gospels and Acts: First, we have reason to grant them integrity as historical documents given the manuscript evidence. Second, we have found they are not so far removed from the events they record as to be unreliable. Third, we find external corroboration for the New Testament reports. Fourth, by virtue of external and internal evidence, we can trust they were written by authors in a position to know the truth about Jesus. Fifth, there would be no reason for these authors to fabricate their Gospels and strong disincentives not to do so. Sixth, the Gospels need not be viewed as contradictory texts concerning Jesus.

Paul As a Witness to Jesus

But we have another witness who presents very earlier material on Jesus: Paul of Tarsus. Almost all biblical scholars accept that Paul wrote Romans, First and Second Corinthians, Galatians, Philippians, 1 Thessalonians and Philemon. Although a strong case can be made that he wrote all the letters of the New Testament attributed to him,[92] we will limit our discussion primarily to these seven letters.

We have already seen the evidence for the *integrity* of the New Testament, and even the most liberal scholars grant that Paul authored the above books, so we are assured of their *authenticity* as well. But what of their *veracity?*

Scholars agree that Paul died by about A.D. 65, so all his letters predate this. F. F. Bruce estimates that all of Paul's letters were written between A.D. 48 and 60.[93] The very early dating of these letters witnesses to their veracity, as does their very character as letters. Historians relish personal letters as primary source material, especially if they contain trivia and lists of details, are written in an unpolished style and were originally for a small audience. Paul's letters fulfill most, if not all, of these requirements and thus evidence historical reliability.[94]

In several places Paul refers to hymns and creeds, which scholars believe predate his writings because they betray features of Hebrew poetry and thought forms and they translate easily into Aramaic, the language in which they would have been spoken in the very early church.[95]

In chapter three we mentioned Philippians 2:6-11, which speaks of the Incarnation ("taking the form of a servant"), suffering ("death on a cross") and exaltation ("the name which is above every name") of Jesus. This is an early church hymn abundant with doctrine that agrees with the Gospel accounts. Other hymns in Pauline writings are found in Colossians 1:15-20, Ephesians 2:14-16, and 1 Timothy 3:16.

Paul also cites early creeds. In discussing the Lord's Supper Paul tells the Corinthians, "For I received from the Lord what I also passed on to you" (1 Cor 11:23). This indicates a previously held early church tradition. In Romans 10:9 Paul repeats what was probably an early baptismal confession: "That if you confess with your mouth, 'Jesus is Lord,' and believe in your heart that God raised him from the dead, you will be saved." In a passage we will inspect more closely in chapter ten, Paul argues for the resurrection of Jesus by saying, "For what I received I passed on to you as of first importance: that Christ died for our sins according to the Scriptures, that he was buried, that he was raised on the third day according to the Scriptures" (1 Cor 15:3-4). Paul is relaying information that had been previously given.

These creeds and hymns lend veracity to Paul's writings for two reasons. First, they reveal a view of Jesus that predates Paul's writings, taking us even closer to the life of Jesus himself. The majority of scholars date them from A.D. 33 to 48.[96] Second, they evidence an emphasis on the death, resurrection and deity of Jesus from an early date. These ideas were not grafted onto a non-supernatural Jesus by the later church. These creeds and hymns represent the "rich Christological content"[97] of the young church's confessions and worship. They cannot be arranged in order from earlier, more simple views, to later, more complex and imaginative ones. Their theology is consistently rich.[98]

New Testament writers such as Peter (1 Pet 3:18-22), the authors of Hebrews (Heb 1:13) and John (Jn 1:1-18) repeat various other hymnic and creedal material as well. Even if there is some debate as to which passages reflect earlier hymns and creeds, their existence and frequency has been positively established, and this more firmly anchors the historicity of the record of Jesus.

The early dates for Paul's writings and the primitive nature of these hymns and creeds also weakens the contention of many New Agers and others that Paul departed from the original spirit of Jesus and invented a Christianity (or Paulinism) of his own design.[99] Although Paul claimed to receive direct revelation from the risen Christ, he is in full agreement with the Gospel accounts of Jesus (whether he knew of these or not). Paul's emphasis is on the glorified Christ (as we will explore in chapter ten), but he by no means ignores the earthly life or teachings of Jesus. For Paul, the outline of Jesus' earthly ministry was a given that he naturally incorporated into his letters. About Jesus Paul declares: he descended from Abraham (Gal. 3:16); he was a descendant of David (Rom 1:3); he was born of a woman (Gal 4:4); he lived under the law (Gal 4:4); he was humble (Phil 2:6-7); he did not please himself, but was insulted (Rom. 15:3); he instituted the Lord's Supper (1 Cor 11:23); he was betrayed (1 Cor 11:23); he was killed by Jews of Judea (1 Thess 2:14-15); he was buried and rose again (1 Cor 15:4-8).[100]

Paul's teaching also deeply reflects the ethics of Jesus at many points, concerning the Lord's Supper (1 Cor 11:23-25; cf. Mk 14:22-25), divorce and remarriage (1 Cor 7:10-11; cf. Mk 10:1-12), practical ethics (Rom 12:9—13:10; cf. Mt 5—7) and other issues. F. F. Bruce puts this in perspective:

> The outline of the gospel story . . . in the writings of Paul agrees with the outlines which we find elsewhere in the New Testament, and in the four gospels in particular. Paul himself is at pains to point out that the gospel which he preached was one and the same gospel as that preached by the other apostles [1 Cor 15:11], a striking claim, considering that Paul was neither a companion of Christ

in the days of his flesh nor of the original apostles, and that he vigorously asserts his independence of these [Gal 1-2].[101] In our inspection of the New Testament[102] witness to Jesus we have found it to pass the tests of integrity, authenticity and veracity. As Jesus put it, the sheep hear the shepherd's voice (Jn 10:16) speaking in the Scriptures. For those who have any sense of historical reality, these factors should lead to respect for the New Testament record of Jesus. We have good reason to trust its testimony as reliable.

The burden of proof, it seems, would be on anyone marshalling an historical case against the evidence of the New Testament that Jesus of Nazareth is the only Christ. This is exactly the strategy of those claiming that Jesus spent his "lost years" in India. This intriguing and increasingly popular claim is the focus of the next chapter.

Notes

[1]Bruce M. Metzger, *Manuscripts of the Greek Bible* (New York: Oxford University Press, 1981), p. 54.

[2]Ibid.

[3]Kurt Aland and Barbara Aland, *The Text of the New Testament* (Grand Rapids, Mich.: Eerdmans, 1987), p. 84.

[4]Ibid., p. 87. See also Bruce Metzger, *The Text of the New Testament* (New York: Oxford University Press, 1964), pp. 36-42.

[5]Metzger, *Text,* pp. 36-42.

[6]Ibid., pp. 42-61.

[7]Ibid., pp. 47-48.

[8]Metzger, *Manuscripts,* p. 54.

[9]Ibid.; Metzger, *Text,* pp. 61-66.

[10]Ibid.; Metzger, *Text,* pp. 30-31.

[11]Metzger, *Text,* pp. 68-86.

[12]See the illustrative chart in J. P. Moreland, *Scaling the Secular City* (Grand Rapids, Mich.: Baker Book House, 1987), p. 135.

[13]Richard Ostling, "Who Was Jesus?" *Time,* August 15, 1988, p. 37.

[14]John Warwick Montgomery, *Human Rights and Human Dignity* (Grand Rapids, Mich.: Zondervan, 1986), p. 139.

[15]Ibid., emphasis his.

[16]Cornelius Hagerty, *The Authenticity of the Sacred Scriptures* (Houston, Tex.: Lumen Christi Press, 1969), p. 303.

[17]John Wenham, *Christ and the Bible* (Grand Rapids, Mich.: Baker, 1984), p. 177.

[18]Ibid.

[19]Stephen Neill and Tom Wright, *The Interpretation of the New Testament 1861-1986* (Oxford: Oxford University Press, 1988), p. 86.

[20]Although he does not come to orthodox conclusions, it is interesting to note that Wilson believes the manuscript evidence for the Gospels is very good. See Ian Wilson, *Jesus: The Evidence* (San Francisco: Harper and Row, 1984), pp. 29-31. He says, "on the whole, errors and textual variations are relatively minor, and the canonical gospels can be judged to be very much as their authors wrote them" (p. 31).

[21]We have argued that every New Testament book has historical integrity. Detailed arguments for the veracity and authenticity of books I do not discuss can be found in Donald Guthrie's *New Testament Introduction* (Downers Grove, Ill.: InterVarsity, 1970).

[22]Paul Barnett, *Is the New Testament History?* (Ann Arbor, Mich.: Servant Publications, 1986), pp. 38-39.

[23]Ibid.

[24]Ibid. Robinson dates 1 Clement at A.D. 70. See John A. T. Robinson, *Redating the New Testament* (Philadelphia: Westminster, 1976), p. 335; see his whole discussion of the dating of post-apostolic writings, pp. 312-35. Robinson's thesis is that every book of the New Testament was written before A.D. 70.

[25]Corinthians by Clement (A.D. 95) and The Epistle of Pseudo-Barnabas (A.D. 130-38) also mention various New Testament books. See Gary Habermas, *The Verdict of History* (Nashville, Tenn.: Thomas Nelson, 1988), pp. 141-42, 144-45.

[26]Although Polycarp, Ignatius and Clement do not refer to every New Testament book, this does not necessarily mean they were not in existence at that time; to argue otherwise would be "the argument from silence" (fallacy). It could be that the other books simply did not warrant the writers' attention or that they did not know of their existence.

[27]On this entire issue, known as the "synoptic problem," see Guthrie, pp. 121-236.

[28]The view of the early church was that Matthew predated Mark and Luke, but this is the minority opinion among modern scholars. Even if Matthew did not predate Mark or Luke, the dating of Acts still gives us the approximate date for Luke.

[29]I am here following the general argument of J. P. Moreland, pp. 151-54. See also Guthrie, pp. 340-45.

[30]Lewis Foster, "Introduction: Acts of the Apostles," in The NIV Study Bible, ed. Kenneth L. Barker (Grand Rapids, Mich.: Zondervan, 1985), p. 1641.

[31]Moreland, p. 154. Even if Luke does not depend on Mark and Matthew, the argument just given still gives us a very early date for Luke and Acts. Early dates can be argued for Mark and Matthew along other lines as well. On this see Guthrie, *New Testament Introduction.*

[32]In logical terms the argument we are using to this point is called the "denial of the consequent." Abstractly put, it runs as follows: If *A* (the antecedent), then *B* (the consequent). Not *B*. Therefore, not *A*. In our terms: If *a later date for Acts* then (likely) *x, y, z*. But we do not find *x, y, z*. Therefore, (likely) no *later date for Acts.*

[33]"Toward a More Conservative Faith: Interview with William F. Albright," *Christianity Today,* January 18, 1963, p. 3.

[34]F. F. Bruce, *The New Testament Documents: Are They Reliable?* 6th ed. (Grand Rapids, Mich.: Eerdmans Pub. Co., 1987), p. 12.

[35]Ibid., p. 14.

[36]Ibid., pp. 30-46.

[37]Ibid., p. 45.

38Ibid., pp. 45-46.

39Ibid., p. 46; see also Craig Blomberg, *The Historical Reliability of the Gospels* (Downers Grove, Ill.: InterVarsity Press, 1987), pp. 31-33.

40Bruce, *New Testament Documents,* p. 46. For a discussion of the reliability of the New Testament witnesses in terms of legal evidence and reasoning see Montgomery, pp. 131-60.

41Barnett, p. 40.

42Ibid., p. 41.

43Ibid.

44Eusebius, *Ecclesiastical History,* 6.14.7.

45Irenaeus, *Against Heresies,* 3.1.1.

46See Leon Morris, *The Gospel of John* (Grand Rapids, Mich.: Eerdmans, 1971), p. 32; see pp. 30-35 for his argument for early dating. See also Barnett, pp. 61-66.

47Blomberg, p. 26.

48Ibid., p. 27.

49For the entire discussion of this issue, see ibid., pp. 25-31, and Moreland, pp. 142-44.

50A. N. Sherwin-White, *Roman Society and Roman Law in the New Testament* (Oxford: Claredon, 1963), pp. 188-91; cited in William L. Craig, *Knowing the Truth about the Resurrection* (Ann Arbor, Mich.: Servant, 1988), p. 96.

51Julius Mueller, *The Theory of Myths, in Its Application to the Gospel History, Examined and Confuted* (London: John Chapman, 1844), p. 26; cited in Craig, p. 95.

52J. B. Phillips, *The Ring of Truth* (New York: The Macmillan Company, 1967), p. 77.

53Ibid.

54Habermas, pp. 154-55.

55Bruce, *New Testament Documents,* p. 94.

56R. T. France, *The Evidence for Jesus* (Downers Grove, Ill.: InterVarsity Press, 1986), p. 147.

57Ibid., pp. 149-50.

58Ibid., pp. 151-52.

59Ramsay, W. M., *The Bearing of Recent Discovery on the Trustworthiness of the New Testament* (London: Hodder and Stoughton, 1915), p. 222; cited in Bruce, *New Testament Documents,* p. 91.

60See Habermas, pp. 152-53.

61Barnett, p. 64; on archaeological insights on Jesus and his day see also James H. Charlesworth, *Jesus within Judaism* (New York: Doubleday, 1988), pp. 103-30.

62For a review of these, see Habermas, pp. 164-69. The entire book is dedicated to uncovering extrabiblical evidence for the life of Jesus.

63Hagerty, p. 230.

64Eusebius, 3.39.16.

65See Bruce Metzger, *The Canon of the New Testament* (Oxford: Clarendon Press, 1987), pp. 51-56. For a discussion of Papias's reference to John the Elder, which some have thought to be different from John the Apostle, see Guthrie, pp. 266-68.

66See Metzger, *Canon,* pp. 153-56, on Irenaeus' view of Scripture.

67Irenaeus, 3.1.1.

68Justin Martyr, *The First Apology of Justin Martyr,* ch. 66, in *The Apostolic Fathers,* p. 185; emphasis mine.

[69]Justin Martyr, *Dialogue with Trypho,* in *The Apostolic Fathers,* ch. 103, p. 185.

[70]Cited in F. F. Bruce, *The Canon of Scripture* (Downers Grove, Ill.: InterVarsity Press, 1988), p. 159.

[71]Ibid. The extant text is mutilated at the beginning and only names Luke and John. We can legitimately surmise that the original mentioned the first and second Gospels as well.

[72]See Hagerty, pp. 234-36.

[73]Ibid., p. 234.

[74]Guthrie, p. 44.

[75]Ibid.

[76]Homer A. Kent, "Introduction: The Gospel According to Matthew," in *The Wycliffe Bible Commentary,* ed. Charles F. Pfeiffer and Everett F. Harrison (Chicago: Moody Press, 1977), p. 929.

[77]Guthrie, p. 44.

[78]For a defense of Matthew's authorship against some modern criticisms see Guthrie, pp. 33-43, and Hagerty, pp. 252-58.

[79]See Barnett, pp. 85-86.

[80]Ibid., p. 84.

[81]Ibid., pp. 83-84.

[82]Ibid., p. 57.

[83]Ibid., pp. 58-59. See also Bruce, *New Testament Documents,* pp. 47-48.

[84]On the importance of eyewitness testimony see Barnett, pp. 49-55, and Moreland, pp. 137-42.

[85]See John A. T. Robinson, *Can We Trust the New Testament?* (London and Oxford: Mowbrays, 1977), p. 8.

[86]David Wells, *The Person of Christ* (Westchester, Ill.: Crossway Books, 1984), p. 14.

[87]France, p. 103.

[88]Will Durant, *Caesar and Christ,* vol. 2, The Story of Civilization (New York: Simon and Schuster, 1944), p. 557.

[89]Ibid.

[90]Joseph Campbell, *The Power of Myth* (New York: Doubleday), p. 211.

[91]See especially, Blomberg, pp. 113-89. See also Gleason Archer, *Encyclopedia of Biblical Difficulties;* and Robert L. Thomas and Stanley N. Gundry, *A Harmony of the Gospels with Explanations and Essays* (San Francisco, Calif.: Harper and Row, 1978), pp. 265-337.

[92]See Guthrie.

[93]Bruce, *New Testament Documents,* p. 76.

[94]Moreland, pp.136-37, and Phillips, p.39

[95]Moreland, p. 148.

[96]Ibid., p. 149.

[97]Bernard Ramm, *An Evangelical Christology* (Nashville, Tenn.: Thomas Nelson Publishers, 1985), p. 114.

[98]Ibid. On the early creeds and hymns see also Habermas, pp. 120-27.

[99]This accusation is leveled by Holger Kersten in *Jesus Lived in India* (Longmead, England: Element Book Ltd., 1986). This book will be critiqued in the next chapter.

[100]See Barnett, p. 131.

[101]Bruce, *New Testament Documents,* p. 79. See also Barnett, pp. 125-36. For a more

detailed treatment of Paul's view of Jesus see F. F. Bruce, *Paul: Apostle of the Heart Set Free* (Grand Rapids, Mich.: Eerdmans, 1979), pp. 95-112. For a defense of Paul's fidelity to the historical Jesus and the non-syncretistic nature of his theology see J. Gresham Machen, *The Origin of Paul's Religion* (Grand Rapids, Mich.: Eerdmans, 1976), particularly pp. 117-69, and Ronald Nash, *Christianity in the Hellenistic World* (Grand Rapids, Mich.: Zondervan, 1984), especially pp. 57-79, 183-99, 241-50.

[102]We have only specifically dealt with the Gospels and several of Paul's writings as passing all three tests of integrity, authenticity and veracity. We have, though, shown that all the New Testament documents have integrity and were early recognized by the church as authoritative. For a more full-orbed defense of the entire New Testament, see Bruce, *The New Testament Documents* and *The Canon of Scripture;* Barnett, *Is the New Testament History?*; Hagerty, *The Authenticity of the Sacred Scriptures;* and John Wenham, *Christ and the Bible.*

Chapter 7
The Lost Years
of Jesus

*W*e all love secrets, especially when we are the recipients of a particularly juicy one. And the more significant the subject matter, the more precious the secret. Hidden wisdom is a scarce and treasured commodity that elevates the initiated into rarified realms. What the masses have lost, the knowers have found. Blessed are the knowers who see through convention to reality, those who solve the mystery of "the lost years of Jesus."

The conventional Christian understanding of Jesus places him in Jewish sandals worn only in ancient Palestine. The Christ came to the Jewish people, as promised by the prophets, to mend the lame, feed the poor, raise the dead, proclaim the kingdom, obey the Father, die as a ransom for many and be raised from the dead as the final demonstration of his unique mission and deity. Before his ascension Jesus charged his disciples to make disciples of all the nations (Mt 28:18-20; Acts 1:8), yet his own earthly ministry was limited to his homeland, Palestine.

In the biblical understanding Jesus need not be a world traveler to be the Savior of the world. Matthew records Jesus' trip to Egypt as an infant, but the significance of this flight from Herod's sword is explained as a fulfillment of the prophecy "Out of Egypt I called my Son" (Mt 2:15; see Hos 11:1). God called Jesus "out of Egypt," not toward Egypt or any other Eastern site.

When Jesus taught in the synagogue in his hometown, many were amazed at his teaching and wondered, "Where did this man get these things? . . . What's this wisdom that has been given him, that he even does miracles! Isn't this the carpenter? Isn't this Mary's son and the brother of James, Joseph, Judas and Simon? Aren't his sisters here with us?" (Mk 6:1-3; cf. Mt 13:53-58). They were shocked that the Jesus they knew, this hometown boy, would teach with power and work miracles.

Despite the fact that Jesus' biblical biography sums up his life between the ages of about twelve to thirty with one sentence in Luke ("And Jesus grew in wisdom and stature, and in favor with God and men" [2:52]), there is no hint that he left Palestine. As a carpenter, he would have no reason to do so. As the Son of Man, he said, "I was sent only to the lost sheep of Israel" (Mt 15:24). Jesus never showed any desire to explore the world in search of greater teaching; in fact he confidently affirmed to the Samaritan woman that "salvation is from the Jews" (Jn 4:22). A natural reading of the Gospel of Luke, for instance, does not reveal a gaping hole in Jesus' life. No years are "lost"; rather, some years are summarized. Given Jesus' later ministry and his interest in theology displayed as a child, we can well imagine him studying the Scriptures while learning the trade of carpentry from his father. Commenting on the supposed "lost years," biblical scholar Edgar Goodspeed assumes that it was no wonder Jesus could use the Hebrew prophets "with such power in his brief ministry; he had studied and pondered them for many years, as no one has ever done, before or since."[1]

In the Gospels the key to Jesus' public ministry is not a sojourn to the East but his baptism. This is the time when God the Father publicly endorsed and commissioned him and when the Holy Spirit came upon him in power. As we saw in chapters two and three, Jesus' subsequent ministry and teaching was not that of a Hindu guru or Buddhist sage. He preached resurrection, not reincarnation. He instructed his disciples to relate to a personal God, not an impersonal principle. He declared and demonstrated himself uniquely to be God in the flesh, not one of many God-realized masters.[2]

Nevertheless, two passages from the New Testament are sometimes used to justify Jesus as a world traveler. The first is John 21:25: "Jesus did many other things as well. If every one of them were written down, I suppose that even the whole world would not have room for the books that would be written."[3] This is thought to sanction ventures eastward by a Jesus bearing little resemblance to the Bible's central character. But a parallel passage adds more clarity to this verse. John 20:30-31 says:

> Jesus did many other miraculous signs in the presence of his disciples, which are not recorded in this book. But these are written that you may believe that Jesus is the Christ, the Son of God, and that by believing you may have life in his name.

John is overwhelmed with Jesus' miraculous power, but he has selected certain accounts in order to trigger belief in Jesus. His statement that all the books in the world could not contain a complete record of Jesus' deeds is not a carte blanche endorsement of anything that might be said about him. In his first letter he warns of anti-Christs who distort the doctrine of Christ (1 Jn 4:1-4). Someone might say that all the biographies the world has to offer on Mother Theresa are not sufficient to record the extent of her loving deeds, but this would in no way open the door to a biography claiming that she spent her teenage years as a glamorous fashion model in France. John is referring to those things Jesus did *when he was with his disciples in Palestine.* This is the normal and natural way to read John 21:25 when compared with John 20:30-31. Lost years are not in question.

Janet Bock refers to John 1:31, where John the Baptist says he did not know Jesus, as evidence that Jesus had been away from Palestine for quite some time. Otherwise, John, Jesus' cousin, would have recognized him.[4] Bock fails to note the obvious fact that John was a recluse who "lived in the desert until he appeared publicly to Israel" (Lk 1:80); he may not have known Jesus at all because he had not grown up with him. Or, probably more likely, given the context of the verse, John would not have known Jesus was *the Messiah* if not for the fact that the Holy Spirit had descended on him (Jn 1:29-34). In any case, lost years and world traveling, again, are not at issue.

Nevertheless, these silent or "lost" years have mystified and preoccupied many who believe that within this biographical blank lies the entire meaning of Jesus.

Enter Nicholas Notovitch

In 1894 a Russian journalist named Nicholas Notovitch published a book in France called *La vie inconnue de Jesus-Christ (The Unknown Life of Jesus Christ)*, which became quite popular and controversial, going through eight editions in one year. Later in that same year three English translations appeared, along with Italian and German translations, followed a few years later by Swedish (1896) and Spanish (1909) translations.[5] Notovitch's story was as exotic as his claims were bold. If he was right, historic, institutional Christianity was wrong about the one they worshiped as Lord.

The controversy centered on a supposedly lost Tibetan document called "The Life of Saint Issa: Best of the Sons of Men," which claims that Jesus left Palestine from ages thirteen to twenty-nine to travel East. Notovitch made this rather short document the heart of his book, bracketing it with essays explaining how he happened to find it and what he made of its significance.

In 1907 Levi Downing offered a channeled book, *The Aquarian Gospel of Jesus the Christ*, which echoed many of Notovitch's claims. (We will deal with Downing in chapter nine.) Several New Age books, such as *The Lost Years of Jesus* by Elizabeth Clare Prophet, *The Jesus Mystery* by Janet Bock, and *Jesus Lived in India* by Holger Kersten, present the claims of Notovitch, Downing and others as serious challenges to established Christianity. With certain variations, they all believe that Jesus was no stranger to the mystic East. He lived there, imbibed the ancient teachings and returned to Palestine an enlightened Master. But it all began with the obscure Russian journalist, Notovitch. Just what did he claim and what was his evidence?

In the preface of *The Unknown Life of Jesus Christ* Notovitch reports that after the Turkish War (1877-1878) he journeyed to India to study "the peoples who inhabit India and their customs, the grand and mysterious archaeology, and the colossal and majestic nature of their country."[6] After various travels he arrived at Ladakh, Tibet, from where he intended to return to Russia. But while there he heard from a chief lama of "very ancient memoirs relating to the life of Jesus Christ,"[7] contained in certain great monasteries. With renewed vigor, Notovitch decided to hunt down this material instead of returning to Russia. While at Leh, the capital of Ladakh, he visited the Himis monastery, where the chief lama informed him that copies of the manuscripts were housed. Notovitch says that, in order not to arouse suspicion, he decided to depart for India.[8]

After his departure Notovitch says he fortuitously broke his leg, which brought him back to Himis for treatment and, ultimately, for the recovery of the "lost" years of Jesus. He claims that upon his request the chief lama brought to him "the manuscripts relating to Jesus Christ and, assisted by my interpreter, who translated for me the Thibetan [sic] language, transferred carefully to my note book what the lama read to me."[9] He says that since he did not doubt the authenticity of the chronicle, which was "edited with great exactitude by the Brahminic, and more especially the Buddhistic historians of India and Nepaul [sic],"[10] he sought to publish a translation.

Notovitch claimed to be so sure of the document's authenticity that he essentially threw down the gauntlet to those who favored the New Testament Gospels, saying his discovery was "compiled three or four years after the death of Jesus, from the accounts of eyewitnesses and contemporaries, [and] has much more probability of being in con-

formity with truth than the accounts of the Gospels," which he held
to be written much later.[11]

So runs a streamlined account of the alleged uncovering of the
document (we will return to other key details later). But what does the
text say?

The Life of Saint Issa

Notovitch published the document under the title, "The Life of Saint
Issa: Best of the Sons of Men," within *The Unknown Life of Jesus
Christ*. It is divided into fourteen chapters with verses within the chapters. It begins with a prologue lamenting "the great crime committed
in the land of Israel" (1:1) of murdering "the great and just Issa, in
whom was manifest the soul of the universe" (1:2). Issa (Jesus) was
incarnated to lead people back to "the one and indivisible Creator
whose mercy is infinite" (1:4).

The next verse speaks of "the merchants coming from Israel" giving
the following account (1:5). A discussion of Israel's bondage in Egypt
follows, speaking of Prince Mossa's (Moses') role in securing the liberation of God's people from Pharaoh. Mossa leads Israel back to
God; but they soon return to idolatry.[12]

We then hear of Israel's unfaithfulness being punished by God
through the Roman oppression. Yet God heard his people's prayers
and decided to "re-incarnate in a human form" (4:1). "The eternal
Spirit" came in human form so "He might teach man to identify
himself with the Divinity and attain to eternal felicity" (4:3).

God spoke through this child and even as a youth Issa gathered a
following by talking of "the only indivisible God" and "exhorting the
strayed souls to repent and purify themselves from [their] sins" (4:8).
Yet at age thirteen, just when he expected to marry, Issa left Jerusalem
with a train of merchants and "journeyed toward the Sindh [India]"
(4:13) in order to perfect "himself in the knowledge of the word of God
and the study of the laws of the great Buddhas" (4:13).

At age fourteen, Issa "came this side of the Sindh and settled among
the Aryas, in the country beloved by God" (5:1). After his fame spread

in the northern Sindh "the devotees of the god Djaine" (5:2) sought him, but he "left the deluded worshippers" (5:3) and went to "Djagguernat, in the country of Orsis," (5:3) where Brahma [sic] priests taught him to comprehend the Vedas, to cure physical ills by prayer, to teach the sacred scriptures, to drive out evil desires from man and remake him in the likeness of God (5:4).

During six years here and in "other holy cities" (5:5) Issa lived and loved the lower Hindu classes and sided with them against the oppressing higher classes. He even "denied the divine inspiration of the Vedas and the Puranas" in favor of the universal law of worshiping God alone (5:12-13). Issa denounced all idolatry, and called down the anger of God on those who worship inanimate objects (5:15-26). God is the "cause of the mysterious life of man, into whom He has breathed part of His divine Being" (5:18).

Although the higher classes of priests and warriors took offense at Issa's rejection of their teaching and sought to kill him, he escaped to "the country of the Gautamides, where the great Buddha Sakya-Muni came to the world, among a people who worshipped the only and sublime Brahma [sic]." (6:2). In other words, Issa moved from Hinduism to Buddhism, although a Buddhist "worshipping Brahma" is anomalous to say the least.[13] He then mastered the Pali language and studied the sacred Sutras (Buddhist scriptures) for six years, after which he could "perfectly expound the sacred scrolls" (6:4).

He then left Nepal and the Himalaya mountains and descended to the valley of Radjipoutan. He later moved to the west and everywhere preached "the supreme perfection attainable by man" (6:5). Issa continued to condemn idolatry among "the Pagans" (6:7-16), warning that those who create idols "will be the prey of an eternal fire" (7:10). Many forsook their idols (7:1).

Issa's next stop was Persia, where he excoriated the Zoroastrians for viewing God as both good and evil and for worshiping the sun (ch. 8). This was less than warmly received by the "Magi," who abandoned Issa on a highway outside the city in the middle of the night, hoping he would become breakfast for wild beasts. Yet he escaped.

Issa, then age twenty-nine, returned to Israel for three years. There he preached high ethical standards of reverence for God, altruism and non-resistance in relation to Roman oppression. He was unopposed by the Jewish religious leadership but was feared by Pilate, who worried that he would incite insurrection. Pilate gave Issa over to the Jewish judges, who found no fault in him and washed their hands in a sacred vessel saying, "We are innocent of the blood of this righteous man" (13:25).

Nevertheless, Pilate prevailed, and Issa was crucified. After a full day on the cross, Issa "lost consciousness and his soul disengaged itself from the body, to reunite with God" (14:4); "thus ended the terrestrial existence of the reflection of the eternal Spirit under the form of a man who had saved hardened sinners and comforted the afflicted" (14:4).

Pilate then ordered that the body be given to relatives, who placed it in a tomb where many came to wail and lament. Three days later Pilate had Issa's body put in another place, fearing a rebellion among the people (14:6). When some of Issa's followers visited the now empty tomb, a rumor spread that "the Supreme Judge had sent his angels from Heaven, to remove the mortal remains of the saint in whom part of the divine Spirit had lived on earth" (14:7).

This caused Pilate to become angry and to impose the death penalty for proselytizing in Issa's name (14:8). Nevertheless, despite persecution, Issa's disciples left Israel and preached to the heathen to "abandon their gross errors, think of the salvation of their souls and earn the perfect bliss" for the immaterial world of the great Creator (14:10). And they met with success (14:11). So ends "The Life of Saint Issa."

Reality According to Issa

The theology of the text is a curious mixture of Judaism, Christianity, Hinduism and Buddhism. The God of Issa seems to be a personal and moral being who demands worship and hates idolatry (hence Judaism), even threatening unrepentant idolaters with hell! The Christian element is present in that some of Issa's teachings are close to those found in the Gospels, particularly when he says he did not come to disown the laws of Moses but to "reestablish them in the hearts of men" (10:21; cf. Mt 5:17-20). Yet the appearance of Issa is closer to the pantheistic Hindu idea of an avatar (periodic manifestation of God) than the Christian view of God uniquely incarnate as a man, because Issa is said to "manifest the *soul of the universe.*" Issa seems most favorably disposed toward Buddhism, which, unlike the other religions he is exposed to, he does not criticize. He leaves Israel with the express purpose of studying "the laws of the great Buddhas" (4:13). Zoroastrianism and Jainism fare far less well.

Notovitch's narrative and the Issa the text presents are drastically detached from the biblical record at many points, but we will only mention a few decisive dissimilarities.

We read of Issa learning from the Hindus how "to cure physical ills by means of prayers" (5:4), but the text gives us no record of him doing so or of any supernatural touch upon his ministry. Issa, unlike Jesus, is a stranger to the miraculous.

In the story of Issa the Jewish religious leaders side with Issa against Pilate, begging him to not execute him. This contradicts all four Gospels, which present both the Jewish leadership and Roman rule as equally responsible for his death. The growing tension between Jesus and the Jewish religious establishment, so keenly felt in the Gospels, is nonexistent in the account of Issa.

Although Issa is somehow a revelation of God, he is not an incarnation in the biblical sense. He is said to be a manifestation of "the soul of the universe" (1:2) and "a saint in whom part of the divine Spirit had lived on earth" (14:7). These descriptions are utterly alien to biblical theology, which declares Jesus to be "the Word made flesh" who himself created the universe (Jn 1:1-18).

Issa and the narration repeatedly speak of sin and the need to repent from sin, especially idolatry, yet Issa is silent about any atoning sacrifice being offered for sin. Rather, "the good he must do to his fellow man [is] the sure means of speedy union with the eternal Spirit" (6:6). "He who has recovered his primitive purity shall die with his transgressions forgiven" (6:6). Issa teaches that part of God dwells in each person (5:18; 9:15), and it is intimated that salvation involves identifying oneself with this indwelling part (4:3).

Issa never presents himself as a ransom given to redeem many from sin (Mk 10:45), nor does he affirm much of anything about himself. The text says Issa "saved hardened sinners" (14:4), but he did this by his example and teaching that leads to repentance, not by giving his life. Issa is more an ethical teacher and preacher than a Redeemer.

The account of Issa's crucifixion occupies only a small fraction of the text, whereas the Gospels emphasize it more than any other aspect of Jesus' life. This betrays the theology: Issa dies a martyr's death, not a Savior's death. His life is more important than his death. His death is the end, not the beginning.

What the Gospels present as the climax of Jesus' ministry and his ultimate vindication, the resurrection, "The Life of Saint Issa" flatly denies. Issa's body was secretly moved by Pilate, after which his followers *mistakenly* assume his body was supernaturally transported to heaven, when in reality it was rotting in an unmarked grave of Pilate's choosing.

The text provides no reason why Pilate would think that moving the body to another grave would discourage an insurrection, nor is any reason evident. But if Pilate feared a mass Christian movement and knew where Jesus' body was located, it would have only made sense to produce the corpse in order to squash all preaching of the resurrection. But history knows nothing of this. (Chapter ten discusses the evidence for and significance of Jesus' resurrection.)

There is a huge chasm between the Jesus of the New Testament and Saint Issa. Notovitch's claims to the contrary,[14] the divergent accounts cannot be harmonized without substantially rejecting one or the other.

But before looking at the evidence for and against Notovitch's claims, we should note that the theology of Issa itself is at odds with much of New Age theology. This is especially ironic considering that New Agers often invoke Issa to support their view of Jesus as a New Ager.

The text seems to speak of God as a personal and moral being, not the impersonal force, principle or vibration of New Age theology. Issa's God is repeatedly angry at humans for their disobedience, particularly concerning idolatry. Hinduism, which provides much of the spiritual muscle of New Age spirituality, takes it on the theological chin several times.

Although Issa speaks of humans as having at least part of the divine spirit in them, he calls people to repent of sin (sin being understood as actions and attitudes that displease a personal God). This is at loggerheads with the human potential aspect of the New Age, which stresses our sinlessness and infinite potential. At one point Issa says that miracles cannot be performed by man (11:7), thus putting him at odds with the paranormal propensity of much New Age thinking.

Further, Issa comes out against divination, saying that "he who has recourse to diviners soils the temple of his heart and shows his lack of faith in his Creator" (11:10). This puts the brakes on any number of New Age divining practices, such as Tarot card reading, casting the I Ching, using crystal divination and psychic readings.

The story of Issa seems unclear on reincarnation. It says that God was in some sense "reincarnated" in Issa, but it also speaks of the Judgment Day as if it were a final judgment. Issa does deny transmigration, saying that God "will never humiliate his child by casting his soul for chastisement into the body of a beast" (6:11). So we can say the text is at least ambiguous on the key New Age doctrine of reincarnation.

"The Life of Saint Issa: Best of the Sons of Men" is really a theological hodgepodge. It does not clearly support many core New Age doctrines, despite the fact that books like The Jesus Mystery, by Janet Bock, claim that Jesus' supposed travels put him firmly in the New Age camp.

Janet Bock and other New Age writers tend to supplement the Notovitch book with various spiritual revelations received by people like Edgar Cayce and Levi Downing during trance states. We will address these sorts of non-historical claims in chapter nine. But what historical evidence do we have for the objective truth of Jesus as Saint Issa?

Issa on Trial

As in previous chapters, we will apply the historical tests of *integrity,*
authenticity and *veracity* to this text, but this time in reverse order for
reasons to emerge as we proceed. What of the nature of the text itself?
Does it appear to be truthful?

Edgar J. Goodspeed, an expert on ancient manuscripts, observes
that "the whole cast of the book is vague and elusive."[15] He also notes,
"It presents no difficulties, no problems—whereas any really ancient
work newly discovered bristles with novelties and obscurities." We saw
this especially in the ferment of scholarly disagreement that ensued
after the discovery of both the Dead Sea Scrolls and the Nag Hammadi texts. Speaking of the text, Goodspeed continues: "Here the
message of Issa is a pallid and colorless morality, amiable and unob-
jectionable enough, but devoid of the flashes of insight and touches
of genius that mark the early gospels."[16]

Goodspeed also recognizes that the text "identifies itself with no
recognizable type of primitive thought" although it "shows a superficial acquaintance with the leading New Testament" accounts.[17] As we
have argued, it is more of a hodgepodge, or theological patch-quilt,
than a well-integrated belief system.

The veracity of the document is also called into question when we
consider some historical inaccuracies concerning world religions. Per
Beskow, a Swedish New Testament scholar, points out that the reference to "the God Djaine" (5:2) discloses "a considerable lack of
knowledge about Indian religions." He goes on:

> The Jains, or Jainas, do not believe in any god at all, but in certain
> *jinas* ("Conquerors"), who are enlightened spiritual leaders. The *a*
> in Jain comes from the same phonetic law that makes the [Hindu]
> worshippers of Shiva into Shavias and the [Hindu] worshippers of
> Vishnu into Vaishnavas.[18]

There is no "God Djaine."

The fact that "The Life of Saint Issa" would err so egregiously
concerning the Jain religion does not bode well for its overall veracity.[19] Nor does another error concerning religious belief.

The document was purportedly reconstructed from manuscripts in a Buddhist monastery and speaks more highly of Buddhism than any other religion. It even speaks of Issa as having been "elected" by Buddha "to spread his holy word" (6:4). Buddha seems to be interchangeable with God in this case. It also speaks of Buddhists worshiping Brahma, which is an odd combination of Hinduism and Buddhism. And it speaks of a jealous Creator God who can punish and forgive sin and who hates idols. This has little to do with historic Buddhism, which is either atheistic or pantheistic and abounds in images of the Buddha as proper objects of religious veneration and contemplation. The "Buddhism" of the text looks more like a syncretistic creation of an attempt to graft elements of Buddhism on to Judaism than it does identifiable Buddhism of history.[20]

It is instructive to know that theories relating Christianity to Buddhism were very much in vogue when Notovitch published his *Unknown Life of Jesus Christ,* and many Westerners sought to synthesize the two religions in novel ways. Historian Carl Jackson, in reviewing this phenomenon, says that Notovitch "may be said to have carried the controversy to its ultimate *reductio ad absurdum"* by his claim that the supposed resemblances between Christianity and Buddhism are accounted for by Jesus studying Buddhism with Buddhists.[21]

It is also rather odd that while certain commonly known English names take on exotic spellings (supposedly following the language of the text) in the document, such as Issa for Jesus (which *is* faithful to the Tibetan),[22] Mossa for Moses, and Romeles for Romans, Pontius Pilate remains unchanged.[23]

So we find several reasons to question the veracity of "The Life of Saint Issa," especially in terms of its disagreement with biblical history and theology.

Concerning its *authenticity,* we have but one verse in the document claiming that the account was written by "the merchants" who presumably accompanied Jesus on his trek from Israel to the East. These merchants are not named, and their identity is neither directly nor indirectly mentioned in the entire text. Neither is there any strong external tradition as to the document's authorship, as we find with regard to the New Testament Gospels (see chapter six). We are thus left in the dark as to where the merchants were from (India or Palestine?),[24] how they gained their facts or their abilities to record the facts, assuming they wrote the document at all.

Thus far, we have found substantial reasons to cast doubt on the veracity and authenticity of this controversial document. But the greatest difficulties are in regard to the issue of *integrity*. Do we have reason to believe this text has been accurately transmitted over the centuries? Or is it a modern invention, a forgery?

F. Max Muller, the great orientalist of the nineteenth century and translator and editor of the multi-volumed *Sacred Books of the East,* subjected the Issa thesis to critical scrutiny soon after its publication. Lest anyone accuse him of ill intentions,[25] in 1882, twelve years before Notovitch's publication, he had written that he "would be extremely grateful if anybody would point out to me the historical channels through which Buddhism influenced early Christianity," because he had been searching in vain for this his entire life.[26] Muller also thought that if the Issa document was legitimate, it would help establish the historicity of Jesus, despite the document's differences from the New Testament accounts.[27]

Muller, writing in 1894, found it exceedingly difficult to believe that a text of this importance was not listed in the Kandjur and Tandjur collections, the "excellent catalogues of manuscripts and books of the Buddhists in Tibet and China" and found it "impossible or next to impossible . . . that this Sutra of Issa, composed in the first century of our era, should not have found a place either in the Kandjur or in the Tandjur."[28] Notovitch responded by saying that those catalogs didn't exhaust the manuscript resources at his disposal at the Himis monastery.[29] Yet how plausible is it that Issa would not be well known in India if, in fact, he had actually been there? We would expect this document to be listed in the major catalogs if Issa had the impact in India that "The Life of Saint Issa" claims he did. Here we should also remember Notovitch's lack of scholarly standing and Muller's world renown.[30]

This brings us to Notovitch's account itself. Even if we take him at face value, we are quite distant from the events supposedly recorded in the Issa document. Notovitch's own words make this clear:

> The two manuscripts, from which the lama of the convent Himis read to me all that had a bearing upon Jesus, are compilations from divers copies written in the Thibetan language, translations of scrolls belonging to the library of Lhassa and brought, about two hundred years after Christ, from India, Nepaul and Maghada, to a convent on Mount Marbour, near the city of Lhassa.[31]

In light of this Goodspeed notes that Notovitch's claims are extremely unscholarly.

> It is evident that the scholar's desire to see the manuscript of the work, or failing that to see a photograph of it or a part of it, or at least to have precise directions about how and where to find it (its place and number in the Himis library) is not in this case to be satisfied.[32]

We are at least thrice removed from the manuscript because Notovitch tells us that, first, the lama read aloud from the manuscripts; second, the interpreter interpreted; and, third, Notovitch recorded it. But Notovitch also admits that he "arranged all the fragments concerning the life of Issa in chronological order and [took] pains to impress upon them the character of unity, in which they were absolutely lacking."[33] Goodspeed complains that "this is just what a scholar would not have done; he would wish to present the fragments just as the manuscripts had them, unaffected by his own views and tastes."[34]

While it is not impossible for a non-scholar to stumble across a valuable manuscript, Notovitch's testimony loses credibility given the many inaccuracies already noted and considering the fact that Notovitch, in the words of one reviewer, was "a man of no known attainments in any direction, certainly not in the direction of biblical history and criticism."[35] Notovitch's lack of scholarship, or even basic biblical knowledge, is painfully evident when he describes the Gospel of Luke as saying that *Jesus* "was in the deserts until the day of his showing in Israel" (1:80), which he believes proves that no one knew where he

had gone until he reappeared sixteen years later.[36] Yet the biblical
reference has nothing to do with Jesus, but with *John the Baptist!*
(Whether anyone claims John went to India, I do not know.)

The ring of truth in relation to Notovitch's account becomes so faint
as to be inaudible when we note that he describes the manuscripts
about Issa as scrolls or books, when, in fact, as Per Beskow points out,
"Tibetan books are neither scrolls nor bound in our way. They consist
of oblong leaves, imitating palm leaves; they are kept loose between
wooden plates, and the whole is kept wrapped in a piece of cloth."[37]
Notovitch was wrong again.

Let us bring together the facts on Issa and Notovitch. The Issa of
the manuscript bears little resemblance to Jesus Christ. The doctrine
of the text is a rather sloppy syncretism that cannot fully support a
New Age platform. Concerning the tests of historicity: The text contains several obvious falsehoods regarding Jainism and Buddhism. We
have no idea who wrote the text outside of a vague reference to un-
identified "merchants." Even if the document is what Notovitch
claims, it is *textually* uncertain with regard to integrity because of (1)
its being transcribed through a translator, (2) its unavailability for
scholarly inspection, and (3) Notovitch's admittedly substantial re-
working of the original material.

Another Gospel Forgery?

Beyond these considerable problems several witnesses came forth
shortly after the publication of *The Unknown Life of Jesus Christ*
claiming Notovitch never discovered the manuscript. A finely detailed
article published in a scholarly journal called *The Nineteenth Century,*
in April 1896, by Professor J. Archibald Douglas recounts his trip to
the Himis monastery to check up on Notovitch's claims.

Douglas says he was open-minded and initially expected to confirm
Notovitch's discovery. He seems to have had no personal or monetary
motive to discredit Notovitch.

Douglas begins by agreeing that Notovitch visited the monastery,
noting that the chief lama remembered several European gentlemen

visiting in 1887 and 1888, which could very well have included Notovitch, a Russian.[38] But Douglas notes that Notovitch's name does not appear on the list of travelers kept at the bungalow in the city of Leh, where Notovitch said he stayed. Douglas did find that a Notovitch was treated there—not for a broken leg, but for a toothache.[39]

A translator was enlisted by Douglas to read extracts from Notovitch's book to the chief lama, in order to elicit his response. The lama's comments were recorded in a statement signed by the lama, Douglas, and the translator, Shahmwell Joldan, late postmaster of Ladakh.

In the document, reprinted in the journal, the lama contradicts all of Notovitch's major assertions. When asked about the Issa document, the Chief Superior Lama replies:

> I have been for forty-two years a Lama, and am well acquainted with all the well-known Buddhist books and manuscripts, and I have never heard of one which mentions the name of Issa, and it is my firm and honest belief that none exists. I have inquired of our principal Lamas in other monasteries of Tibet, and they are not acquainted with any books or manuscripts which mention the name of Issa.[40]

When asked if the name Issa was held in high respect by Buddhists, the lama replied, "they know nothing even of his name; none of the Lamas has ever heard it, save through missionaries and European sources."[41] The lama further denied that any Westerner had stayed there to nurse a broken leg (contra Notovitch);[42] he denied having spoken with Notovitch about the religions of the ancient Egyptians, Assyrians and people of Israel (contra Notovitch) and even denied knowing anything about these religions;[43] he likewise denied that the monastery contained any Buddhist writings in the Pali language (contra Notovitch).[44] Per Beskow confirms this, saying (contra Notovitch) that "Pali, which is the sacred language of Theravada Buddhism, has never been used in Tibet, and the Tibetan translations have usually been done from Sanskrit or from Chinese."[45]

Douglas reports that when parts of Notovitch's book were read to the lama he burst out with, "Lies, lies, nothing but lies,"[46] and on another occasion asked Douglas if Notovitch could be punished by law for his untruths.[47]

Douglas also finds suspect Notovitch's reference to using a resident *(shikari)* from a nearby village as an interpreter, because such a person is always a simple peasant, unable to handle the theological and philosophical concepts found in Notovitch's book.[48]

Notovitch later claimed that the lama lied to Douglas because he was afraid the precious manuscripts would be stolen by Westerners. Only Notovitch's "Eastern diplomacy" put him on the good side of the lama.[49] But this is implausible. Even if the lama had confessed to the existence of such a manuscript, he would not have needed to reveal its location in the large collection. He could certainly have refused to show it, sell it or donate it to foreigners. I would also assume that the monasteries had adequate means to keep their precious documents secure. Further, if the monks were so reticent, how did Notovitch, visiting there for the very first time, gain access to the manuscripts, despite his "Eastern diplomacy"? We should remember that Douglas was accompanied by the postmaster of Ladakh, someone surely on better terms with its citizens than Notovitch, a total stranger.

Elizabeth Clare Prophet tries to strengthen the case that the monks feared the manuscripts would be stolen. She quotes from a passage from *The Cultural Heritage of Ladakh* to the effect that because the Himis monastery attracted so many visitors, the monks had a supercilious, if not contemptuous, attitude toward them and seemed convinced that all the foreigners would steal from them if possible. The passage also goes on to say that the monastery experienced some quite serious losses of property "in recent years," which were being investigated when the writers were there. It was found, though, that foreigners were not responsible.[50] This fact, Prophet avers, lends credence to Notovitch's idea that his own "Eastern diplomacy," not possessed by Douglas, won him a peek at the manuscripts.

This argument has at least three serious weaknesses. First, the reference to supposedly stolen property is only in "recent years." The

Notovitch incident dates to 1887, which is presumably not "recent." Second, the original quote from *The Cultural Heritage of Ladakh* goes on to mention something crucial omitted by Prophet: that "Hemis [sic] suffers greatly from the absence of its head lama."[51] It is just such a head lama that plays a prominent role in both Notovitch's and Douglas's accounts. Surely, the Himis of today is different enough from that of 1887 to render Prophet's selective quotation mute with regard to defending Notovitch. Third, the very book she cites concerning Himis and the region of Ladakh has no reference to Notovitch, Jesus, Christ or Issa in its index. If the Notovitch story had any credibility, wouldn't it be mentioned in this source? This is an indicting omission.

We should consider one more item before delivering a verdict on Notovitch: Could the Issa story have been created out of his imagination if he named the specific site at which he claimed to have found the manuscript? Prophet[52] and Notovitch himself[53] say it is unlikely that a liar would make such particular claims. But is it?

Notovitch could have easily realized that very few people actually have access to an obscure Tibetan monastery. He could have expected that his book would be in print for many months, while he pocketed considerable royalties, before someone checked him out. (This, in fact, is just what happened.) He may have even made contingency plans to use if he were challenged, such as the "Eastern diplomacy" response. Furthermore, he himself backtracked after Douglas's and Muller's criticisms. In the preface to the edition reprinted by Prophet, he confessed that there was probably no one manuscript about Issa but that the story had been gathered from various books in the monastery,[54] a revision of his earlier comments.[55]

So what is the verdict on Notovitch and his *Unknown Life of Jesus Christ?* Beskow calls his "discovery" the "best known Gospel forgery of modern times."[56] Goodspeed, Douglas and Muller agree. Albert Schweitzer calls it a "fictitious" life of Christ and "a bare-faced swindle and an impudent invention."[57] This verdict is, I believe, accurate.

But Elizabeth Clare Prophet's book *The Lost Years of Jesus* adds three other witnesses who claim to have seen the documents and, in the case of one Swami Abhedananda, made a translation of them. The reader can consult her arguments for the details,[58] but at least four salient and stubborn facts remain.

First, the Issa manuscripts remain unavailable for scholarly inspection. Second, no one has come up with an adequate picture of the document that reveals its distinctive features and unique identity.[59] Prophet includes a photo of a monk holding some kind of scroll with the caption, "These books say your Jesus was here"[60] but this hardly qualifies as sound evidence, especially since "books" is the wrong word to use (as noted above). Third, these anecdotal claims do nothing to rehabilitate Notovitch's inaccuracies and implausibility. The arguments given above stand fast. Fourth, and most importantly, the reliability of "The Life of Saint Issa" must be compared with the biblical record of Jesus. As discussed in chapter six, the New Testament marshals impressive credentials. It has historical *integrity,* which Issa lacks. It has historical *authenticity,* which Issa lacks. It has historical *veracity,* with Issa lacks. In the bright light of this threefold argument for the New Testament, it is safe to say that the burden of proof is on "The Life of Saint Issa," a burden that is very difficult to bear. To put it another way, 5,366 ancient Greek New Testament manuscripts in the hand are worth more than (at most) one inaccessible and idiosyncratic manuscript in the Tibetan bush (see chapter six).

Given the above considerations, *even if* it could be established that a *bona fide* manuscript of "The Life of Saint Issa" exists, this, in itself, would not prove it to be true to fact. Such a manuscript could easily be understood as a legendary fabrication attempting to synthesize material previously known about Jesus through the spread of Christianity with other religious teachings.[61]

Did Jesus Die in India?
While Notovitch's "discovery" leaves the body of Issa decomposing in Palestine, other New Age revisionists have him surviving the crucifixion and retiring in India. After dying there, he was supposedly interred in a tomb in Kashmir. Ironically, one article defending this view begins

by citing Notovitch as a source, even though his account of Issa does not permit Jesus returning to India.[62]

Before dealing with these claims, we should again keep in mind the case for the historical reliability of the New Testament. Any historical claim that contradicts this record in any important way needs to assume the burden of proof. The New Testament, of course, records that Jesus died on the cross, was buried, rose again and ascended to heaven. We will deal specifically with the historicity and significance of the resurrection of Jesus in chapter ten, but we should remember from chapter three that Jesus' death *on the cross* was integral to his life and mission. He was a man born to die and emphasized his destiny throughout his ministry in different ways. Therefore, to claim that he did not die on the cross is to question the entire biblical portrait of Jesus. But how is this done?[63]

A popular notion is that Jesus was crucified, but did not expire on the cross; instead he only appeared to die. He then was brought to a tomb where he revived, only to leave Palestine and head eastward. This is a new twist on an old idea called the swoon theory.

First, it is maintained that Jesus was not on the cross long enough to have died from crucifixion. Richard Walters says, "Writings on crucifixion state that, when the person crucified was in normal health, in no case did death occur with [sic] 12 hours." He concludes that "it is improbable that Jesus died after just three hours on the cross."[64] Second, some claim that Jesus was drugged when someone put a sponge up to his mouth to drink. This caused the appearance of death that deceived those present.[65] Third, the fact that blood spurted out from Jesus' side when it was pierced by the Roman's sword is thought to be another indication he was still alive.[66]

Before moving to the claims of Jesus' tomb being in India, we should briefly address these three arguments.

As a general point, one has to wonder why those who trust the Gospel accounts enough to affirm that Jesus was crucified depart from the narratives when they clearly report that Jesus was dead as dead could ever be. Why believe at one point and doubt at another? If critics do not establish sufficient criteria as to their doubts, their rejection of Jesus' death is simply ad hoc.

More specifically, first, there *was* sufficient time for Jesus to die on the cross. We must not view the crucifixion in isolation from what preceded it. As Michael Green notes:

> It is incredible that Jesus, who had not eaten or slept before his execution, who was weakened by a loss of blood through the most brutal flogging [see 1 Pet 2:24], who was pierced in both hands and feet, could have survived unaided had he been alive when taken down from the cross.[67]

Jesus was so weakened from his beatings that he was unable to carry his cross all the way to Golgotha, the execution site (Mt 27:32). The authors of a technical article called "The Physical Death of Jesus Christ," in the *Journal of the American Medical Association,* remarked that the time of survival for Roman crucifixions "ranged from three or four hours to three or four days and appears to have been inversely related to the severity of the scourging."[68]

Pilate showed surprise that Jesus died so rapidly (Mk 15:44), but he did not question that Jesus was, in fact, dead. The Romans were no beginners when it came to crucifixion. The squad of four soldiers broke the legs of the two men crucified with Jesus (a practice that would hasten death), but did not bother to break Jesus' legs because they saw he had already expired.

Second, the theory that Jesus arranged to be given some potion to feign death is problematic in several ways. The Gospel of John reports that Jesus was given a drink *in full view of the Roman guards* before he expired (Jn 19:28-29). It was their job to be executioners, not accessories to a hoax. They had a vested interest in being accurate coroners because "had the centurion, had the governor made a mistake over the execution of a messianic pretender, their jobs and probably their lives would have been on the line."[69] Surely, they would have been wise to such a ploy. Moreover, if we assume that Jesus somehow arranged for his last-minute rescue, he is no less than a grand impostor and not worthy of any respect, because he preached the necessity and finality of his own death. We might then say he rivaled Houdini, but we could never view him with religious veneration, let alone worship. Third, the fact that blood and water came from his side is positive evidence for his death. The Roman soldiers pierced his side because they wanted to make doubly sure he was dead; this was standard practice to insure death.[70] What followed confirmed Jesus' death, as explained in the aforementioned article in the *Journal of the American Medical Association*. Here is the conclusion of the authors:

Clearly, the weight of historical and medical evidence indicates that Jesus was dead before the wound to his side was inflicted and supports the traditional view that the spear, thrust between his right ribs, probably perforated not only the right lung but also the pericardium and heart and thereby ensured his death. Accordingly, interpretations based on the assumption that Jesus did not die on the cross appear to be at odds with modern medical knowledge.[71]

Various authors have spoken of legends in Eastern lands claiming Jesus as their own. A tomb thought by some to contain Jesus' remains is in Kashmir, India, supposedly occupied by a mysterious Yuz Asaf.[72] But here again, a heavy burden of proof rests on such a view, given the historical reliability of the New Testament and considering the fact that Jesus could not have lived through the crucifixion. The resurrected and ascended Christ proclaims in the book of Revelation, "I was dead, and behold I am alive for ever and ever!" (Rev 1:18). Paul is confident that "since Christ was raised from the dead, he cannot die again; death no longer has mastery over him" (Rom 6:9).

Those who claim that Jesus ended up in India must also explain the existence of the primitive church's faith in the resurrected and ascended Lord. And what sort of a teacher would Jesus be if he escaped to India while permitting an entire religion to be hinged on a threefold falsehood, namely his death, resurrection and ascension?

But the real evidence against Jesus' death in India is a developed argument for his bodily resurrection and ascension. Jesus cannot be both rotting in Kashmir and ruling in Heaven. We must save this for our chapter "Jesus and the Cosmic Christ."

One more revisionist historical view casts doubt on the biblical Jesus. Many claim Jesus was a member of the mystical Essene community and that his life and teachings can be explained by this connection. Was Jesus an Essene? Is this the great secret of the New Testament? We will address this question in the next chapter.

Notes

[1]Edgar J. Goodspeed, *Modern Apocrypha* (Boston: The Beacon Press, 1956), p. 7.

[2]For a detailed comparison of Jesus and present-day Indian gurus see Vishal Mangalwadi, *The World of the Gurus* (New Delhi, India: Nivedit Good Books Distributors Pvt. Ltd., 1977).

[3]The story of Elizabeth Caspari's supposed contact with the "Life of Saint Issa" uses this verse as a defense in Elizabeth Clare Prophet, *The Lost Years of Jesus* (Livingston, Mont.: Summit University Press, 1984), p. 317.

[4]Janet Bock, *The Jesus Mystery* (Los Angeles: Aura Books, 1984), pp. 116-17.

[5]See Goodspeed, p. 3, and for exact bibliographic information on the French and American publications, Per Beskow, *Strange Tales about Jesus* (Philadelphia: Fortress Press, 1985), p. 121.

[6]Nicholas Notovitch, *The Unknown Life of Jesus Christ,* translated by J. H. Connelly and L. Landsberg (New York: R. F. Fenno and Company, 1890), p. 7. (This stated publication date is, in all likelihood mistaken, since the first editions did not come out until 1894.) I have chosen to cite this edition because it appears to be less condensed in translation than the edition translated by Virchand R. Gandhi and revised by G. L. Christie (Chicago: Progressive Thinker Publishing House, 1907). This edition includes some unusual spellings that I will not correct when quoting. I will, on some occasions, refer to Prophet's *Lost Years,* which reprints another edition of *The Unknown Life* (which appears to be the edition translated by Violet Crispe [London: Hutchinson and Co., 1895]; but this is never directly stated). This includes a preface added by Notovitch, in response to his critics, which is not available in the editions to which I have direct access.

[7]Notovitch, p. 8.

[8]His exact reasoning for this is never spelled out.

[9]Notovitch, p. 10.

[10]Ibid., pp. 10-11.

[11]Ibid., pp. 229-30.

[12]The brief story diverges from the account in Exodus at many places that need not concern us.

[13]If Buddhists worship anything, it is Buddha, not Brahma.

[14]In a section called "To the Publishers" in a later edition of *The Unknown Life of Jesus Christ* which is reprinted in Prophet, *The Lost Years,* pp. 95-96, Notovitch, responding to his critics, says: "Was it [my intention] to invalidate the authority of the Gospels and the whole New Testament? Not in the least degree. In the French journal *La Paix,* I concisely affirmed my belief in the orthodox Russian religion, and I hold to that affirmation. . . . But the doctrine contained in these Thibetan [sic] verses is the same

as that of the Gospels, and the facts only differ in outward seeming." This contradicts what he says above about the Issa text being more reliable than the New Testament. (See footnote 11.)

[15]Goodspeed, p. 8.

[16]Ibid.

[17]Ibid.

[18]Per Beskow, *Strange Tales about Jesus* (Philadelphia: Fortress Press, 1985), p. 59.

[19]For more on Jainism see Walter Kaufmann, *Religion in Four Dimensions: Existential, Aesthetic, Historical, Comparative* (New York: Readers Digest Press, 1976), pp. 297-301. Kaufman does point out that the founder of Jainism is sometimes worshipped, but this goes against his stated teachings. Jainism is primarily known as atheistic, or at least as a non-worshiping agnosticism. God, if there be one, is not the prime focus of religious devotion. Therefore, the statement "the god of the Djaines" is not an accurate summary of their beliefs because the role of deity in Jainism is peripheral at best. It is not known as monotheistic.

[20]See Arid Romarheim, *Various Views of Jesus Christ in New Religious Movements— A Typological Outline* (unpublished manuscript), pp. 12-13. This is available from Christian Research Institute, Box 500, San Juan Capistrano, CA 92693.

[21]Carl Jackson, *Oriental Religions and American Thought* (Westport, Conn.: Greenwood Press, 1981), pp. 149-50.

[22]See Beskow, p. 58.

[23]See F. Max Muller, "The Alleged Sojourn of Christ in India," *The Nineteenth Century*, no. CCXII (October 1894), p. 518.

[24]Ibid.; Muller thought it very unlikely that the same "Jewish merchants who arrived in India immediately after the Crucifixion knew not only what had happened to Christ in Palestine, but also what happened to Jesus, or Issa, while he spent fifteen years of his life among the Brahman." Notovitch responded that the merchants were indigenous Indians who had returned from Palestine on business. See Notovitch in Prophet, p. 96.

[25]As does Holger Kersten, *Jesus Lived in India* (Longmead, England: Elementt Book, Ltd., 1986), pp. 36-37. Kersten's response is little more than an ad hominem attack on Muller.

[26]Max Muller, *India, What Can it Teach Us?* (London, 1883), p. 279; quoted in Albert Schweitzer, *The Quest for the Historical Jesus* (New York: The Macmillan Company, 1973), p. 291.

[27]Muller, "The Alleged Sojourn," p. 518. Muller did not adequately understand, it seems, the vast differences between Issa and Jesus, but, nevertheless, his comment shows that he was not predisposed to reject the document as spurious.

[28]Ibid.

[29]Notovitch in Prophet, p. 94.

[30]As an appendix to his article, Muller included a letter to him from an English woman familiar with the Himis monastery who wrote from Leh, Ladakh on June 29, 1894. It claimed that Notovitch's story was a complete fabrication (Muller, pp. 521-22). A more detailed case for fabrication will be made below.

[31]Notovitch, "The Alleged Sojourn," p. 226.

[32]Goodspeed, p. 9.

[33]Notovitch, p. 229.

34Goodspeed, p. 10.
35From a review of *The Unknown Life of Jesus Christ,* in *The Biblical World* 4, no. 2 (August 1894):147.
36Notovitch, pp. 244-45.
37Beskow, p. 121.
38J. Archibald Douglas, "The Chief Lama of Himis on the Alleged 'Unknown Life of Christ,' " *The Nineteenth Century* 230 (April 1896), pp. 668-69.
39Ibid., p. 669.
40Ibid., p. 671.
41Ibid., p. 672.
42Ibid., p. 671.
43Ibid., pp. 671-72.
44Ibid., p. 672.
45Bcskow, p. 59.
46Douglas, p. 672.
47Ibid., pp. 669-70.
48Ibid., p. 674.
49Notovitch in Prophet, pp. 91-92.
50David L. Snellgrove and Tadeusz Skorupski, *The Cultural Heritage of Ladakh— Volume One: Central Ladakh* (Boulder, Colo.: Prajna Press, 1977), p. 127; quoted in Prophet, pp. 37-38.
51Snellgrove and Skorupski, p. 127.
52Prophet, pp. 35-36.
53Notovitch in Prophet, p. 93.
54Ibid., p. 94.
55Notovitch, pp. 151-52.
56Beskow, p. 58.
57Schweitzer, p. 328.
58Beskow makes this comment about one of the supposed other witnesses of the manuscript: "Professor Nicholas Roerich, painter and amateur archaeologist, traveled in Ladakh in the 1920s and believed that he had found traces of *The Life of Saint Issa*. Unfortunately, his examples from living folk traditions lend no added reliability, for the first part of his account is taken literally from Notovitch's *Life of Saint Issa,* chapters 5-13 (only extracts but with all the verses in the right order). It is followed by "another version" (pp. 93-94), taken from chapter 16 of Downing's *Aquarian Gospel.* There is a vague possibility that visiting enthusiasts from Europe had already spread these stories to Ladakh, and that they had taken root in popular belief. But Roerich's literal quotations rather suggest that he inserted them only because he found them attractive. He was of a romantic nature and seems not to have taken a great interest in more tangible facts" (pp. 62-63).
59For instance, the Nag Hammadi manuscripts have been photographically reproduced in scholarly volumes in the original Coptic language.
60Prophet, p. 312.
61See Ron Rhodes, "The Jesus of the New Age Movement," *Christian Research Journal,* Fall 1989, p. 20. Although this chapter resembles Rhodes's article in several ways, the overwhelming majority of my research and writing was completed before his article was published. Any similarity between this chapter and his article, besides the one

noted above, is a matter of coincidence and not of literary dependence.

[62]Richard Walters, "Christ, Christian, Krishna," *New Frontier,* December 1988, p. 5.

[63]See Kersten, pp. 124-78; Kersten also argues from evidence derived from the Shroud of Turin that Jesus did not die on the cross. The legitimacy of the Shroud is certainly a debatable issue, but for material on the Shroud as supporting the death of Jesus on the cross, see Kenneth E. Stevenson and Gary R. Habermas, *Verdict on the Shroud* (Ann Arbor, Mich.: Servant Books, 1981), pp. 133-42.

[64]Walters, p. 7.

[65]Ibid.

[66]Ibid.

[67]Michael Green, *The Empty Cross of Jesus* (Downers Grove, Ill.: InterVarsity Press, 1984), p. 93. On the speed of Jesus' death, see also James Charlesworth, *Jesus within Judaism* (New York: Doubleday, 1988), pp. 122-23.

[68]William D. Edwards, Wesley J. Gabel, Floyd E. Hosmer, "On the Physical Death of Jesus Christ," *Journal of the American Medical Association* 255, no.11 (March 21, 1986):1460.

[69]Green, pp. 93-94.

[70]William Lane Craig, *Knowing the Truth about the Resurrection* (Ann Arbor, Mich.: Servant Books, 1988), p. 33.

[71]Edwards et al., p. 1463.

[72]Walters, p. 46; Kersten, pp. 179ff. For further criticism of this view, see Beskow, pp. 63-64, 122-24.

Chapter 8
Was Jesus
an Essene?

*A*nother strategy to revise the Jesus of traditional Christian understanding is to situate him in a spiritual environment closer to his home than the mystic East. This portrait finds Jesus not in Eastern environs but influenced by, or even a member of, the Essene community located on the shores of the Dead Sea in Palestine. Although it existed during the time of Jesus, this ancient Jewish religious group is not mentioned by the New Testament. Yet it has a strong spiritual allure for many modern spiritual seekers.

In some New Age circles the Essenes are viewed as a kind of halfway house between orthodox Judaism and Eastern mysticism. They are revered as having captured the hidden essence of Jewish religion, while the other Jewish parties of the day got lost in external legalities. The Essenes, for many, represent a "third way" of Jewish spirituality closely akin to modern New Age enthusiasms. In various esoteric or mystery organizations such as Theosophy, Anthroposophy and Rosicrucianism, the Essenes are seen as members of the Great White Brotherhood or Lodge, a mystical brotherhood tracing back to earlier mystery religions.[1]

Manly P. Hall, a prolific author on spiritual themes, asserts that the Essenes "were a link between pagan and Christian mysticism, and were absorbed into the new faith or into orthodox Jewish communities as the result of the conflict between Christians and orthodox Jews."[2] One writer calls them "a new age religious sect in matters of belief and philosophy."[3] Shirley MacLaine waxes exuberant on the Essenes, views them as prototypical New Agers, finds Essenism in the best of all world religions and confidently identifies Jesus as an Essene.[4] The early Theosophist Annie Besant in *Esoteric Christianity* affirms that Jesus was groomed for ministry by studying in Essene environs.[5] The medium Edgar Cayce affirmed much of the same in his trance readings.[6]

Prior to 1947, what was known of the Essene community was gleaned from the Jewish philosopher Philo (c. 20 B.C.-A.D. 50); Jewish historian Josephus (A.D. 37-c. 100); Pliny the Elder, writing in the period A.D. 73-79; and Hippolytus, the Christian writer of Rome at the early part of the third century. As with Nag Hammadi, we no longer have to rely on secondary sources to understand this religious movement of antiquity. The discovery of the Dead Sea Scrolls in 1947 dwarfs even the Nag Hammadi discoveries and has been the center of much more critical attention and acclaim. Primary documents have been unearthed dating from about the first century B.C. and the first century A.D. The Essenes can now speak for themselves. By comparing the classical sources on the Essenes with the documents found beginning in 1947 at the Dead Sea, most scholars have concluded that the community at Qumran was an Essene group.[7] But who exactly were the Essenes?

What Did the Essenes Believe?

Although the word *Essene* covers a sect which spanned many decades and not all Essenes had the same status or exact beliefs, a general picture does emerge from our sources.[8]

The Essenes at Qumran were largely a group of ascetics who separated themselves from the orthodox Judaism of the temple because of its perceived religious laxity; they viewed themselves as a remnant voice, crying "in the desert" (Is 40:3), preparing for a new era of righteousness. They lived communally with strict standards of religious and ceremonial discipline, especially regarding ritual purity. And they were deeply rooted in the Old Testament Scriptures, which they transcribed and wrote commentaries on. In fact, among other writings, the Dead Sea Scrolls contain fragments from all the books of the Hebrew Bible except Esther, giving us manuscripts 1,000 years older than those previously known.[9]

But can the material on the Essenes culled from the Dead Sea Scrolls and the secondary sources support the notion that these people were substantially New Age in their orientation and that Jesus was either an Essene or had strong affinities with the sect?

The Dead Sea Scrolls themselves are comprised of biblical commentaries, apocryphal writings, pseudepigrapha and writings relating to the Essene community's rules of order.[10] Interestingly, although the community possessed scriptures other than Old Testament texts, it seems that only books presently in our Old Testament were deemed worthy of interpretive commentary.[11] Pfeiffer notes that "scholars who have examined the manuscripts assert that the Biblical scrolls are written in a style of writing that is distinctive, as if to mark them off for special consideration."[12] This is instructive because, despite various non-Jewish elements that can be discerned in the Dead Sea Scrolls, the predominating world-view is that of *Jewish monotheism, not pantheistic monism.*[13] Confessional poetry from The Community Rule (the rule of order for the Qumran Essenes) displays a deep sense of remorse over sin in the face of a personal and holy God:

> As for me,
> I belong to wicked mankind,
> to the company of ungodly flesh.

My iniquities, rebellions, and sins,
    together with the perversity of my heart,
belong to the company of worms
    and to those who walk in darkness.
For mankind has no way,
    and man is unable to establish his steps
since justification is with God
    and perfection is out of His hand.[14]

The hymnwriter finds himself to be a sinful person in the company of sinful humanity, whose only hope of justification lies in a personal God who is in no sense identified with the self. This directly contradicts the New Age teaching that God is a principle, not a person.[15] Many other similar passages are found in this book, as well as in the Thanksgiving Hymn, that emphasize human sinfulness, God's holiness and the necessity of God's action for humans to be justified in God's sight. In the Thanksgiving Hymn the writer says that "a creature of clay" is "in iniquity from the womb" (cf. Ps 51:5) and "in guilty unfaithfulness until old age."[16] This is hardly New Age theology.

New Age teaching professes that we, as divine beings at various levels of manifestation, create our own reality and control our own destiny. Such affirmations of autonomy are absolutely alien to the Essenic theology of the scrolls. For the Essenes, God is the sovereign Lord and moral governor of the universe who knows the beginning from the end and who is bullied by no one. The Community Rule declares:

For without Thee no way is perfect,
    and without Thy will nothing is done.
It is Thou who hast taught all knowledge
and all things come to pass by Thy will.
There is none beside Thee to dispute Thy counsel
    or to understand Thy holy design,
or to contemplate the depth of Thy mysteries
    and the power of Thy might.[17]

Such declarations certainly chafe at New Age ambitions.[18]

Although it is often claimed that the Essenes believed in reincarnation, the Dead Sea documents do not support or confirm this. It is questionable whether they held to a Pharisaical view of the physical resurrection or to a more Greek-inspired view of the immortality of the soul, but, in any case, reincarnation was not in view.[19] John Hick further explains this in responding to a statement, by theologian Leslie Weatherhead,[20] that Josephus believed that the Essenes definitely taught reincarnation.

He [Weatherhead] is referring to Josephus' *Jewish Wars,* book II, ch. 8, para. 14. This reads "[It is said that] on the one hand all souls are immortal, but on the other hand those of good men only are changed into another body *(metabainein eis heteron soma)* but those of evil men are subject to eternal punishment." However there is nothing here to indicate that the change into another body is reincarnation, i.e., being born again as a baby on earth. It seems more likely that Josephus had in mind the resurrection of the body.[21]

Hick grants that the reference could be to the idea of some kind of "spiritual body," but still denies that this entails reincarnation.[22]

The evidence points to the Essenes' belief in heaven and hell as final destinations. The Community Rule speaks of the "eternal joy in life without end, a crown of glory and a garment of majesty in unending light"[23] for the just and "eternal torment and endless disgrace together with shameful extinction in the fire of the dark regions"[24] for sinners. This again is far less mellow and much more black and white than most New Age scenarios.

The historical evidence recovered at the Dead Sea, along with secondary sources, shows the Essenes to deviate from mainstream Judaism at some points but not at the level of their essential world view. The Essenes were fiercely monotheistic. Despite their having greater interest in angelic beings than other Jewish sects, they worshiped the Creator alone. Despite their emphasis on receiving special knowledge and status in relation to other Jews, they attributed this to God's grace, not to mystical intuition. Despite probably being influenced by

Greek and possibly Persian thinking to some degree, any foreign influence was secondary to the teachings of their sacred Jewish Scriptures. Moses was the lawgiver, not Plato. And despite some tendencies
to exalt the spiritual over the material, the Essenes were still essentially
Jewish monotheists, not Gnostics.

These factors alone begin to damage the program to paint Jesus in
New Age colors by dipping into the Essenes' theological palate. *Even
if* we could connect Jesus with the Essenes (which we will dispute
below), this would not, in itself, convert Jesus into a pantheistic mo-
nist believing in human perfectibility and reincarnation.

But can a connection be made between the Essenes and Jesus? If so,
what kind of a connection would it be?

Was John the Baptist an Essene?

We need to start with John the Baptist, Jesus' forerunner and, according to Jesus, a prophet worthy of high honor. John is often thought
by many New Agers either to be an Essene or to have strong connec-
tions with the group, because of the location of his stay in the wilderness, his ascetic life, and his practice of baptism. Did Jesus, then,
endorse an Essene?

The Gospels record John as coming from the wilderness (Lk 1:80;
3:2). This is likely to be near the Qumran community. John may have
been somewhat influenced by the Essenes, but he ultimately stands
apart from them. His clothing was not the white linen of Essenes but
was made of camel's hair. His diet of locusts and wild honey was also
more austere than the Essenes.[25] A life of ascetic renunciation was
known among the Jews outside of the Essenes through the Nazarite
vow (1 Sam 1:11, 28), and Luke even seems to pattern his recounting
of John's early life after the Hannah/Samuel story of the Old Testament.[26] Furthermore, since John's parents, Zechariah and Elizabeth,
were of the priestly line, it is highly unlikely that they would commit
their young son to an order so hostile to the established priesthood
in Jerusalem.[27]

John's baptismal practice and theology were also at odds with the practices of the Essenes. Although the Qumran community appropriated to itself Isaiah 40:3 ("A voice of one calling: 'In the desert prepare the way for the LORD; make straight in the wilderness a highway for our God"), their interpretation differed greatly from John's. The Essenes retreated into the wilderness to prepare the way of the Lord by searching the law of Moses and purifying themselves so as to be united with the godly and separate from the ungodly. John preached from the wilderness, delivering a message of repentance in order to prepare the public at large for the coming of the Messiah.[28] F. F. Bruce notes that:

> John chose for the inauguration of his ministry the most public part of the wilderness of Judea, the crossing of the Jordan north of the Dead Sea, where traffic between Judaea and Peraea passed this way and that; and he addressed his message to all who would hear, including the "men of the pit" from whom the pious sectaries of Qumran swore to keep aloof.[29]

John is presented by Luke, not as a monk but as a prophet (Lk 3:2) who directly receives the word of the Lord. This puts him some distance from Essenic understanding.

John's practice of baptism differs from the Essenes' baptism also, in that his was an act signifying immediate repentance as a kind of initiation, whereas Essenian ritual bathing was administered only after a probationary period and then on a daily basis, not one time only as practiced by John. John's baptism was messianic; he was preparing people for Jesus. The Essenes' washings were unrelated to any messianic or religious figure per se.[30]

If John the Baptist had ever been an Essene, he certainly must have left the ranks of the remnant before his public ministry or he must have been an incredibly poor student.[31]

The Case for Jesus As an Essene

The question now becomes, Can we establish a positive connection between Jesus himself and the Essenes? Is it the case, as often put, that Christianity is the Essenism that succeeded?

The Dead Sea Scrolls never mention Jesus of Nazareth by name, nor does the New Testament mention the Essenes,[32] even though the events of the Gospels, Acts and much of the rest of the New Testament overlap with the Qumran community's existence, which probably came to a violent end some time around A.D. 70 with the fall of Jerusalem. Therefore, no direct evidence on Jesus is available. In this sense the Dead Sea Scrolls differ from the Nag Hammadi texts, which, although composed later than and derivative of the New Testament documents, do explicitly mention Jesus.

Some have tried to identify Jesus with an important leader (or founder) of the sect referred to in the Dead Sea Scrolls as the Teacher of Righteousness. Yet this is more imaginative than historical, as many scholars have pointed out. Besides the fact that the Teacher of Righteousness is usually dated as having lived a century or more before Jesus, the defining aspects of the biblical Jesus, such as his miracles, sinless life, crucifixion and resurrection, are absent from what little we learn of the Teacher of Righteousness.[33] Yet we can consult the teachings of the scrolls, and information derived from secondary sources, in order to find similarities and dissimilarities between the Nazarene and the Essenes.

If John differed from the Essenes by virtue of his stricter asceticism, Jesus differed from both in that he was accused of being a glutton and drunkard (Mt 11:19). Although Jesus encouraged his disciples to fast when needful, he laid down no rule regarding it, nor did he seem particularly to encourage it during his public ministry. He refused the devil's offer of turning stones into bread, but refused few dinner invitations afterward, and even turned water into wine at a wedding feast (Jn 2:1-11). Jesus was often found dining with tax collectors and Pharisees alike, using his conviviality as a means for teaching about the kingdom of God. Such activities would have scandalized even the most libertine of the Essenes.

Josephus related that the Essenes, unlike the other religious sects of the day, thought "that oil is a defilement; and if any of them be anointed without his own approbation, it is wiped off his body."[34]

Jesus allowed himself to be anointed with costly oil before his crucifixion (Mk 14:3-9), commissioned his disciples to anoint with oil (Mk
6:13) and advised putting oil on one's head when fasting (Mt 6:17).

Jesus also differed from his austere Jewish brothers in that he
brought his message to all the people face to face. He was no monk
who retreats, but a prophet who confronts. "For the Son of Man came
to seek and save what was lost" (Lk 19:10, emphasis mine), and this
required walking mile after dusty mile on the streets and roads of
Palestine for about a three-year period. Jesus was a door-to-door
preacher, not a behind-closed-doors recluse. He urged his followers to
forsake all to follow him, yet they found themselves in the middle of
everyday life as "fishers of men."

Jesus, the leader, did not divide his followers into strict hierarchical
order, as was the order of Qumran. Nor did he require any probationary period for kingdom service. He drew disciples to himself by the
sheer force of his moral magnetism, and repelled those who would not
comply. He cultivated disciples on a personal, non-institutionalized
basis. When the twelve disciples began to jockey for power, he said
the greatest is the servant of all (Mt 23:11). Although it seems Jesus
developed deeper relationships with some disciples than others, there
was no official ranking. The Essenes, however, divided members into
four classes: priests, Levites, lay members and applicants.[35]

Unlike the Essenes, Jesus did not identify himself and his band of
followers with the kingdom of light and give up on all others as children of darkness. Although Jesus did demand a decision concerning
himself and his kingdom—a decision which would put a person on one
side of the eternal fence or the other—he didn't write off all those not
yet his disciples. He pursued people in the hope of their becoming his
disciples, and he trained his disciples to do the same. Jesus moved
toward the lost, not away from them, even lamenting over Jerusalem's
rejection of his mission (Mt 23:37). This is different in spirit from the
overall view of the Dead Sea documents, which taught that only the
Essenes were saved, and they were to remain separate from the un-
saved. (The Essenes did seek some converts, but their identity was

wrapped up in exclusivism.)

The Essenes were avid law keepers and viewed the Pharisees as too lax on the law. They retreated into the wilderness to become immune from such lawless infections. Jesus never flouted the law of Moses and affirmed its principles, yet he targeted a legalism that exalted the law over the Lawgiver and that replaced a heartfelt obedience to God with a mechanical legalism. Although we saw earlier that the Qumran community could emphasize the grace of God in salvation, their views on the law differed from Jesus' in several ways.

The Dead Sea document called The Damascus Rule says, "No man shall assist a beast to give birth on the Sabbath day. And if it should fall into a cistern or a pit, he shall not lift it out on the Sabbath."[36] After declaring himself the Lord of the Sabbath, Jesus argued against the Pharisees' view of the Sabbath by asking, "If any of you has a sheep and it falls into a pit on the Sabbath, will you not take hold of it and lift it out? How much more valuable is a man than a sheep! Therefore it is lawful to do good on the Sabbath" (Mt 12:11-12). We do not know if Jesus was actually speaking against the Essenes, but his argument does not square with their teaching. Neither would his revolutionary statement, "The Sabbath was made for man, not man for the Sabbath" (Mk 2:27), have won him favor with Essene audiences.

Jesus' views on ritual purity and impurity also put him in a different category than Essenian rigorism. James Charlesworth speaks of the "Essenes' virtual paranoia about becoming unclean."[37] Especially ostracized were the lepers. The Temple Scroll says, "In every city you shall set aside areas for those stricken with leprosy, with plague and with scab, who shall not enter your cities and profane them."[38] Jesus *touched* lepers and made them whole (Mt 8:2-3). He also deliberately stayed at the home of Simon the leper (Mk 14:3).

The Essenes looked forward to messianic redemption from God. Jesus claimed to be that redemption in the flesh. He fulfilled the law as the Son of God and announced the kingdom of God as coming in his own person. Christianity was built on this premise. Frank Moore

Cross underscores this by observing that what distinguished the Essenes and the early Christians was "the 'event' of Jesus as the Christ, his exaltation, his resurrection, the gift of his Spirit."[39] He goes on to note that:

The Christian faith is distinguished from the ancient [Jewish] faith which brought it to birth in its knowledge of a new act of God's love, the revelation of His love in Jesus' particular life and death and resurrection.[40]

These fundamental differences between Jesus and the Essenes cannot be diluted by the similarities that can be found. Yet even the similarities can be understood as coming, not from the direct influence of the Essenes, but by virtue of the common Jewish theological influence on both Jesus and the Essenes. F. F. Bruce explains the commonalities of Jesus and various Jewish groups without demoting Jesus' uniqueness:

It is easy to go through the recorded teachings of Jesus and list parallels—some of them quite impressive—with what we find in the Qumran texts. . . . It is idle to feel alarm at this, as though the originality of Jesus and the divine authority of Christianity were imperiled by such a recognition. For He accepted the same Biblical revelation as did the Qumran converters and the rabbis in the mainstream of Jewish tradition, and it would be surprising if no affinity at all were found between their respective interpretations of that revelation, on which their respective teachings were based.[41]

It is not impossible that Jesus as a Jew of his day knew of, and in some cases may have been influenced by, the Essenes' teachings to the degree that he used some of their phrases or recognized good aspects of their lives.[42] But this is conjectural, because he never mentioned the Essenes by name. And even if some influence is granted, it does not mean that Jesus was an Essene or that his theology was largely indebted to the Essenes. Speaking of the uniqueness of Jesus, Charlesworth says, "It is startling to discern how true it is that the genesis and genius of earliest Christianity, and the one reason it was distinguishable from Judaism, is found essentially in one life and one person."[43]

According to the classical secondary sources and the Dead Sea Scrolls, the Essenes were not the proto-New Agers they are often thought to be. Even if it could be established that they were forerunners of the New Age, the reliability of the New Testament picture of Jesus (see chapter six) is such that Jesus cannot be fit into an Essenian mold. Yet several books claim to reveal other information on the Essenes not normally recognized. While the basic historical reliability of the Dead Sea Scrolls and other material on the Essenes is generally not questioned, these exotic documents need closer inspection.

Szekely and *The Essene Gospel of Peace*

In her recent book *Going Within,* Shirley MacLaine speaks of "Edmond Bordeaux Szekaly's [sic] translations from the original Hebrew and Aramaic texts" concerning the Essenes, and later says that "of course, Jesus was an Essene teacher and healer."[44] Although she does not mention it outright, MacLaine was probably influenced by Szekely's edition of *The Essene Gospel of Peace,* purportedly a record of the life of Jesus as an Essene Master,[45] which he claims has sold hundreds of thousands of copies over its long publication history.

Szekely claims to have discovered an Aramaic manuscript buried in the Secret Archives of the Vatican library while doing research there in 1923-1924. Two other manuscripts are said to duplicate this manuscript: one in Old Slavonic, said to be in the National Library of Vienna, and Hebrew fragments that had resided in the now destroyed Benedictine Monastery in Cassino, Italy. Before scrutinizing the historical reliability of these documents, we need to understand the Jesus that Szekely finds in them.

The Essene Gospel of Peace, Szekely's supposed translation of this Aramaic manuscript, was first published in 1937, with second and third installments published in the 1970s. Jesus is portrayed as giving many long discourses having to do mainly with health concerns and the sacredness of the earth. He says:

Your Mother is in you, and you in her. She bore you: she gives you

life. It was she who gave you your body, and to her shall you one
day give it back again. Happy are you when you come to know her
and her kingdom; if you receive your Mother's angels and if you
do her laws, I tell you truly, he who does these things shall never
see disease. For the power of the Mother is above all. And it de-
stroys Satan and his kingdom, and has rule over all your bodies and
all living things.[46]

The Earthly Mother plays just as important, if not more vital, a role
in the Essene Jesus' theology as the Heavenly Father. Jesus advises the
needy to purify their bodies and receive the natural gifts of the Mother. Instead of healing miraculously with a word of command, as in the
Gospels, Jesus leads the sick into natural cures:

And many unclean and sick followed Jesus' words and sought the
banks of the murmuring streams. They put off their clothing, they
fasted, and they gave up their bodies to the angels of the air, of
water, and sunshine. And the Earthly Mother's angels embraced
them, possessing their bodies both inwards and outwards. And all
of them saw all evils, sins and uncleanness depart in haste from
them.[47]

In another poetically put, but descriptively precise passage, the Essene
Jesus encourages his followers to let "the angel of water . . . baptize
you also within" in order to become free from sin. He means this quite
literally, because the text goes on to explain how to administer a
sacred enema.[48]

The Essene Jesus teaches that God's law is not to be found in the
Scriptures, which are only humanity's product, but in nature. The
"living word" is found "in the grass, in the tree, in the river, in the
mountain, in the birds of heaven, in the fishes of the sea; but seek it
chiefly in yourselves."[49]

Meat eating is not an option for the Essene Jesus who preaches that
everything beyond "the fruits of the trees, the grain and grasses of the
field, the milk of the beasts and the honey of the bees" is "of Satan."[50]

The Essene Gospel of Peace: Book Two, published four decades
after the first book, contains three pages called "Fragments from the

Essene Gospel of John" that give a new gloss on Jesus' view of being
born again (cf. John 3). The Essene Jesus says that unless "a man be
born of the Earthly Mother and the Heavenly Father, and walk with
the Angels of the Day and the Night he cannot enter into the Eternal
Kingdom."[51]

The theology of the texts is pantheistic, monistic and earth-centered.
The Essene Jesus is a Cosmic Naturopath who waxes lyrical about the
healing power of various angels of water, air, sun and so on sent by
the Earthly Mother. His idea of sin is not that of moral transgression
but physical mistreatment. Sin is flushed out by natural processes, not
atoned for by the death of Jesus himself.

Szekely synthesizes the supposedly Essenian material in another
book called *The Essene Jesus* and subtitled *A Revelation from the
Dead Sea Scrolls.*[52] According to Szekely, all religions teach the same
truths at the esoteric level, and the Essene Jesus is the esoteric Master
missed by the masses.[53] He claims that Jesus said he was "no longer
a man but had become as God"[54] and that Jesus saved mankind not
by his death but by his life and teachings on cosmic and natural law,[55]
or to put it better, "he did not save mankind, but showed mankind
the path to salvation" because "each must save himself; no one else
can save him."[56]

Szekely and the Evidence

The above should be sufficient to give the New Age flavor of Szekely's
"Essene Jesus." Before examining the case for the documents, we
should realize that both Szekely's version of the Essenes and his picture of Jesus are highly unorthodox. His mystical, nature-loving Essenes bear little resemblance to the Essenes of the Dead Sea Scrolls
and the classical sources. Szekely's Essenes have no awareness of sin
as an ethical category and are more concerned with the Earthly Mother than with the Heavenly Father. ("Earthly Mother" is a designation
never found in the writings of the historical Essenes.) Despite the fact
that the Essene Jesus uses biblical terminology and phraseology such
as "Verily . . ." and "Happy are they . . ." and biblical passages are

interspersed in the material, the theology is antithetical to the New Testament. Jesus is presented as a nature-healer, not the Savior; instead of eating the Passover lamb, he requires vegetarianism; he reveres the Earthly Mother more than his Heavenly Father (making him a bi-theist instead of a monotheist); he never speaks of sin as an offense against a holy God, but as a physical imbalance; he is evolved highly enough[57] to have become as God, but this is not his unique status.

Clearly, then, the burden of proof is on Szekely to disprove not only the scholarly world's view of the Essenes, but also the historic Christian understanding of Jesus as the Christ. Can he withstand and overthrow this burden through the strength of his evidence?

We immediately run into trouble concerning the integrity and authenticity of Szekely's purported texts. We have only his word on their existence. There is no external corroboration. He claims one complete Aramaic manuscript of *The Essene Gospel of Peace* is lodged in the Secret Archives of the Vatican and that he translated it during a stay there.[58] Translating a large ancient manuscript in a dead language is not as simple as Szekely makes it sound. Yet he says he "read" it and left shortly thereafter. He makes no mention of taking photographs. But as Beskow notes, "Not even today with sophisticated phototechnology, would it be possible to produce copies useful for a scholarly edition in such haste."[59] Neither does Szekely give any scholarly details concerning the nature of the manuscript, whether it was a scroll or a codex.

Beskow notes that an official at the Secret Archives informed him that no such manuscript is housed there and that there is no record of Szekely's visit there.[60] He even documents a letter from the Prefect of the Secret Archives to this effect.[61]

Szekely claims he presented his finds at the University of Paris in 1925, but he says his thesis has been lost, and he does not mention the name of his advising professor.[62]

We are given precious little information on the supposed Old Slavonic manuscript, which Szekely says belongs to the National Library of Vienna. It is not even mentioned in his book dealing with the discovery of *The Essene Gospel of Peace*. Beskow notes that manuscripts in official libraries invariably have code numbers, and if Szekely had been working with this manuscript for fifty years it would be a moral obligation to let others know where it can be found.[63] But he never did. Beskow also observes that it is not uncommon for the National Library of Vienna to receive inquiries about Szekely's material; but it is not to be found there.[64]

Szekely further claims that Hebrew fragments of the document were found in Mount Cassino, which has since been destroyed in World War 2. Although Szekely published a Hebrew edition of *The Essene Gospel of Peace,* he did not translate it, annotate it or explain how it was reconstructed from the original fragments, procedures required in scholarly circles to establish credibility.[65]

To sum up, there is little evidence for the veracity of Szekely's supposed find. It is contradicted repeatedly by other much better attested sources both from the Dead Sea Scrolls and the New Testament. Stylistically, *The Essene Gospel of Peace* does not read like ancient Jewish literature; it resembles Romantic impressions more than biblical narrative or poetry.[66] Concerning authenticity, recent editions do not say who wrote *The Essene Gospel of Peace* (except that the author was an Essene). But Szekely claims to have a fragment from "the *Essene Gospel of John,*"[67] which is little more than a rewriting of part of John with the addition of "the Earthly Mother" and other Szekelian trademarks. As for the integrity of the document, Szekely asserts his best texts supposedly date to the third century; but we have no way of verifying their *existence,* let alone their integrity. If these manuscripts actually existed as Szekely claimed, it seems unlikely that he would not have revealed them to the scholarly world, because their import would rival the Dead Sea Scrolls and the Nag Hamaddi manuscripts. Yet he never did so.[68]

Many more criticisms could be leveled regarding inconsistencies in Szekely's writings, logical gaps, the general unreliability of his claims and his predilection to inflate his own achievements,[69] but we will conclude with Beskow:

The Gospel of Peace is a sheer forgery, written entirely by Szekely himself. It is one of the strangest frauds we know of in the biblical field, as it has been carried through by stages during a whole lifetime and has been built into an entire body of research based on imagination only.[70] Given the immense weight of evidence stacked so high against Szekely, it is now appropriate to mention that many of his dozens of books dealt with health foods and natural healing. Titles listed in his books include *The Book of Living Foods, Scientific Vegetarianism, Healing Waters* and *Treasury of Raw Foods.*[71] It is easy then to see him cooking up an "Essene Jesus" as the Cosmic Naturopath who advances Szekely's agenda for health.

Szekely's Essene Jesus is attractive to many, Shirley MacLaine among them, because the sting of the biblical Jesus is entirely lacking. The Essene Jesus provokes no controversy, makes no enemies, issues no ethical demands, and never divides the world into those who are for him and those who are against him. He is a mellow metaphysician and an organic physician who bears no cross, sheds no blood and startles no disciples as the resurrected Lord. Instead he, fictitious though he may be, validates the message of the New Age.[72]

Another view of Jesus comes not from supposedly historical manuscripts but descends from spiritual elevations by means of those metaphysically attuned to the higher source, whether it be the Akashic Records, the Collective Unconscious or an assortment of Ascended Masters. This "Jesus of the spirits" is the subject of our next chapter.

Notes

[1]See for instance H. Spencer Lewis, *The Mystical Life of Jesus* (San Jose, Calif.: Supreme Grand Lodge of AMORC, 1974), pp. 23-42. He says some rather ominous things about Jesus and the Essenes being pure white Aryans.

[2]Manly P. Hall, *The Mystical Christ* (Los Angeles, Calif.: The Philosophical Research Society, Inc., 1951), p. 39.

[3]Richard Walters, "Christ, Christian, Krishna," *New Frontier,* Dec. 1988, p. 7.

[4]Shirley MacLaine, *Going Within* (New York, N.Y.: Bantam, 1989), pp. 178-81.

[5]Annie Besant, *Esoteric Christianity* (Wheaton, Ill.: The Theosophical Publishing House, 1966), p. 89.

[6]Edgar Cayce, *Edgar Cayce's Story of Jesus,* ed. by Jeffrey Furst (New York, N.Y.: Berkley Books, 1976), pp. 130-58.

[7]See James Charlesworth, *Jesus within Judaism* (New York, N.Y.: Doubleday, 1988), pp. 62-63; and F. F. Bruce, *New Testament History* (Garden City, N.Y.: Doubleday, 1980), pp. 115-21.

[8]See Charlesworth, p. 63.

[9]G. Vermes, *The Dead Sea Scrolls in English,* 3rd edition (London: Penguin, 1988), p. xiv, comments on how the findings relate to the reliability of the Old Testament: "With this newly discovered material at their disposal, experts concerned with the study of the text and transmission of the Scriptures are now able to achieve far greater accuracy in their deductions and can trace the process by which the text of the Bible attained its final shape. Moreover, they are in a position to prove that it has remained virtually unchanged for the last two thousand years."

[10]A few fragments from horoscopes were also found. Vermes thinks that rather than indicate an astrological concern to predict the future, these fragments are probably "horoscope-like compositions" used as "literary devices." See ibid., p. 305.

[11]Charles F. Pfeiffer, *The Dead Sea Scrolls and the Bible* (Grand Rapids, Mich.: Baker Book House, 1984), p. 112.

[12]Ibid., p. 111.

[13]Charlesworth, p. 71.

[14]Quoted in Vermes, p. 79.

[15]H. Spencer Lewis, p. 30, the Rosicrucian writer, lists as the first of ten principles of Essenism: "God is principle. . . . God is not a person, nor does He appear to the outer man in any form of cloud or glory."

[16]Vermes, p. 177.

[17]Ibid., p. 80.

[18]See ibid., pp. 42-43.

[19]On the Qumran Essene views of the afterlife see ibid., pp. 55-56.

[20]Leslie Weatherhead, *The Christian Agnostic* (Nashville, Tenn.: Abingdon Press, 1965), p. 296.

[21]John Hick, *Death and Eternal Life* (San Francisco, Calif.: Harper and Row, 1980), p. 395.

[22]Ibid.; Hick says this "idea can be found in Jewish apocalyptic writings (for example, 2 Enoch 8:5; 65:10; 2 Esdras 2:39, 45)."

[23]Vermes, p. 65.

[24]Ibid., p. 66.

[25]William Sanford LaSor, *The Dead Sea Scrolls and the New Testament* (Grand Rapids, Mich.: William B. Eerdmans Publishing Company, 1983), p. 146.

[26]Ibid., p. 148.

[27]Ibid., p. 146.

[28]Ibid., p. 147.

[29]F. F. Bruce, *New Testament History,* p. 154.

[30]LaSor, pp. 150-51.

[31]Josephus discusses John the Baptist and mentions nothing of an Essene connection, even though he was well acquainted with the Essenes. See *Antiquities of the Jews,* 18.5.2.

[32]Charlesworth, p. 57.

[33]See LaSor, pp. 206-13; and Edwin M. Yamauchi, *The Stones and the Scriptures* (Philadelphia, Penn.: J. B. Lippincott Company, 1972), pp. 140-45. Vermes, p. xvi, makes this interesting comment on the Teacher of Righteousness in relation to Jesus: "And although the Teacher of Righteousness clearly sensed the deeper obligations implicit in the Mosaic Law, he was without the genius of Jesus who laid bare the inner core of spiritual truth and exposed the essence of religion as an existential relationship between man and man, and between man and God."

[34]Josephus *The Wars of the Jews,* 2.8.3.

[35]Hans Küng, *On Being a Christian* (Garden City, N.Y.: Doubleday, 1976), p. 198.

[36]Vermes, p. 95.

[37]Charlesworth, p. 72.

[38]Vermes, p. 145.

[39]Frank Moore Cross, Jr., *The Ancient Library of Qumran and Modern Biblical Studies* (Grand Rapids, Mich.: Baker Book House, 1980), p. 242.

[40]Ibid., p. 243.

[41]F. F. Bruce, *Second Thoughts on the Dead Sea Scrolls* (Grand Rapids, Mich.: Wm. B. Eerdmans, 1980), p. 144.

[42]See Charlesworth, pp. 68-71, discussion of Jesus' statement "Blessed are the poor in spirit" (Mt 5:3) as possibly having some reference to the Essenes. Although Charlesworth finds some possible positive influence by the Essenes on Jesus, he does not think Jesus was an Essene or that Essenism substantially contributed to Jesus' dynamic. For a different view of Jesus and the Essenes' understanding of "the poor," see Cross, p. 241.

[43]Charlesworth, p. 74.

[44]MacLaine, pp. 179-80. The proper spelling is *Szekely,* not *Szekaly.*

[45]Her undocumented comments seem to come straight from the introduction to *The Essene Gospel of Peace: Book Three* (San Diego, Calif.: Academy Books, 1977), pp. 11ff.

[46]Edmond Bordeaux Szekely, *The Essene Gospel of Peace: Book One* (USA: International Biogenic Society, 1981), p. 9.

[47]Ibid., p. 24.

[48]Ibid., pp. 15, 16.

[49]Ibid., p. 13.

[50]Ibid., p. 41.

[51]Edmond Bordeaux Szekely, *The Essene Gospel of Peace: Book Two* (San Diego, Calif.: Academy Books, 1977), p. 97.

[52]This does not claim to be a translation from an ancient manuscript.

[53]Edmond Bordeaux Szekely, *The Essene Jesus* (San Diego, Calif.: Academy Books, 1977), p. 7.

[54]Ibid., p. 34.

[55]Ibid., p. 49.

[56]Ibid., p. 50.

[57]Ibid., p. 7.

[58]See Edmond Bordeaux Szekely, *The Discovery of the Essene Gospel of Peace* (San Diego, Calif.: Academy Publishers, 1975).

[59]Per Beskow, *Strange Tales about Jesus* (Philadelphia: Fortress Press, 1985), p. 84.

[60]Ibid., p. 89.

[61]Ibid., p. 129.

[62]Szekely, *The Discovery,* p. 45.

[63]Beskow, p. 88.

[64]Ibid., pp. 88-89.

[65]For more on this see Beskow, pp. 85-86.

[66]See Beskow, p. 90.

[67]The first edition in 1937 of *The Essene Gospel of Peace* was titled *The Gospel of Peace by the Disciple John.* Curiously, references to authorship do not appear in the later editions. See Beskow, p. 83.

[68]Beskow, p. 88.

[69]See ibid., pp. 81-91, for Beskow's entire fair, careful and devastating critique.

[70]Ibid., p. 89.

[71]Of the fifty-one titles by Szekely listed in his more recently published books, at least twelve deal with health matters.

[72]Beskow, pp. 42-50, discusses and refutes another less well-known, supposedly Essene manuscript on Jesus called *The Essene Letter.* This document emphasizes that Jesus did not die on the cross. For a discussion of this claim see chapter seven.

Chapter 9
Jesus
of the Spirits

*T*his is a course in miracles. It is a required course. Only
the time you take it is voluntary." So begins the increasingly popular
three-volume, 1200-page *A Course in Miracles*. The short introduction
concludes with, "Nothing real can be threatened. Nothing unreal exists. Herein lies the peace of God."[1] Over 160,000 sets of the expensive
A Course in Miracles have been sold since its publication in 1975.[2] The
books list no author, but they claim to be transcribed from the voice
of Jesus himself.[3]

This Jesus says, "There is nothing about me that you cannot attain."[4] And also: *"There is no death because the Son of God is like
his Father. Nothing you can do can change Eternal Love. Forget your
dreams of sin and guilt and come with me instead to share the resurrection of God's Son."*[5] The *Course* further teaches that "it is impossible to kill God's Son; nor can his life in any way be changed by sin

and evil, malice, fear, or death."[6] Therefore, "all your sins have been forgiven because they carried no effect at all."[7]

A Course in Miracles has had close to miraculous success in its short career, in no small measure because of its asserted authorship and its adornment with biblical terminology. The books claim to cut through the illusions that enslave us and to reveal our true spiritual condition. Speaking of Jesus, it asks, "Is he the Christ? O yes, along with you."[8] Jesus became the Christ by seeing "the face of Christ in all his brothers" so that "he became identified with Christ, a man no longer, but one with God."[9]

Beyond History

In earlier chapters we have seen Jesus as the Gnostic revealer, Jesus as the world traveler and Jesus as the Essene mystic. The New Age lays claim to these revisions of the orthodox picture of Jesus of Nazareth by appealing to certain historical documents. In other words, the arguments are framed with factual claims within the realm of verifiable history. The Nag Hammadi library was unearthed, inspected and consulted to derive the Gnostic Jesus, a Jesus we found did not exist. "The Life of Saint Issa: Best of the Sons of Men" was hailed by Notovitch in his Unknown Life of Jesus Christ as establishing Jesus' trips Eastward, a life we found unknown because nonexistent. The Dead Sea Scrolls and other documents are said to reveal Jesus as a proto-New Age Essene, an assertion that also falls flat. In analyzing each of these claims, and finding them wanting in the very historical dimension they invoke, we have applied various historical tests for reliability.

Yet the New Age movement is pregnant with revelations about, and even from, Jesus or the Christ that are untethered to any terrestrial record. A Course in Miracles cites no footnotes and speaks of no historical corroboration. These revelations allegedly issue from the spiritual world, either from disincarnate entities or from more impersonal cosmic records. These messages may relate historical events but are not derived from historical sources such as archaeology, manuscripts or oral tradition per se. They are believed to have been intuited, received, transcribed or channeled from higher levels of Being not normally accessible.

Channeling has recently become a centerpiece for New Age interests, with hundreds of channelers (or channels) claiming secret contact with a plethora of paranormal teachers. These range from Ramtha, a 35,000-year-old warrior spirit hosted by J. Z. Knight; to Lazaris, a more mellow entity hosted by Jach Pursel; to Jesus or the Christ, hosted by assorted channelers. Channeling, otherwise known as mediumship or spiritism, is an ancient phenomenon that seems to come in waves of interest over the centuries. Rather than surveying this vast subject, we will cite proponent Jon Kilmo's concise definition of channeling as:

> The process of receiving information from some level of reality other than the ordinary physical one and from beyond the self as we currently understand it. This includes messages from any mental source that falls outside one's own ordinary conscious or unconscious and is not anyone else incarnate on the physical plane of reality.[10]

Both the modality of channeling and the entities channeled vary considerably. Some claim that channeling is a kind of "voluntary possession" in which the entity takes complete control of the human. After the channeled message the channeler has no recollection of what his or her vocal chords were doing during this time. Others claim a more cooperative endeavor such as hearing a voice, seeing a vision or being strongly impressed in some manner that does not swallow up the channeler's personality *in toto* in the delivery process.[11]

Many of the thousands of modern channelers make mention of Jesus at least in passing, hailing him as a great spiritual master of one sort or another. Yet the myriad messages converge on Jesus as an example of Christ Consciousness rather than as the unique Lord and Savior. Consequently, notions of human limitation, sin, death as the result of sin, and hell are rejected in favor of the self as intrinsically divine and unlimited.[12] For example, Ramtha says that "for two thousand years, we have been called *sinful creatures*. That stigma automatically takes away our ability to remind ourselves that we are great, or that we are equal with God or Christ or Buddha, or whomever."[13]

Rather than chronicle a welter of words about Jesus from the panoply of paranormal pronouncements, we will explain and assess three channeled sources that significantly center on Jesus and the Christ, namely, *A Course in Miracles, The Aquarian Gospel of Jesus the Christ,* and the Edgar Cayce readings. All of these sources highly esteem Jesus as the Christ and present themselves as essentially Christian. The questions then arise: On what basis can they make this claim, and why should anyone believe them?

Jesus According to *A Course in Miracles*

We have already tasted a portion of *A Course in Miracles,* but we need a larger serving to understand its appetizing elements. The human transcriber of the revelations was Helen Schucman who, after several visionary experiences, began to hear an inner voice in 1965 say, "This is a course in miracles. Please take notes." After protracted protests, Schucman, a Jewish atheist, began a seven-year process of recording what eventually became the three-volume set and the basis of a worldwide organization known as the Foundation for Inner Peace.[14] Although Schucman died in 1981, the teachings she received have skyrocketed in popularity since then, with over 300 groups formed in the United States to study the set.[15]

The *Course* teaches that we are all at least potentially Christs, that Jesus is not touched by evil, that he never died, that sin and guilt are unreal and that there is no death. Despite these unorthodox assertions, the teaching repeatedly uses biblical terminology. Atonement, according to the *Course,* has nothing to do with blood sacrifice. It says, "The crucifixion did not establish the Atonement; the resurrection did."[16] The Jesus of the *Course* says, "I was not 'punished' because *you* were bad. The wholly benign lesson the Atonement teaches is lost if it is tainted with this kind of distortion in any form."[17] More terms are also redefined:

I have been correctly referred to as "the lamb of God who takes away the sins of the world," but those who represent the lamb as a blood stained symbol do not understand the meaning of that symbol. Correctly understood, it is a very simple symbol that speaks of my innocence.[18]

This Jesus goes on to say that the idea of "taking away the sins of the world" means to show people their true, original innocence, and "innocence is wisdom because it is unaware of evil, and evil does not exist."[19] Further, true perception sees that "sin does not exist."[20]

The overall perspective of the *Course* is that humans are imprisoned by the illusion of a separate ego that is distinct from God. We are not separate from God either by being created by God or because of sin against God. Sin, evil, guilt and any separation from God are ultimately unreal, as is death itself: "There is no death, but there is belief in death."[21] Consequently, Jesus is not viewed as the Savior from sin's penalty or as one who defeated death by his own death on the cross. *Sacrificial* atonement is unnecessary for innocent beings. Humans suffer from ignorance of their true reality, not from any inherent moral problem. Christ is not to be worshiped; rather, "Christ waits for your acceptance of Him *as yourself.*"[22] This Jesus also says, "I have stressed that awe is not an appropriate reaction to me because of our inherent equality."[23] Given all this, it should not be surprising that the *Course* would recommend that every person say to himself or herself, "my salvation comes from me. It cannot come from anywhere else."[24]

The "miracle" of *A Course in Miracles* is a shift in perception that sees all things as one and divine without sin, guilt and death. It has nothing to do with a supernatural intervention in human affairs. Judith Skutch, cofounder and president of the Foundation for Inner Peace, sums this up: "By not seeing anyone else as guilty, and by extending love instead of fear, we can begin to recognize the truth about our real identity as a sinless Son of God."[25]

According to proponent Robert Perry, the *Course* is "intended not as a restatement, but as a purification, of traditional Christianity." This is "most easily seen in its use of Christian terminology . . . [which is] changed to reflect a purified and more universal perspective."[26] Skutch is forthright in admitting that the *Course* "combines a lot of Eastern themes and approaches them within a more familiar Western framework—the strongest of which is the nondualistic."[27] This means that "our only reality lies in spirit, with God as our source,"[28] and the physical world is not ultimately real. For this reason, she refers to the *Course* as "Christian Vedanta."[29] (Vedanta is a rigidly monistic and pantheistic tradition of Hinduism.)

Many of those associated with the *Course* seem to accept its teaching because they believe it to be compatible with biblical doctrine. Yet a strong promoter of the *Course,* Kenneth Wapnick, commented at a seminar on the *Course* that if the Bible were the literal truth, the *Course* would have to be viewed as inspired by demons.[30] He clearly and correctly saw an incompatibility.[31]

Others seem to embrace the *Course* because they view it as superior to a dead Christianity unable to meet people's needs. The benefit they derive from the *Course* is all the proof they require. Yet while the message of sinlessness, Christhood and unconditional love seems appetizing, the experience of these realities demands work. "Salvation is nothing more than 'right-mindedness,'. . . which must be *achieved* before One-mindedness is restored."[32] "Salvation is your happiest *accomplishment.* "[33]

One must unflinchingly deny all guilt in order to earn salvation from the illusion of guilt. Dean Halverson's analysis of the *Course* brings this into perspective:

> While it may be true that guiltlessness is unconditional, *manifesting guiltlessness* is the condition for overcoming the illusion of guilt. Thus living a guiltless life is the condition that must be met for that illusion to be banished and for salvation to be achieved.[34]

The existential price for exchanging the biblical view of Jesus Christ's atoning death on behalf of sinful humanity for the *Course*'s "atonement" of remembering one's true innocence is the hard psychological labor of convincing oneself that sin, guilt, and death do not exist. The only thing left to feel guilty about is guilt itself. But one should not fret too much over an illusion, no matter how incorrigible that illusion may seem. It will give way . . . someday.

The *Course* has been viewed as a "purification" of Christianity, but it more resembles an inversion of every aspect of the message of Jesus delivered by the Bible. Atonement is inverted to mean there is no need for reconciliation with a holy God through Jesus' death and resurrection. Sin is rejected as unreal; harboring the illusion of guilt, sin and death is the real problem. Any supposed separation from God is merely an illusion, a dream; nevertheless, the illusion is universally compelling and demands the solution offered by the *Course*.

Dean Halverson nicely contrasts the cleavage between the biblical view and the perspective of this other Jesus:

> In the *Course's* plan for salvation, *we* pay for the Son of God's mistake. In the Bible's plan for salvation, *Jesus Christ,* the one and only Son of God, pays for our sin. In the *Course,* salvation is earned through the perfect demonstration of our awareness of sinlessness and unity with God. In the Bible, salvation is a gift that cannot be earned; it can only be received by trusting in the completed work of Jesus Christ.[35]

The ultimate reality for the *Course* is a God who is an impersonal oneness; final salvation means being absorbed into this abstraction in a realm beyond distinctions, words and events.[36]

Comparing this picture with the crucified Jesus' words to the thief on the cross beside him puts the issue in sharp perspective. After the man confessed to Jesus that he was being punished justly, he cried out and said, "Jesus, remember me when you come into your kingdom" (Lk 23:42). Jesus replied, "I tell you the truth, today you will be with me in paradise" (Lk 23:43). Repentance and faith were required of the thief. His sin was real. His pain was real. His literal death would soon be real. Jesus' pain was more real than any ever experienced before or since. He too would truly die, only to rise again. But this thief, because he was redeemed by Jesus' sacrifice, would be with Jesus himself in a real paradise, not beyond distinctions, words or events, but full of undiluted Life himself.

Another Gospel presents a Jesus whose life is an example of what all may attain; it is the Gospel for the Aquarian Age.

An Aquarian Gospel

"Then hear, you men of Israel, hear! Look not upon the flesh; it is not king. Look to the Christ within, who shall be formed in every one of you, as he is formed in me."[37] So speaks the Jesus of another channeled source that has become a New Age classic. First published in 1907, *The Aquarian Gospel of Jesus the Christ* has interested a score of seekers wanting a greater knowledge of Jesus than given in the Bible. The book has the appearance of "a fifth Gospel" in that it is divided into chapters and verses much like modern translations of the Bible.[38] The subject matter overlaps the biblical accounts at certain places, but the document makes no claim on historical tradition. Although *The Aquarian Gospel* finds Jesus in India (as well as Greece and Egypt), it is unlike Notovitch's effort in that it does not appeal to any lost physical manuscript. Rather, it is purported to be a receipt of a heavenly revelation to one Levi H. Downing (who preferred to be called simply Levi).

Although Levi is listed as the author, he is better understood as the receiver because the book is, according to the title page, "transcribed from the Akashic Records." Levi (1841-1911) had a Christian background, but as a boy he is said to have become sensitive to the "finer ethers and believed that in some manner they were sensitized plates on which sounds, even thoughts, were recorded."[39] He "entered into the deeper studies of etheric vibration" and after forty years spent in meditation and study "found himself in that stage of spiritual consciousness that permitted him to enter the domain of superfine ethers and become familiar with their mysteries."[40] These "ethers" are also known as the Akashic Records, which Levi says refers to "the Primary Substance" or "Universal Mind" in which everything that has ever happened is recorded. This spiritual substance is not relegated to any one part of the universe; it is everywhere present, but only accessible to those trained to pick up the higher frequencies.[41] Levi wrote *The*

Aquarian Gospel "between the early morning hours of two and six—the absolutely quiet hours,"[42] thus becoming the nocturnal notary of the Akashic accounts.

Other sensitives, particularly those connected with Theosophy, have appealed to the Akashic Records for hidden wisdom about Jesus and the universe (including, as we will see, Edgar Cayce and Rudolf Steiner). Klimo describes it as a "nonphysical 'cosmic memory bank' of all that has occurred, which can be tapped by certain individuals, physical and non-physical."[43]

The Aquarian Gospel differs from the *Course* in that it was received, not from a personal spirit, but extracted from an impersonal record. It also makes factual claims about the historical Jesus, something the *Course* finds no need to do, since matter is viewed as illusory anyway.

Who Is the Aquarian Jesus?

In the introduction to the book, Levi clearly spells out the relationship between Jesus of Nazareth and the Christ:

Orthodox Christian ecclesiastics tell us that Jesus of Nazareth and the Christ were one; that the true name of this remarkable person was Jesus Christ. They tell us that this man of Galilee was the very eternal God clothed in flesh of man that men might see his glory. Of course this doctrine is wholly at variance with the teaching of Jesus himself and of his apostles.[44]

In order to anchor this rather bold assertion, Levi must place his purported revelation above the New Testament, which clearly teaches that "Jesus and the Christ were one." The Aquarian Jesus is less a Savior than a magus, a world traveler in search of religious wisdom and initiation into deeper mysteries.[45] His journeys take him to India, Tibet, Persia, Assyria, Greece and Egypt. Levi's account of Jesus in India echoes Notovitch's in places, as when Jesus visits Leh, the capital of Ladak. There Notovitch claims to have found "The Life of Saint Issa" at the Himis monastery. Yet the account differs from Notovitch's in several ways.

First, the Aquarian Jesus is much more Eastern than the Jewish-

Christian-Buddhist mix of Notovitch. We find him clearly teaching
reincarnation as the explanation for musical prodigies. He says, "In
one short life they surely could not gain such a grace of voice, such
knowledge of harmony and tone." Instead, he says, "these people are
not young" because "ten thousand years ago these people mastered
harmony" and "they have come again to learn still other lessons from
the varied notes of manifests."[46]

Second, the Aquarian Jesus is not like Notovitch's teacher of wisdom, who became a martyr, but is instead an initiate into the esoteric
mysteries. In Egypt Jesus visits the temple in Heliopolis to be received
as a pupil of Egyptian wisdom. He passes through six degrees of
initiation—sincerity, justice, faith, philanthropy, heroism, and love
divine—before entering the Chamber of the Dead. Here, clothed in
purple, Jesus receives the seventh and highest degree from the hiero-
phant who says:

> Brother, man, most excellent of men, in all the temple tests you
> have won out. Six times before the bar of right you have been
> judged; six times you have received the highest honours man can
> give; and now you stand prepared to take the last degree. Upon
> your brow I place this diadem, and in the Great Lodge of the
> heavens and earth you are THE CHRIST. This is your great Pass-
> over rite. You are a neophyte no more; but now a master mind.[47]

Third, the Aquarian Jesus, unlike Issa, performs miracles and is resurrected from the dead. In fact he even appears to various people in
India, Persia, Greece, Rome and Egypt. Yet the resurrection appearances are much closer to spiritistic "materializations" than the New
Testament accounts of Jesus' resurrected body.

The essential message of the Aquarian Jesus is the Christhood of
all people. He says near the end of the book:

> You know that all my life was one great drama for the sons of men;
> a pattern for the sons of men. *I lived to show the possibilities of
> man.* What I have done all men can do, and what I am all men shall
> be.[48]

The possibilities of man are great, according to the Aquarian Jesus, because "all things are God; all things are one."[49] Although the Aquarian Gospel sometimes speaks of Jesus giving his life for man, the real message is that Jesus is a prototype of Christ Consciousness, not the unique Lord and Savior. This Jesus says he will resurrect "just to prove the possibilities of man."[50] The resurrected Jesus addresses a royal feast in India and says, "You shall go to all the world and preach the gospel of the omnipotence of man."[51]

Because *The Aquarian Gospel* makes historical claims, despite its supposedly spiritual and non-historical origin, it can be checked for accuracy through outside sources. Much of the text repeats material found in the Gospels, either verbatim or in altered form. Other material has no Gospel parallels, but some can be compared with general historical knowledge.

The Akashic account opens by affirming that "Herod Antipas was the ruler of Jerusalem" during the birth of Jesus.[52] This is close, since the ruler at that time was a Herod, but not close enough, because it was Herod *the Great*. Non-biblical sources say Herod *Antipas,* Herod the Great's son, ruled after and not during the time of Jesus' birth. The synoptic Gospels tell us Herod Antipas put John the Baptist to death (Mt 14:1-12) and tried Jesus (Lk 23:6-15).

The Aquarian Jesus is found studying in a temple in Lassa, Tibet, with one Meng-ste, "greatest sage of all the farther East."[53] This is reminiscent of Meng-tse (notice Levi's reversal of the fifth and sixth letters) sometimes known as Mencius, the Chinese sage. If this is Levi's reference, he is off by three hundred years, because Mencius died in 289 B.C.[54]

Jesus is said to have traveled from Tibet to Lahore.[55] This is interesting since the city is "not known in history until the seventh century A.D."[56] Another anachronism pops up when Jesus appears "fully materialized" to magian priests in Persepolis.[57] This city was destroyed by Alexander the Great in 330 B.C. and never rebuilt.[58]

Although *The Aquarian Gospel* mixes in much biblical material (as well as material from the apocryphal *Gospel of James*),[59] it contradicts the New Testament record many times, especially concerning Jesus' supposed sojourns East. The theology from the Akashic Records is also at odds with the biblical records, which we have argued are reliable historical documents. The Aquarian Jesus is a pattern for the destiny of all people and the harbinger of a new Aquarian age of self-realization. He is not the unique incarnation of a personal God who dies for the sins of humanity and who alone provides redemption. To give credence to this *Aquarian Gospel,* one must jettison the New Testament as untrue and overlook several obvious historical anachronisms.

The Sleeping Prophet's Jesus

Edgar Cayce (1877-1945), known as the "sleeping prophet," was one of the foremost mediums of the century. For over four decades he gave "readings" on medicine, lost civilizations, the future and Jesus himself. These readings have gone public through many popular books. The Association for Research and Enlightenment (A.R.E.) continues to disseminate his materials widely.

As a child Cayce experienced various visions and would enter a trance state to memorize his school lessons. In 1900, after an untreatable paralysis of the throat, a friend named Al Layne helped him re-enter the trance state during which he said, "Yes, we can see the body" (which indicated other beings speaking of their view of Cayce's body). The voice diagnosed the problem as bad circulation, and Cayce recovered after Layne suggested his body heal itself.[60] So began Cayce's psychic career.

Cayce's readings were given during this deep trance state and originally only concerned matters of personal health. He would amaze those who came to him with the effectiveness of the often unorthodox prescriptions and recommendations given while he was unconscious. After thirteen years of medical readings, someone asked Cayce questions of a more metaphysical nature. Cayce was initially shocked upon awaking to find that his readings were deviating considerably from what he himself had taught in Sunday school and what he believed was taught in the Bible. Concerning his readings that taught reincarnation, he said:

What the readings have been saying, is foreign to all I've believed
and taught, and all I have taught others, all my life. If ever the Devil
was going to play a trick on me, this would be it.[61]
Cayce, nevertheless, continued to entertain metaphysical questions in
his trance readings, many of which concerned Jesus. The answers
reveal a Jesus decidedly unorthodox.

Reincarnation is the linchpin of Cayce's world view, and the readings repeatedly assert that Jesus had been incarnated many times before "becoming the Christ." When asked to list "the important incarnations of Jesus in the world's history," Cayce replied, "In the
beginning as Amilius, as Adam, as Melchiezek [sic], as Zend, as Ur,
as Asaph, as Jeshua—Joseph—(Joshua)—Jesus."[62] On another occasion Cayce said thirty incarnations were required for Jesus to become
the Christ.[63] Cayce also affirmed that Jesus first knew that he would
be the Savior "when he fell, in Eden."[64]

Like *The Aquarian Gospel,* the Cayce readings also find Jesus head-
ing eastward to India, Persia and Egypt. In India Jesus learned of
"those cleansings of the body related to preparation for strength in the
physical as well as the mental man."[65] In Persia he learned of "the
unison of forces as related to those teachings of that given by Zu and
Ra."[66] Cayce chimes in with *The Aquarian Gospel* in saying that Jesus
visited the temple in "Hilleopolis [sic] for the period of attaining to
the priesthood; in the taking of the examinations there."[67] Cayce
differs from Levi in saying that Jesus did not study with Greek phi-
losophers because he "never appealed to the worldly wise."[68] But the
key point is that Jesus was an initiate who gradually attained a realization of Christhood.

When asked the significance and meaning of the words *Jesus* and
Christ Cayce replied:

Jesus is the man—the activity, the mind, the relationships that he
bore with others. . . . He grew faint, He grew weak, and yet gained
in strength which He had promised in becoming the Christ. . . . Ye
are made strong in body, in mind, in soul and purpose, by that power
in Christ. The power, then, is in the Christ. The pattern is in Jesus.[69]

Although some of the readings sound biblical, the overall context is that of souls gradually reaching perfection through a long series of reincarnations. According to Cayce, "Jesus who became the Christ" may serve as a metaphysical boost for those on this journey, but Jesus is not the Savior who insures eternal salvation for those who come to him by faith. It is revealing that at one place Cayce says that the "whole gospel of Jesus Christ" is the great commandment to completely love the Lord and our neighbor as ourselves.[70] This is not the *gospel* at all but the demand of the *law*, which, according to the New Testament, no one can perform adequately to merit eternal life.

Cayce saw all knowledge as residing within. Understanding the creation of souls to be emanations of God or "portions of [God] himself,"[71] he could agree with the statement, made by one of his questioners during a reading, that the Christ-Consciousness is "described as the awareness within each soul, imprinted in pattern on the mind and waiting to be awakened by the will, of the soul's oneness with God."[72] He also said, "All ye may know of God is within your own self."[73]

The Cayce material, although thoroughly imbued with biblical language, offers a Jesus foreign to the New Testament record. Instead of Jesus being the Christ from birth, as the Gospels report, he became the Christ through successive incarnations and occultic initiation. Instead of being the first and last incarnation of the eternal Word (Jn 1:1-2, 18), Cayce's Jesus evolves upward through thirty earthly advents. Cayce's Jesus omits or misinterprets the many biblical references to a final judgment immediately after death (Mt 25:31-46; Heb 9:27). More will be said on this in the next chapter.

Cayce was thought to have filled in the gaps of the biblical record by consulting the Akashic Records with his subconscious mind.[74] Hugh Lynn Cayce believed that such records "may be the source of a much truer and more complete understanding of the life of Jesus than the Bible alone."[75] But how should we assess portraits of Jesus withdrawn from the Akashic Records or vouchsafed from personal channeled entities?

Channeling and Trustworthiness

It is interesting to note that while both Levi Downing and Edgar Cayce supposedly consulted the same cosmic memory bank, they withdrew contradictory facts about Jesus. Levi sees him in Greece. Cayce says not. Of course, this in itself doesn't necessarily discredit the Akashic source, but it makes one wonder how to choose between competing claims, especially if one is unable to access the cosmic Source oneself.

The deeper question involves the reliability of these channeled messages, whether from Ramtha, Jesus, the Akashic Records, the Collective Unconscious, the Universal Mind, or whomever.

A clue to evaluating this is given by a follower of Rudolf Steiner, the German occultist, who also tapped into the Akashic Records for an unorthodox view of Jesus. In describing Steiner's rather complex views of Jesus, Stewart Easton explains the ultimate basis of Steiner's school of thought (called Anthroposophy):

> We must emphasize once again that anthroposophy must rest its case on the truth of Steiner's revelations from the Akasha Chronicle and that his teachings represent in no sense an interpretation of the Bible.[76]

Easton is more honest about Steiner's revisionism than many who consult channeled material. Acceptance of Steiner's neo-Gnostic view (that is, Jesus is separate from the Christ, the Christ came upon Jesus at his baptism, Christ is the higher self of all people and that reincarnation is a reality)[77] must rest on the reliability of the supposed supernatural source, not on historical warrant.

But in staking this claim all contrary historical evidence must be denied with a wave of the Akashic wand. We found *The Aquarian Gospel* wanting in historical aptitude at several embarrassing points, which should lead us to question its general veracity. And the Cayce readings prophesied many events which failed to materialize, such as a shifting of the earth's axis in 1936 and the rise of Atlantis in 1968 or 1969.[78] (The very existence of Atlantis as a lost continent is highly suspect historically as well.)[79]

This puts channeled materials in a precarious position logically. If claims are made regarding recorded history, the channeled assertions can be verified or falsified. But if the claims are independent of historical authorization or disqualification, we are left with brute trust that the rarified realms are dispensing truth. For instance, *A Course in Miracles* redefines the person and work of Jesus *in toto* without giving any historical detail about Jesus of Nazareth. Why should we believe this claim, supposedly from Jesus himself, over the abundant historical evidence for the reliability of the New Testament?

If one has jettisoned any normal historical testing of channeled pronouncements, there is the further difficulty of accurately identifying the channeled source and testing its veracity. Emanuel Swedenborg, the famous seer of the eighteenth century, was well acquainted with the spirit world, having experienced detailed visions recorded later in book form. Nevertheless, he cautioned those courting the spirits:

> When Spirits begin to speak with a man, he ought to beware that he believes nothing whatever from them; for they say almost anything. Things are fabricated by them, and they lie . . . they would tell so many lies and indeed with solemn affirmation that a man would be astonished . . . if a man listens and believes they press on, and deceive, and seduce.[80]

The same sentiment was expressed in less solemn tones in a book satirizing much of the New Age movement (and written by a New Ager). An ad for TCT Ultima II, "a cosmic aptitude test" for evaluating channeled entities, reads:

> Just because they're dead doesn't mean they're smart. Channeling, like anything else, requires that the consumer be discriminating and careful. THERE ARE IDIOT ENTITIES, spooks from the other side who are tired of talking to each other. They're desperate to gab, and will do so whether or not their information is valuable or even true.[81]

The TCT Ultima II can be administered to determine "whether the entity you consult is a brilliant mind from afar or just another astral couch potato."[82]

This humorous lampoon from within the New Age nonetheless underscores a serious problem: how can the accuracy of the channeled messages be gauged?

Christianity, the Supernatural and History

Some have called the Bible a channeled document, but it is significant to realize that it, unlike channeled documents, claims to be both supernaturally inspired by a personal God and rooted in space-time factuality. As mentioned in chapter six, the apostle Paul was initially converted through a supernatural vision of the risen Christ. Yet Paul also speaks of historical details of Jesus' life that completely agree with those given in the Gospels, and he cites Christian hymns and creeds which predate his own letters. And although historic Christianity views Paul's writings and the rest of the Bible as inspired by God, this does not make the authors wholly passive or mean that they received their material through divine dictation. Rather, the Sovereign Spirit so directed their lives as to guide them into the truth, truth that was rooted in history.[83] The God-inspired visions recorded in Scripture always relate in some way to historical events and do not contradict previously revealed truth, even if the manner in which God relates to his people develops over time from the Old Testament to the New Testament. There is a continuity in the revelations, as seen in a revelation to the apostle John.

In the book of Revelation John says he was "in the Spirit" when he heard a voice say, "Write on a scroll what you see and send it to the seven churches" (Rev 1:10-11). John then beheld the following vision of the exalted Jesus Christ arrayed in heavenly glory as the great High Priest:

> I turned around to see the voice that was speaking to me. And when
> I turned I saw seven golden lampstands, and among the lampstands
> was someone "like a son of man," dressed in a robe reaching down
> to his feet and with a golden sash around his chest. His head and
> hair were white like wool, as white as snow, and his eyes were like
> blazing fire. His feet were like bronze glowing in a furnace, and his

voice was like the sound of rushing waters. In his right hand he held seven stars, and out of his mouth came a sharp double-edged sword. His face was like the sun shining in all its brilliance. (Rev 1:12-16)

John relates that the vision overwhelmed him such that he fell at his feet as a dead man. Yet the figure placed his right hand on John and responded: "Do not be afraid. I am the First and the Last. I am the Living One; I was dead, and behold I am alive for ever and ever! And I hold the keys of death and Hades" (Rev 1:17-18).

The exalted Christ then goes on to give specific messages to seven different churches. This is clearly a vision that John received when he was "in the Spirit," yet there is no indication that John lost conscious control of any of his senses. He was overwhelmed by the majesty of Christ and freely worshiped him. What Christ says perfectly accords with what John already knew from Jesus' earthly ministry. Jesus is supreme, the First and the Last (cf. Jn 1:1-3); he was crucified (Jn 19:30), but he was resurrected (Jn 20), and is now ascended (Jn 14:12); he holds the keys to the future (Jn 14:1-4). We find a continuity between the earthly and heavenly Jesus. New information will be disclosed in the rest of the book of Revelation, but none that contradicts the teachings of Jesus or his apostles.

In another context the apostle John warns his hearers concerning the spiritual world and gives a test for weeding out, not "astral couch potatoes" or "idiot entities," but antichrists:

Dear friends, do not believe every spirit, but test the spirits to see whether they are from God, because many false prophets have gone out into the world. This is how you can recognize the Spirit of God: Every spirit that acknowledges that Jesus Christ has come in the flesh is from God, but every spirit that does not acknowledge Jesus is not from God. This is the spirit of the antichrist, which you have heard is coming and even now is already in the world. (1 Jn 4:1-3)

John targets any spiritual manifestation that denies the Incarnation. Earlier in his letter he says:

> Who is the liar? It is the man who denies that Jesus is the Christ. Such a man is the antichrist—he denies the Father and the Son. No one who denies the Son has the Father; whoever acknowledges the Son has the Father also. (1 Jn 2:22-23)

John teaches that lying spirits populate the supernatural world and that discernment is demanded. The touchstone for discernment is the doctrine of the Incarnation. Jesus is, and forever remains, *the* Christ; one cannot be rightly related to God without confessing this fundamental fact. In his Gospel John records Jesus as saying, "I am the way and the truth and the life. No one comes to the Father except through me" (Jn 14:6). For John no one can lay hold of God without recognizing Jesus as the unique and final revelation from God. Other voices speak other than the truth.

Jesus himself repeatedly warned that false teachers, false prophets and false Christs would lead many astray (Mt 7:15-23; 24:23-25). He said to judge them by their fruits. Any spiritual communication that denies the essential message of the gospel, according to the biblical Jesus, bears bad fruit. It is both false and dangerous.

As we saw in chapter two, Jesus also clearly believed in the reality of the devil and the demonic realm as a source of confusion, deception and spiritual derangement. He says more about the devil than does anyone else in the entire Bible. He called the devil a liar and the father of lies (Jn 8:44), and taught his disciples to pray, "deliver us from the evil one" (Mt 6:13). One cannot read the Gospels without feeling the conflict between Jesus and the devil. The demonic cannot be edited from the Gospels without doing historical, theological and literary violence. Michael Green notes that:

> We have to give full weight to the tremendous moral earnestness of his teaching and living in this whole area of the satanic. His teaching is bound up with it. His exorcisms are bound up with it. His death is bound up with it. At all the major points in his life and ministry the conflict with Satan is of cardinal importance.[84]

We see in the Gospels that demons can exert tremendous control over individuals, causing illnesses and insanity, as well as giving supernatural strength and causing other manifestations. We also find in the book of Acts that a slave girl had a spirit that was used profitably in fortune-telling for her masters. The apostle Paul recognized this and cast out the spirit "in the name of Jesus Christ" (Acts 16:16-18).

These verses and other biblical texts recognize that the devil and demons can impart certain information to those they influence. They can deceive and counterfeit the truth. Yet even a supernatural demonstration, such as a prediction of the future, is no guarantee of the veracity of the message (Deut 13:1-4). Paul, who was converted through a heavenly vision, warned his readers to test the spirits, irrespective of their apparent grandeur. In defending the gospel message to the Galatian church he said:

> I am astonished that you are so quickly deserting the one who called you by the grace of Christ and are turning to a different gospel—which is really no gospel at all. Evidently some people are throwing you into confusion and are trying to pervert the gospel of Christ. But even if we or an angel from heaven should preach a gospel other than the one we preached to you, let him be eternally condemned! (Gal 1:6-8)

In contending for the gospel in another church that was heeding spiritual error, Paul says:

> But I am afraid that just as Eve was deceived by the serpent's cunning, your minds may somehow be led astray from your sincere and pure devotion to Christ. For if someone comes to you and preaches a Jesus other than the Jesus we preached, or if you receive a different spirit from the one you received, or a different gospel from the one you accepted, you put up with it easily enough. (2 Cor 11:3-4)

Paul later goes on to affirm that the bearers of this false Jesus and false gospel are false apostles, and this is no wonder, "for Satan himself masquerades as an angel of light" (2 Cor 11:14).

Not only do the channeled messages invariably and insistently deny the biblical Jesus, they repeat a message first offered in the Garden of Eden when the serpent seductively and successfully offered a temptation to the unfallen couple, saying that disobedience to God was not harmful because they would not die but would be as God themselves (Gen 3:1-5). The serpentine seduction succeeded, resulting in spiritual death. The entities and impersonal cosmic sources—Akashic or otherwise—which are influencing the New Age, are simply replaying the same old serpentine message from Genesis chapter three, which is the essence of sin and rebellion against God. The apostle John identifies the serpent as the devil himself (Rev 12:9).

What or who, then, is behind this "Jesus of the spirits"? The evidence points to an overarching spiritual liar armed with ingenuity and craftiness, commanding a number of subordinates and able to recycle one basic message in an appealing number of versions—but unable to speak the saving truth. John Ankerberg and John Weldon ask, "Isn't it interesting that [Satan's] spirits have not deviated from their master's first lies? If channeled beings are not demons, the consistency and persistence of these themes throughout the history of spiritistic revelations is nothing short of amazing."[85]

Every channeled word may not be breathed by Satan or other seductive spirits, but as with the fortune-telling slave girl in Acts, we should note that spirits can directly intervene with their messages. But sometimes other, less supernatural, explanations can account for the phenomenon of channeling.

Conscious fraud should not be ruled out in many cases, especially when histrionics and recycled New Age verbiage seem to exhaust the "mystery" of the channeling event. One ex-follower of Ramtha reported in *Newsweek* that J. Z. Knight could impersonate Ramtha without going into her characteristic, traumatically induced trance. She said: "We thought she did a better job of doing Ramtha than Ramtha. In fact, we couldn't tell the difference."[86] One linguist also subjected the accents of several channeled entities (who claimed previous embodiment on earth) to linguistic analysis and found them to be pseudo-accents, better understood as the channeler's invention than an entity's intervention.[87]

Other manifestations of channeling may be explained by some kind of dissociative mental disorder resulting in a secondary personality.[88] Some instances of channeling may be explained in terms of conscious or unconscious self-hypnotism. In these kinds of cases, it is more likely that the channelers are expressing a non-supernatural message spun out of their own subjective disorders rather than delivering a direct demonic message.[89]

One option not open to those who believe the biblical Jesus is that the channeled interpretations of Jesus are trustworthy. The channeled material may agree with the biblical record on generalities or inessentials, but on essentials such as the unique and unrepeatable Incarnation, the sacrificial death of Jesus, his bodily resurrection and his cosmic rule, they take the predictable esoteric detours. A clear case is a statement channeled from "the Christ" who says of his embodiment as Jesus: "It was not my intention to be deified and to be called a savior of mankind. My role was that of way-shower."[90] In light of this kind of misrepresentation, Brooks Alexander's comments are not too harsh:

> The practice of spiritism is terminal because it represents the ulti-
> mate confusion of values. It trades humanity's privilege of intimacy
> with God for sheer fascination with a liar who secretly hates all that
> is human and all that humans hold dear.[91]

Yet some will still protest that material derived from channeled and other New Age sources "works" where traditional Christianity does not. We have suggested that the "good news" of the channeled sources may not be as good as it initially sounds because of the effort involved in attaining the ever-elusive Christ Consciousness. But more needs to be said about this. So we will next consider the fundamental message of the biblical Jesus in relation to the Cosmic Christ of the New Age. Can the orthodox Jesus meet the human need for spiritual reality so sought after in the New Age?

Notes

[1]*A Course in Miracles: Text* (Farmingdale, N.Y.: Foundation for Inner Peace, 1981), "Introduction," n. p.

[2]Dean C. Halverson, "A Course in Miracles: Seeing Yourself As Sinless," *Spiritual Counterfeits Journal* 7 (1987):18. I am indebted to this article for much of my analysis.

[3]*A Course in Miracles: Manual* (Farmingdale, N.Y.: Foundation for Inner Peace, 1981), p. 56.

[4]*Course: Text,* p. 5.

[5]*Course: Manual,* p. 84; emphasis in text.

[6]*Course: Manual,* p. 83.

[7]Ibid.

[8]Ibid.

[9]Ibid.

[10]Jon Klimo, *Channeling* (Los Angeles, Calif.: J. P. Tarcher, 1987), p. 345.

[11]For an elaboration of this see Klimo, pp. 185-201.

[12]For a description of the various teachings see Klimo, pp. 146-67.

[13]Ramtha (with Douglas James Mahr), *Voyage to the New World* (New York, N.Y.: Ballantine Books, 1987), pp. 180-81; emphasis in text.

[14]For a brief version of this story, see Robert Perry, *An Introduction to a Course in Miracles* (USA: Miracle Distribution Center, 1989), pp. 8-16.

[15]Halverson, p. 18.

[16]*Course: Text,* p. 32.

[17]Ibid.

[18]Ibid., p. 33.

[19]Ibid.

[20]*Course: Manual,* p. 81.

[21]*Course: Text,* p. 46.

[22]Ibid., p. 187.

[23]Ibid., p. 13.

[24]*A Course in Miracles: Workbook* (Farmingdale, N.Y.: Foundation for Inner Peace, 1981), p. 119.

[25]Rama Jyoti Vernon, "Exploring a Course in Miracles," *Yoga Journal,* January/February 1983, p. 40.

[26]Perry, pp. 4-5.

[27]Quoted in Vernon, p. 40.

[28]Ibid.

[29]Ibid.

[30]Referred to in Halverson, p. 23.

[31]See "A Matter of Course: Conversation with Kenneth Wapnick," *Spiritual Counterfeits Journal* 7 (1987):8-17.

[32]*Course: Text,* emphasis mine, p. 53.

[33]*Course: Workbook,* emphasis mine, p. 70.

[34]Halverson, p. 24; emphasis mine.

[35]Ibid., p. 26.

[36]See Halverson, p. 27.

[37]Levi H. Downing, *The Aquarian Gospel of Jesus the Christ* (Marina Del Ray, Calif.: DeVorss & Co., Publishers, 1981), p. 110 (68:13).

[38]It should be remembered that chapters and verses were only incorporated into the biblical books in the medieval period. Manuscripts before this time do not have them.

[39]Downing, p. 14.

[40]Ibid.
[41]Ibid., pp. 16-17.
[42]Ibid., "Who Was Levi?" n. p.
[43]Klimo, p. 344.
[44]Downing, p. 13.
[45]Per Beskow, *Strange Tales about Jesus* (Philadelphia: Fortress Press, 1985), p. 79.
[46]Downing, p. 76 (37:11-15).
[47]Ibid., pp. 96-97 (55:4-7).
[48]Ibid., p. 265 (178:45, 46); emphasis mine.
[49]Ibid., p. 64 (28:4).
[50]Ibid., p. 255 (172:21).
[51]Ibid., p. 260 (176:19).
[52]Ibid., p. 33 (1:1).
[53]Ibid., p. 74 (36:3).
[54]Edgar J. Goodspeed, *Modern Apocrypha* (Boston: The Beacon Press, 1956), p. 18.
[55]Downing, pp. 76-77 (37:1ff.).
[56]Beskow, p. 76.
[57]Downing, p. 261 (176:22).
[58]Beskow, p. 80.
[59]Goodspeed, p. 17.
[60]For a detailed and well-documented treatment of Cayce's life history see Gary North, *Unholy Spirits* (Ft. Worth, Tex.: Dominion Press, 1986), pp. 193-206.
[61]Quoted in Thomas Sugrue, *There Is a River* (rev. ed.; New York, N.Y.: Holt & Co., 1948), p. 247; cited in North, p. 204.
[62]Jeffrey Furst, ed. *Edgar Cayce's Story of Jesus* (New York, N.Y.: Berkley Books, 1976), pp. 39-40.
[63]Ibid., pp. 76-77.
[64]Ibid., p. 47.
[65]Ibid., p. 192.
[66]Ibid., pp. 192-93.
[67]Ibid., p. 193.
[68]Ibid., p. 194.
[69]Ibid., p. 196.
[70]Ibid., p. 76.
[71]Ibid., p. 33.
[72]Ibid., p. 73.
[73]Ibid., p. 53.
[74]Ibid., p. 51.
[75]Hugh Lynn Cayce, *Edgar Cayce on Jesus and His Church* (New York, N.Y.: Paperback Library, 1970), p. 12.
[76]Stewart C. Easton, *Man and World in Light of Anthroposophy* (USA: Anthroposophic Press, Inc., 1975), p. 199.
[77]See Easton's chapter, "Anthroposophy and Christianity," pp. 173-216, for a summary of Steiner's views on Jesus, the Christ and Christianity.
[78]For documentation of Cayce's false prophesies see Andrew Neher, *The Psychology of Transcendence* (Englewood Cliffs, N.J.: Prentice-Hall, 1980) pp. 159-61. Neher concludes, "In view of Cayce's extremely poor batting average for his prophecies that can

be followed up, there seems little reason to regard him as a great prophet," p. 161.

[79]See Karla Poewe-Hexham and Irving Hexham, "The 'Evidence' for Atlantis: Addressing New Age Apologetics," *Christian Research Journal,* Summer 1989, pp. 16-19.

[80]Samuel M. Warren, *A Compendium of the Theological Writings of Emanuel Swedenborg* (New York: Swedenborg Foundation, 1977), p. 618; quoted in John Ankerberg and John Weldon, *The Facts on Spirit Guides* (Eugene, Ore.: Harvest House, 1988), p. 12.

[81]Chris Kolham, illustrated by Robert Engman, *In Search of the New Age* (Rochester, Vt.: Destiny Books, 1988), p. 49.

[82]Ibid.

[83]For a rich and learned discussion of the meaning of biblical inspiration see Carl F. H. Henry, *God, Revelation, and Authority* (Waco, Tex.: Word Books, 1980) 3:129-493.

[84]Michael Green, *I Believe in Satan's Downfall* (Grand Rapids, Mich.: Eerdmans, 1981), p. 28.

[85]Ankerberg and Weldon, pp. 34-35.

[86]George Hackett with Pamela Abramson, "Ramtha, a Voice from Beyond," *Newsweek,* December 15, 1986, p. 42. This confession, if true, does not necessarily mean that every Ramtha session was a fraud, only that Knight was capable of producing the effect by herself. Another ex-follower I saw on a television program in 1987 said he believed Knight was legitimately in touch with Ramtha at first but later lost contact with him and relied on impersonation.

[87]Sarah Grey Thomason, " 'Entities' in the Linguistic Minefield," *Skeptical Inquirer,* Summer 1989, pp. 391-96. See also Marjory Roberts, "A Linguistic 'Nay' to Channeling," *Psychology Today,* October 1989, pp. 64-65.

[88]See Brooks Alexander, *Spirit Channeling* (Downers Grove, Ill.: InterVarsity Press, 1988), pp. 16-19. For a more detailed treatment see Graham Reed, "The Psychology of Channeling," *Skeptical Inquirer,* Summer 1989, pp. 385-90.

[89]For explanations of this sort see Elliot Miller, *A Crash Course on the New Age* (Grand Rapids, Mich.: Baker, 1989), pp. 167-69. His treatment of channeling is quite thorough and covers important aspects not covered in this chapter; see pp. 141-82.

[90]The Christ, *New Teachings for an Awakened Humanity* (Santa Clara, Calif.: Spiritual Education Endeavors Publishing Company, 1986), p. 50. For a redefinition of Jesus' life on earth, see the entire chapter, pp. 45-60.

[91]Alexander, p. 29.

Chapter 10
Jesus and the Cosmic Christ

*M*any *who have caught the New Age vision have reject*-ed orthodox Christianity yet remain attracted to if not entranced by Jesus. The New Age is hospitable to Jesus as a Gnostic Revealer, a well-traveled, mystical magus, an Essene initiate or a Christ-conscious master. Yet "old age" orthodox views of Jesus are often rejected as "dogmatic," "narrow" or "anthropomorphic." Christ Consciousness cannot be chained to one solitary incarnation. Jesus, along with many others, deserves the highest praise as a god-realized man; he does not deserve worship as the unique and final incarnation of the Creator.

But has the New Age rejected Jesus as the one and only Christ for the right reasons? Can the biblical understanding of the Christ answer the spiritual longings of those seeking Universal Reality? Can Jesus be both the unrepeatable incarnation of God on earth and the Cosmic Christ?

The New Age yearns for no less than a Cosmic Christ. As noted New Age spokesman David Spangler declared, "Naturally, any old Christ will not do, not if we need to show that we have something better than the mainstream Christian traditions. It must be a Cosmic Christ, a universal Christ, a New Age Christ."[1] He goes on to say that these concepts take us beyond "purely anthropomorphic associations and thought-forms about the Christ."[2]

For Spangler and the New Age in general, the Christ is a universal Presence working within all humanity to raise it to a higher level of evolutionary attainment. Christ is not as much a person as "a cosmic principle, a spiritual presence whose quality infuses and appears in various ways in all the religions and philosophies that uplift humanity and seek unity with spirit."[3] The Second Coming has already occurred in the "inner planes of Earth" through the Christ life impregnating and inspiring evolutionary advancement. This Second Coming "is not a person; it is a life which quickens a comparable Christ life within each of us."[4]

Matthew Fox, a controversial Roman Catholic priest, has heralded "the coming of the Cosmic Christ." While claiming to be within the orthodox orbit, Fox decries what he calls "Jesus-olatry" in which people "concentrate so much on Jesus that they miss the Cosmic Christ and the divinity within the creation."[5] Jesus, for Fox, is one of many manifestations of divine Wisdom.[6] In fact when Jesus identified himself as the "I am" of Exodus 3:14 (Jn 8:58), Fox claims he "shows us how to embrace our own divinity" because "the Cosmic Christ is the 'I am' of every creature."[7] He also says "we are Cosmic Christs."[8] Fox's Cosmic Christ leads to a Christic (deified) cosmos and a "deep ecumenism" wherein all religions may tap into the Cosmic Christ without reference to Jesus of Nazareth.[9] The theological chasm between this Cosmic Christ and the biblical Christ should become evident in the following discussion.[10]

What Spangler, Fox and others strive for is a total explanation for reality and a comprehensive significance for existence. In Spangler's system of thought, Jesus plays a crucial role in tuning into the Christ

Consciousness and releasing evolutionary powers into the divine realm. Yet the Christ Consciousness is an *impersonal* principle, operative not only in Jesus but in all people and religions to varying degrees. Fox's vision is similar, though couched in more orthodox terms. But is the New Age Christ "something better" than the Christ of mainstream Christianity?

Uniting the Personal and the Cosmic
The "cosmic" properly refers to the entire cosmos. If something is cosmic it has a universal or comprehensive meaning, significance and value. The cosmic is the opposite of the pedestrian, the mundane, or the constricted. To be cosmic is to relate to all things in robust fashion.

Many in the New Age have taken the biblical teaching of the Incarnation to be a constricting view of God: Christ is limited to but one person, not unlimited as the inner reality of all people. But the New Age Christ is an impersonal cosmic process or principle. Historic Christianity unites both the cosmic and the personal in Jesus Christ.

In an earlier chapter we mentioned the prologue to John's Gospel, which reads:

In the beginning was the Word, and the Word was with God, and the Word was God. He was with God in the beginning. Through him all things were made; without him nothing was made that has been made. In him was life, and that life was the light of men. (Jn 1:1-4).

We have highlighted repeatedly that this "Word became flesh" (Jn 1:14), which is the personal Incarnation of God in Jesus. But our attention now turns more to the meaning of "Word" and its cosmic significance.

As we briefly alluded to earlier, "Word" is from the Greek word *Logos,* from which we derive our word "logic" and all words ending in -ology: psychology, theology, sociology and so on. It was used in a variety of ways in Greek philosophy, but generally referred to an immanent and *impersonal* ordering principle in the cosmos that provided coherence, making it a uni-verse instead of a multi-verse. Theologian Carl Henry notes that, for the Greeks, "the concept of the logos comprehends at once the interrelationship of thought, word, matter, nature, being and law."[11] R. C. Sproul notes that "the Apostle John dropped a theological bombshell on the philosophical playground of his day by looking at Jesus and talking about Him not as an impersonal concept, but as the incarnation of the eternal Logos."[12] John harnesses this word so rich in philosophical meaning for a unique purpose. Jaroslav Pelikan explains:

> "Logos of God" when applied to Jesus Christ meant far more than "Word of God," more even than divine revelation; there were many other Greek vocables that would have sufficed to express that much and no more, and several of them were being used in the New Testament and in other early Christian literature. Employing the specific name Logos implied in addition to this that what had come in Jesus Christ was also the *Reason and Mind of the cosmos.*[13]

John borrows a term, but does not parrot its previous meaning. God is the Logos. God is uncreated logic in his very being and provides the order, regularity, law and intelligibility to the cosmos—not as some impersonal World Soul, but as its personal Creator: "Through *him* all things were *made;* without *him* nothing was *made* that has been *made"* (Jn 1:3; emphasis mine). The Maker is not one with the made; yet the Maker, the Logos, insures that the cosmos not sink into chaos. To put it another way, the Logos is the cosmic or universal support system for all the qualities and quantities of created being. More vividly, "In him was life, and that life was the light of men" (1:4). John further affirms, "The true light that gives light to every man was coming into the world" (Jn 1:9).

Truly the Logos has cosmic significance. The Logos is not provincial, pedestrian or constricted. Carl Henry packs quite a philosophical wallop when he says that "the Logos of the Bible is personal and self-revealed, transcendent to man and the world, eternal and essentially divine, intrinsically intelligible, and incarnate in Jesus Christ."[14] In other words the Logos is "the foundation of all meaning, and the transcendent personal source and support of the rational, moral, and purposive order of created reality."[15] The Logos is indispensably involved with all the cosmos, but it is not identified as the cosmos or part of the cosmos, Matthew Fox and others to the contrary.[16] Why do mathematical constructs relate to external reality so successfully? How can we calculate the trajectory of a spaceship to the moon and back without ever having been there before? Because of the Logos. Why do chemical reactions obtain uniformly under similar conditions? Because of the Logos. How can humans from various races speaking various languages communicate with each other rationally at the United Nations? Because of the Logos. Why do all societies affirm, in one form or another, the golden rule in morality?[17] Because of the Logos. Why have all societies throughout history had some understanding of a spiritual realm surpassing the physical world? Because of the Logos.

Although Paul does not use the term *Logos,* his thinking also centers on this concept in the book of Colossians where he presents the Cosmic Christ.

He is the image of the invisible God, the firstborn over all creation. For by him all things were created: things in heaven and on earth, visible and invisible, whether thrones or powers or rulers or authorities; all things were created by him and for him. . . . And he is the head of the body, the church; he is the beginning and the firstborn from among the dead, so that in everything he might have the supremacy. For God was pleased to have all his fullness dwell in him. (Col 1:15-19)

By the term "firstborn," Paul refers to Christ's exalted cosmic status, as the firstborn Jewish male had an exalted social status; that is, Paul is referring to Christ's metaphysical priority, not to his being the first thing created. No, he himself created all things for himself. Not only that, he is "the firstborn from among the dead," through his resurrection, the final proof of his supremacy.

The writer of Hebrews speaks of the same Cosmic Christ:

In the past God spoke to our forefathers through the prophets at many times and in various ways, but in these last days he has spoken to us by his Son, whom he appointed heir of all things, and through whom he made the universe. The Son is the radiance of God's glory and the exact representation of his being, sustaining all things by his powerful word. (Heb 1:1-3)

The Son is equal to God: He is the heir of all things and the agent of creation who also sustains the entire cosmos without *being* the cosmos. He is the Cosmic Christ indeed.

All of these enthusiastic biblical writers undeniably and insistently unite the Cosmic Christ with the personal Jesus. They are not lauding an impersonal and abstract principle. They are exalting a Cosmic Person, who, though eternal, was born as a human, lived a perfect life, died for others, was raised from the dead and now is enthroned as "King of kings and Lord of lords." Jesus himself announced his cosmic rule shortly before his Ascension. Matthew tells us that Jesus said, "All authority in heaven and on earth has been given to me" (Mt 28:18). We have seen in chapters two and three that Jesus repeatedly affirmed his deity and the full prerogatives of such. He would judge all the world at the end of time. He existed eternally before his Incarnation. He gives eternal life to all who come to him. Death could not defeat him, but he would defeat death through his resurrection. These are cosmic affirmations uttered from the human lips of Jesus. The universal is declared and recognized in the singular person of Jesus.

In answering the question of why God "did not manifest himself by means of other and nobler part[s] of creation, and use some nobler instrument, such as sun or moon or stars or fire or air, instead of mere man,"[18] Athanasius replied that God was not interested in putting on a display. He had already shown something of himself in his creation (see Rom 1—2).

> But for Him Who came to heal and to teach the way was not merely to dwell there, but to put Himself at the disposal of those who needed Him, and to be manifested according as they could bear it, not vitiating the value of the Divine appearing by exceeding their capacity to receive it.[19]

If God originally created humans "in his image and likeness," human personality is a fitting mode for the supreme divine manifestation. Because we had become blinded and could not "recognize Him as ordering and ruling creation as a whole,"[20] God made himself even more tangible, available, and recognizable in the Incarnation. Athanasius expands on this:

He takes to Himself for [his] instrument a part of the whole, namely a human body, and enters into that. Thus he ensured that men should recognize Him in the part who could not do so in the whole, and that those who could not lift their eyes to His unseen power might recognize and behold Him in the likeness of themselves. For, being men, they could naturally learn to know His Father more quickly and directly by means of a body that corresponded to their own and by the Divine works done through it.[21]

Christian philosopher C. C. J. Webb echoes this concern by averring that:

A religion which involves as part of its essence a sacred history is . . . at a higher level than one which, while setting forth certain universal principles, moral or metaphysical, is ready to symbolize them by anything that comes to hand, as it were, and is comparatively indifferent to the particular symbol chosen. Thus a religion which, having developed a theology, regards the narratives which are associated with it as mere illustrative stories, ranks below one which regards them as the actual forms which the universal principles have taken and could not but have taken in [the] world.[22]

In John's words, "The Word became flesh and made his dwelling among us. We have seen his glory, the glory of the One and Only, who came from the Father, full of grace and truth" (Jn 1:14). The Cosmic Christ appeared in the person of Jesus just when the cosmos was ripe for the revelation. Paul says that "when the time had fully come, God sent his Son" (Gal 4:4). Not only did Jesus, the Christ, fulfill a manifold of Jewish prophecies concerning his life, death and resurrection,[23] he also appeared when the message of the gospel could have free reign in the ancient world because of three factors.

First, the Roman Empire provided a highly efficient and comprehensive system of roads, facilitating ease of travel throughout all provinces controlled by Rome.[24] Good news could spread easily.

Second, because of the *Pax Romana,* or Peace of Rome, travelers could move from one province to another with little concern for anything such as a passport or visa. The general ambiance of peace provided a fit medium for the dissemination of new ideas across borders.[25]

Third, prior to the Roman conquest, Alexander the Great had brought Greek to his empire. By the time of the Roman Empire, Koine Greek had become the world language. This was a common form of Greek spoken by the masses and the language in which the New Testament was written. A. T. Robertson notes that inscriptions in Koine have been found throughout Asia, Egypt, Greece, Italy, Sicily and on various islands. The Roman senate and imperial governor had their decrees translated into this language to be distributed throughout the empire. Robertson continues:

> It is significant that the Greek speech becomes one instead of many dialects at the very time that the Roman rule sweeps over the world.
> . . . Paul wrote to the church at Rome in Greek, and Marcus Aurelius, the Roman Emperor, wrote his *Meditations* . . . in Greek. It was the language not only of letters, but of commerce and everyday life. . . . It was really an epoch in the world's history when the babel of tongues was used in the wonderful language of Greece.[26]

The world was ready for the Revelation.

Yet how can Christianity affirm both the Cosmic Christ and the personal Jesus? Is not the insistence on Christ being incarnate once-for-all in the person of Jesus more limiting than the expansive claims of the New Age that the impersonal Christ Consciousness is equally accessible to everyone?

Some reflection of our discussion of Jesus in chapters two and three should begin to explain this. We found that Jesus made many exclusive claims about himself. He gave no hint of there being other redeemers or that humans could somehow redeem themselves through a process of self-discovery. Rather, he claimed to be sent "to seek and to save what was lost" (Lk 19:10) and "to give his life as a ransom for

many" (Mk 10:45). Yet his exclusiveness is not a provincial or enfee-
bling feature of Jesus; he had the credentials to single himself out from
all others. He not only made bold claims, but he backed up those
claims in everything he did, whether it be healing the sick, working
miracles, loving the downtrodden, sacrificing himself on a bloody
cross or rising from the dead as Lord.

Despite the central focus on this particular Jesus as *the* Christ, as
the sole Savior and Lord, Jesus himself proclaimed a universal message. It was not universal in the vague, indiscriminate sense that all
religious aspirations lead equally to God, but universal in that the
Incarnation is meant for all people and the message of the gospel must
penetrate the entire planet. Jesus was born of a Jewish woman in
Palestine and began his outreach to these chosen people, but he also
reached out to others, such as the Roman centurion who amazed Jesus
with the strength of his faith (Lk 7:1-10). When asked if only a few
people would be saved, Jesus replied, "Make every effort to enter
through the narrow door, because many, I tell you, will try to enter
and will not be able to" (Lk 13:24). He then said that many of his own
people will be cast out because they rejected their Messiah, but people
"will come from east and west and north and south, and will take their
places at the feast in the kingdom of God" (Lk 13:29).

The universality of Jesus' message is further seen before his ascension when he said to his disciples, "But you will receive power when
the Holy Spirit comes on you; and you will be my witnesses in Jerusalem, and in all Judea and Samaria, *and to the ends of the earth* (Acts
1:8, emphasis mine; cf. Lk 24:46-48). Matthew, a witness to Jesus'
farewell speech, would later record these words of Jesus that beckon
all to come to him:

Come to me, *all* you who are weary and burdened, and I will give
you rest. Take my yoke upon you and learn from me, for I am
gentle and humble in heart, and you will find rest for your souls.
For my yoke is easy and my burden is light. (Mt 11:28-30, emphasis
mine).

Jesus, the personal Incarnation of God, was not a vessel too small for

the Cosmic Christ. As Paul said, "For God was pleased to have *all* his
fullness dwell in him" (Col 1:19, emphasis mine). The New Age seeks
in a universal, impersonal force that which is located in the limitless
loving person of Jesus Christ, in whom "all things hold together" (Col
1:17).

Myth Becomes Fact

Throughout the history of the world human beings have enshrined
their weariness and burdens in their art, symbols, religions and myths.
The human condition is subject to pain from which we seek deliverance. We said previously that humanity's spiritual awareness, at whatever level, is due to the quickening power of God, the Logos. He
reveals something of himself even in the midst of a fallen world, a
world where humans made in the divine image nevertheless choose to
disobey their Creator.

John says that the Logos "enlightens every man." Read in the context of the entire Gospel, John cannot mean that every person knows
the Logos as the Incarnation and as Savior and Lord. Many, in fact,
remain in darkness. As Jesus said, speaking of himself, "Whoever
believes in him is not condemned, but whoever does not believe stands
condemned already because he has not believed in the name of God's
one and only Son" (Jn 3:18).

What John means is that the Logos makes knowledge of God possible for all people. We can further observe that something of God is
revealed even in religious systems, symbols and myths that do not
overtly recognize Jesus as the way, the truth and the life. William
James noted that all religions share two structural similarities: They
recognize that the human situation is not the way it ought to be and
that this must in some sense be rectified.[27] From a biblical viewpoint,
this can be explained in terms of human sinfulness. Humans know that
they have fallen short of their standards and that their conscience has
been defiled. Guilt is a universal problem. Something is wrong. Something must be done about it.

Any fair-minded analysis of world religions and mythologies will reveal that the way in which the human problem is described and the solution that is prescribed differs significantly.[28] Yet there are similarities in theme and basic concern. From the vantage point of the Logos doctrine, this is no surprise. God has so built us that even in our rebellion against him, our need for redemption is revealed. The Logos makes it so. John Warwick Montgomery's rich analysis is worth quoting in full:

> Suppose that the fallen race had kept a primordial realization of its separation from God through sinful self-centeredness and of its specific need for redemption through the divine-human conquest of the evil powers arrayed against it. Suppose within each human heart this realization were etched beyond effacement. The sinner would, of course, repress this knowledge, for his sin would be too painful to bear and his egotism would not want to face redemption apart from works-righteousness. Though "the invisible things of God are clearly seen," so that men are "without excuse," they become "vain in their imagination" and their "foolish hearts are darkened" (Rom 1:20-21). The darkening of the heart would quite naturally take the form of a repression of the natural knowledge of God's redemptive plan to the subconscious level, where it could be ignored consciously; but its eradication from the psyche could never occur. Under these circumstances, redemptive knowledge would surface not in a direct fashion but by way of symbolic patterns—visible not only to the sensitive psychoanalyst but also to the folklorist whose material "bubbles up" collectively from the subconscious of the race.[29]

In viewing Christ as the Logos we can explain the universal patterns of human thought throughout the ages: the quest for a lost paradise, the reality of dark forces both within and without, the need for forgiveness and restoration, and the desire for a redeemer to make that restoration a reality. Even though human sin may cloud the Meaning behind the universe, its witness is inextinguishable.

As C. S. Lewis noted, the Cosmic Christ fulfills these human desires in concrete historical and personal fashion. The mythic themes of human history find their answer in Jesus. Lewis says:

> The heart of Christianity is a myth which is also a fact. The old myth of the Dying God, *without ceasing to be myth*, comes down from the heaven of legend and imagination to the earth of history. It happens—at a particular date, in a particular place, followed by definable historical consequences. We pass from a Balder or an Osiris, dying nobody knows when or where, to an historical Person crucified (it is all in order) *under Pontius Pilate*. By becoming fact it does not cease to be myth: that is the miracle.[30]

It should be clear that by "myth" Lewis means the deep, universal and provocative themes of religion, literature and symbolism that disclose the depths of the psyche. They evidence the incorrigibly human concern with spiritual matters. Yet myth became fact. The blurry longing became particular in a way more shockingly real and alive than anyone could have imagined.[31] Christ lived among us, died and rose again from the dead.[32] The riddle of redemption is solved, the scattered pieces of the jigsaw puzzle are brought together in Christ, the Logos.

Resurrection and the Cosmic Christ

We earlier argued that in light of the historical reliability of the New Testament documents, we can be sure that Jesus did in fact die on the cross, contrary to some New Age teaching. We also said that if the biblical accounts of the resurrection and ascension are accurate, all discussion of Jesus retiring to India are scuttled. We now turn to the greatest reason to believe that Jesus is the Cosmic Christ: his singular defeat of death itself through resurrection.

First, the New Testament considers the resurrection as a matter of paramount significance to everything else it says. It is no incidental item or cosmic hiccup. Bernard Ramm notes that:

> The resurrection with the incarnation and atonement is planted at the very heart of the gospel and plan of redemption. So crucial is the resurrection to the writers of the New Testament that Peter attributes all the blessings of redemption to it (1 Pet 1:3); Paul

avows that without it the work of Christ is undone (1 Cor 15:7), and that the confession of the resurrection is integral to salvation (Rom 10:9-10).[33]

It should be obvious to any attentive reader that the entire New Testament reverberates with the reality of Jesus' resurrection from the dead. The Gospels record Jesus teaching that he must be betrayed, killed and rise again. Then they all testify that his tomb was empty and that he appeared to his disciples as he said. The book of Acts records the preaching of the resurrected Christ as its central fact. The various New Testament letters and the book of Revelation would melt into nothingness without a resurrected Jesus. The resurrection is attested to by four separate Gospels, the history of the early church (Acts), by the Letters of Paul, Peter, John, James, Jude and the Letter to the Hebrews. There is a diversity of witnesses. And since the New Testament volumes show considerable fitness in terms of historical reliability (chapter six), this is a good prima facie reason to accept the resurrection as factually true.

Second, there is solid historical evidence for the empty tomb of Jesus. Luke, whom we have found to be a trustworthy historian, tells us that the early church began to preach the resurrection in Jerusalem about seven weeks after Jesus' death. The preaching was heard by those familiar with Jesus and his crucifixion. If Jesus' tomb had not been empty, the apostle's preaching could have been stopped dead in its tracks simply by producing Jesus' body. Both the Jewish religious leadership and the Roman political leadership would have had a vested interest in doing so. But they did not. The apostles feared nothing of the sort and boldly proclaimed a risen Jesus as the central theme of all the sermons recorded in Acts.[34] Furthermore, the Jewish concept of resurrection would not allow for any non-bodily, spiritual resurrection; a Jesus with rigor mortis was not a resurrected Jesus in any sense.[35]

If Jesus had in fact been killed and buried, it would be very likely that his tomb would be venerated as that of a saint, as was the custom in that day. In the Palestine of Jesus' day there were at least fifty such

venerated tombs. Luke tells us that women followed Joseph of Arimathea to the tomb of Jesus, probably to mark the spot for later
tribute. Yet the church commemorates an empty tomb, not an occupied one.[36]

It is also significant that the early Jewish polemic against the Christians presupposed an empty tomb. The New Testament (Mt 28:11-15)
itself records that the Jews spread the word that the disciples stole the
body. But the idea of a corpse heist was highly implausible because
of the guard set around the tomb, the difficulty in identifying the
disciples as the thieves if they somehow sneaked past the guards without getting caught and because we could only find it ludicrous that
these thieving disciples would then flatly preach a lie seven weeks later
in Jerusalem.[37]

Third, there is good historical evidence for the post-crucifixion appearances of Jesus. Probably the earliest written account of the resurrection comes from the quill of the apostle Paul in 1 Corinthians 15,
where he says:

> For what I received I passed on to you as of first importance: that
> Christ died for our sins according to the Scriptures, that he was
> buried, that he was raised on the third day according to the Scrip-
> tures, and that he appeared to Peter, and then to the Twelve. After
> that, he appeared to more than five hundred of the brothers at the
> same time, most of whom are still living, though some have fallen
> asleep. Then he appeared to James, then to all the apostles, and last
> of all he appeared to me also, as to one abnormally born. (vv. 3-8)

We noted earlier that verses 3 and following are thought to be an early
Hebrew-Christian creed that Paul is relating. Jewish New Testament
scholar Pinchas Lapide lists eight separate "linguistic items" that
"speak in favor of the fact that Paul in this oldest faith statement
about the resurrection does not pass on his own thoughts but indeed
delivers what he himself has 'received' from the first witnesses." These
include the section's un-Pauline style, its "Aramaic and Mishaic Hebrew way of narration," the use of the Aramaic "Cephas" instead of
Simon, and other key elements.[38]

These features of Paul's passage would date the original creed for the burial and resurrection of Jesus during the A.D. 30s, considerably before the writing of Paul's letter at approximately the A.D. mid-50s.[39] The affirmation of the death and resurrection of Christ was so firmly established just a few years after his death as to be formulated in a creed, a brief summary and confession of the community's essential beliefs. This points away from the notion of the resurrection as a legendary development of a later period, especially when considering that Paul speaks of those *now living* who had seen the resurrected Jesus. (See also the discussion of legend in chapter six.) The witnesses were alive and available. This is either one of the greatest bluffs in the history of religion or a confident assertion of verifiable fact.

Although it may not strike modern readers as anomalous, the fact that the Gospels report that women first witnessed the crucifixion and saw the risen Jesus firms up the historicity of these accounts. This is because women were not considered reliable witnesses in that culture[40] (which is likely why Paul did not insert them in his list in 1 Corinthians 15). Therefore, the accounts that list women as primary eyewitnesses to the resurrection have the ring of authenticity, not contrivance.[41] It is unlikely that if the disciples had fabricated the story, they would have given the women disciples the crucial roles of witnesses of the risen Jesus.

We should also remember that all the reports of the resurrected Jesus in the Gospels, while possibly later than Paul's list of eyewitnesses, are still too close to the events at hand to admit legendary accretions, as we discussed in chapter three.[42]

Thus far, we have dealt with *documentary evidence* for the resurrection, reasons based on various written sources claiming to present accurate information about the primary events themselves. Yet there is also strong *circumstantial evidence* for the historicity of the resurrection that appeals to certain events that are best explained by the resurrection.

First, if this resurrection did not actually occur, how can we account for the origin and rapid spread of Christianity across the face of the ancient world? How did the same disciples—who could not pray but one hour for their Lord before his crucifixion and who scattered after his capture—be the same evangelists who braved persecution and martyrdom for a resurrected Jesus. What intervened?

Christianity, while promoting an ethical message and an overall world view, was born out of the afterglow of the resurrection of Jesus. This was the fire of its motivation and the fiber of its courage. The uniqueness of the infant Christian message was rooted in the resurrection. Noting that the origin of Christianity cannot be explained in non-supernatural terms, C. F. D. Moule affirmed that "the birth and rapid rise of the Christian church *therefore remain an unsolved enigma for any historian who refuses to take seriously the only explanation offered by the Church itself.*"[43] Lapide has called the resurrection "the birth certificate of the church."[44]

We discover another line of evidence in the sacraments of the early church. The symbol and sacrament of baptism is based on the analogy that just as Jesus died and was raised to life, the believer dies to sinful ways and is raised to a new life in Christ (see Rom 6:3ff.). Baptism presupposes and is meaningless without resurrection. Another sacrament is that of the Lord's Supper as a symbol of Jesus' life given for the believer. Michael Green notes that this was no "memorial feast in honor of a dead founder"; believers "broke bread with *agalliasis,* exultation (Acts 2:46) because they believed the risen Lord was in their midst as they took the tokens of his death for them."[45] Both sacraments, he adds, "would have been a complete travesty had the earliest Christians not believed that Jesus rose from the dead."[46]

The early church also began meeting on Sunday, the first day of the week, very quickly after the death of Jesus (Acts 20:7). This practice went against the religious grain of Jewish observance that honored Saturday, the seventh day, as the Sabbath. The Gospels do not record Jesus advocating a new holy day, yet the church began to meet on Sunday in honor of their risen Lord. This deep change in spiritual observance is best explained by the resurrection itself.

Is it likely that despite these lines of evidence, the early church and the purported eyewitnesses of the risen Jesus sincerely believed they saw him, but in fact were sincerely deceived? The most common defense of this notion is that the resurrection appearances were hallucinations of some sort and not objectively real. The New Testament certainly presents all the appearances as objective, physical realities. It is impossible to defend the idea that such a diversity of persons, at different times and places, were all subject to the same hallucination. Hallucinations are not a group phenomena to begin with but are individual aberrations. They also are occasioned through intense wish-fulfillment, whereas the disciples gave Jesus up for dead and were quite shocked at the first reports of his resurrection (Lk 24:1-11; Jn 20:24-26).[47] The hallucination theory also leads to the unlikely conclusion that the very existence of Christianity is based on mental illness and that its earliest converts preached, quite literally, a message of madness.[48] Lapide tellingly comments:

> If the defeated and depressed group of disciples overnight could change into a victorious movement of faith, based only on autosuggestion or self-deception—without a fundamental faith experience—then this would be a much greater miracle than the resurrection itself.[49]

Although Lapide remains a non-Christian Jew,[50] he affirms the reality of the resurrection and says "the resurrection belongs to the category of the truly real and effective occurrences, for without a fact of history there is no act of true faith."[51]

When taken together these multiple lines of evidence, both documentary and circumstantial, lead us to a Christ-less tomb, a dead man found alive and a dynamic group of followers who turned the ancient world upside down. In light of this firm foundation any exotic speculations about Jesus' interment in India must be dismissed as mere romantic legend. Again, the burden of proof simply presses the life out of such claims.[52]

Resurrection Not Reincarnation

The fact of Jesus' resurrection also nails shut the possibility of reincarnation. He did not teach it and he did not live it. As mentioned earlier, Jesus taught the bodily resurrection of the dead at the end of history, not a process of multiple incarnations of one soul in many bodies. His reference to John the Baptist being Elijah (Mt 11:14; 17:3) should be recognized in its context as a figure of speech meaning that John had a ministry like Elijah's. John himself denied being literally Elijah (Jn 1:21); and the Old Testament prophet himself never died (2 Kings 2:9-18), so he could not have come back in the body of John anyway.[53]

Jesus rose from the dead, according to Paul, as "the firstborn from among the dead, so that in everything he might have the supremacy" (Col 1:18) as Cosmic Lord. He also says that Jesus Christ "was declared with power to be the Son of God by his resurrection from the dead" (Rom 1:4). When the ascended Jesus appeared to his disciple John, he announced, "I was dead, and behold I am alive for ever and ever!" (Rev 1:18). Jesus was not reincarnated; he was incarnated, once for all. Jesus will not reincarnate, because he is resurrected and now enthroned. Yet he will reappear in his glory at the end of the age. He promises his followers, not a gradual salvation through the school of reincarnation, but a resurrected life through faith in him. "I am the resurrection and the life. He who believes in me will live, even though he dies; and whoever lives and believes in me will never die" (Jn 11:25-26).

Only the Cosmic Christ can credibly make such claims, one who himself defeated death by passing through it bruised, bloody and broken only to reverse its reality through resurrection. No other world religion boldly claims a founder resurrected in literal, physical form as the cornerstone of their faith. Wilbur Smith notes that the millions and millions of Jews, Buddhists and Muslims "agree that their founders have never come up out of the dust or the earth in resurrection."[54]

The significance of Jesus' bodily resurrection is not exhausted by the idea of a resuscitated corpse. Those whom Jesus raised from the dead eventually died again. Jesus was raised immortal in a resurrected body, freed from all the constraints of a fallen world, just as his followers one day will be at his physical return (Acts 1:8; 1 Cor 15:12-

58). He could eat with his disciples and also vanish from their sight only to return again at another time. His hands still bore the marks of the crucifixion, but those hands would never bleed again. The writer of Hebrews says:

Because Jesus lives forever, he has a permanent priesthood. Therefore he is able to save completely those who come to God through him, because he always lives to intercede for them. Such a high priest meets our need—one who is holy, blameless, pure, set apart from sinners, exalted above the heavens. (Heb 7:24-26)

Because Jesus lives forever exalted above the heavens, he has a *permanent priesthood.* In biblical thought Jesus is, and always remains, the one and only Christ for all ages. He has no successor and no peer, because he is enthroned above all. He is the once for all Incarnation of God. Paul agrees with Hebrews by affirming that Christ is enthroned at the right hand of the Father "in the heavenly realms, far above all rule and authority, power and dominion, and every title that can be given, not only in the present age but also in the one to come" (Eph 1:20-21).

A Resurrected Jesus and Resurrected Lives

Another powerful kind of evidence can be added to the historical case we have marshalled: the evidence of transformed or resurrected lives. Jesus' first disciples were transformed from weak, dispirited followers without a leader into dynamic evangelists for the risen Christ. Tradition reports that most of the original apostles died martyr's deaths for the sake of their faith. Saul of Tarsus, infamous as the avowed enemy of the young church, was transformed into Paul the apostle, the church's greatest emissary (Acts 9). Countless others since have been touched by the life of the risen Christ by recognizing Jesus Christ as Lord and Savior, turning away from their self-centered ways and turning toward him in faith and obedience.

Jesus explained this transformation in the most radical terms, solemnly saying, "I tell you the truth, no one can see the kingdom of God unless he is born again" (Jn 3:3). Jesus further explained this by saying, "Just as Moses lifted up the snake in the desert, so the Son of Man must be lifted up, that everyone who believes in him may have eternal life" (Jn 3:14-15). Jesus taught that out of love, God sent his "only Son" so that anyone who believes in him will not be destroyed but have eternal life (Jn 3:16). This eternal life explains the contagion of Christian preaching and living in the book of Acts and throughout the history of Christianity. Countless millions, myself included, have agreed with the apostle Paul who said, "Therefore, if anyone is in Christ, he is a new creation; the old has gone, the new has come!" (2 Cor 5:17). Countless millions, myself included, have also exulted with the apostle John who exclaimed, "How great is the love the Father has lavished on us, that we should be called children of God! And that is what we are!" (1 Jn 3:1). This love cannot be earned but only humbly received by faith as a gift from God through Jesus.

These adopted children of God, having been personally transformed, are also to pray that God's kingdom will come to earth in transforming power (Mt 6:10). Jesus taught that cosmic perfection must await his personal Second Coming at the end of the age. Nevertheless, those born again of the Spirit are commissioned to demonstrate the love of God in the entirety of society, as millions have done throughout history by founding hospitals, freeing slaves, caring for the poor and promoting education. If Jesus is the Cosmic Christ, his rule extends to every area of life and his followers should have a global concern to make his reality known.[55]

Christianity, hypocrisy aside,[56] teaches that the resurrected Christ has impelled his followers to love him and their neighbors. Arguing against the complaint that Christianity was unfit to inspire social change, G. K. Chesterton observed, "The Christian ideal has not been tried and found wanting; it has been found difficult and left untried."[57] We have yet to see what a society can do if it turns in obedience to this Cosmic Christ.

The Cross Not a Code

New Age interpretations to the contrary, the Cosmic Christ is not the arcane discovery of Gnostic illumination. The Cosmic Christ is the concrete Jesus. The Christian message is not an esoteric extraction of the subtle gold underneath the superficial dross of the New Testament. It is the clear and direct message of Jesus himself. Jesus kept no secrets, ultimately. He had a perfect sense of timing and did not divulge everything about himself or his mission at once. But he appeared to make the Father known (Jn 1:18) and to regather lost sheep (Mt 9:36), not to befuddle the masses with a message that only the esoterically initiated could fathom.[58] Though Paul sometimes used the word "mystery" to refer to what cannot be completely grasped by finite beings, he also used it to refer to what is now in fact *revealed* for human benefit, as when he said that God *"made known* to us the mystery of his will according to his good pleasure, which he purposed in Christ" (Eph 1:9; emphasis mine; cf. 3:3-9; Rom 16:25).[59]

In essence, there is no esoteric Christianity. What you see in the biblical Jesus, in his life, death and resurrection, is what you get—or what you reject. His message is universal and applicable to all. By virtue of the biblical record we have consulted and defended in these ten chapters, esoteric Christianity must be judged as an oxymoron, a contradiction in terms. It is a concept invented by those outside the Christian orbit in the hope of finding a world view entirely alien to the biblical documents. The Bible nowhere gives any indication of being written in a mystical code. Few human documents, outside of military intelligence, can be accurately understood or handled as coded messages.[60] The New Testament presents not a code, but a cross.

This cross is the key to unlocking the message of Jesus and to entering the new age he promised to inaugurate in history and finally consummate at the end of history. It is not a new age of sleeping gods and goddesses awakening to the Christ Consciousness, but of erring creatures coming to the cross of Christ for forgiveness and new life in him. It is a new age of a growing community of Jesus' followers willing to live for him and to lay down their lives for others, just as Jesus laid down his life for them. It is a community of people willing up their own crosses in their pursuit of his kingdom, all the while depending on Christ himself for both the power and peace that comes from redemption. It is a community of those united, not in their deity, but in their experience of forgiveness and new life in Jesus the Christ. It is, finally, a community of those awaiting Christ's Second Coming. This is not the reincarnation of Jesus or the collective unleashing of humanity's true deity, but the resurrected Lord's triumphant return to earth at the end of the age, when all shall be brought to culmination (Acts 1:11; 3:21; Phil 3:20-21). Then those redeemed by the blood of the Lamb will join the great angelic chorus in proclaiming:

Worthy is the Lamb, who was slain,

to receive power and wealth and wisdom and strength

and honor and glory and praise! (Rev 5:12)

Notes

[1]David Spangler, *Reflections on the Christ* (Glasgow, Scotland: Findhorn, 1978), p. 107.

[2]Ibid.

[3]David Spangler, *Conversations with John* (Middleton, Wis.: Lorian Press, 1983), p. 5; quoted in Ron Rhodes, "The Christ of the New Age Movement," *Christian Research Journal*, Summer 1989, p. 12.

[4]David Spangler, *Revelation: The Birth of a New Age* (San Francisco, Calif.: The Rainbow Bridge, 1977), p. 141.

[5]Sam Keen, "Original Blessing, Not Original Sin: A Conversation with Matthew Fox," *Psychology Today*, June 1989, p. 57.

[6]Matthew Fox, *The Coming of the Cosmic Christ* (San Francisco, Calif.: Harper and Row, 1988), p. 147.

[7]Ibid., p. 154.

[8]Ibid., p. 138.

[9]Ibid., pp. 228-33. Fox does give a special place to Jesus but said in response to the question "Is Christianity the only way to God?": *"I believe God is not bound by any one way* but that God has sent Jesus as a very special way precisely to make the way easier and more accessible for all people." Philip Harnden, "Matthew Fox: Playful Prophet of Creation Spirituality," *The Other Side*, May 1987, p. 15; emphasis mine.

[10]For a critique of Fox's theology and his controversy with the Roman Catholic Church see Robert Brow, "The Taming of a New Age Prophet," *Christianity Today*, June 16, 1989, pp. 28-30.

[11]Carl Henry, *God, Revelation, and Authority* (Waco, Tex.: Word Books, 1979) 3:193.

[12]R. C. Sproul, *Who Is Jesus?* (Wheaton, Ill.: Tyndale House, 1988), p. 46.

[13]Jaroslav Pelikan, *Jesus through the Centuries* (San Francisco, Calif.: Harper and Row, 1987), p. 62; emphasis his.

[14]Henry, p. 194.

[15]Ibid., p. 195.

[16]Fox calls his view *panentheism,* instead of pantheism, meaning: "all things in God and God in all things" (*The Coming of the Cosmic Christ,* p. 57). This deifies the cosmos. This is to be distinguished from biblical *theism* which affirms both the transcendence and immanence of God, yet without deifying the created and now fallen world. See Romans 1:18-32.

[17]See C. S. Lewis, *The Abolition of Man* (New York: Macmillan, 1976), on this.

[18]St. Anthanasius, *The Incarnation of the Word of God* (New York, N.Y.: The Macmillan Company, 1946), p. 78.

[19]Ibid.

[20]Ibid., p. 79.

[21]Ibid.

[22]C. C. J. Webb, *Studies in the History of Natural Theology* (1915), pp. 29-30; quoted in Stephen Neill, *Christian Faith and Other Faiths* (London: Oxford University Press, 1961), p. 89.

[23]See John Ankerberg, John Weldon, and Walter Kaiser, *The Case for Jesus the Messiah* (Chattanooga, Tenn.: The John Ankerberg Evangelistic Association, 1988).

[24]Lawrence Waddy, *Pax Romana and World Peace* (London: Chapman and Hall Limited, n.d.), pp. 122-23, cited in John Warwick Montgomery, *Faith Based on Fact* (Nashville, Tenn.: Thomas Nelson Inc., 1978), pp. 192-93.

[25]Ibid.

[26]A. T. Robertson, *A Grammar of the Greek New Testament in the Light of Historical Research,* 4th ed. (London: Hodder & Stoughton; N.Y.: George H. Doran, 1923), pp. 54-55; cited in Montgomery, p. 197. On the suitability of Greek for the New Testament as a revelation of God see Norman Geisler and William E. Nix, *A General Introduction to the Bible* (Chicago, Ill.: Moody Press, 1986), pp. 329-30.

[27]William James, *The Variety of Religious Experience* (New York, N.Y.: Random House, n.d.), p. 498.

[28]See Norman Anderson, *Christianity and World Religions: The Challenge of Pluralism* (Downers Grove, Ill.: InterVarsity Press, 1984).

[29]John Warwick Montgomery, *Myth, Allegory and Gospel* (Minneapolis, Minn.: Bethany Fellowship, Inc., 1974), pp. 25-26.

[30]C. S. Lewis, *God in the Dock* (Grand Rapids, Mich.: Eerdmans, 1979) pp. 66-67. See the entire essay "Myth Becomes Fact," pp. 63-67, for insightful comments.

[31]For another Christian view of mythology as pointing toward something beyond itself see G. K. Chesterton, *The Everlasting Man* (Garden City, N.Y.: Image Books, 1955), pp. 103-18.

[32]For a discussion of how Christian historical claims differ from non-historical mythical ideas see Carl Henry, *God, Revelation and Authority* (Waco, Tex.: Word, 1976) 1:44-69.

[33]Bernard Ramm, *Protestant Christian Evidences* (Chicago: Moody, 1967), p. 185.

[34]C.S. Lewis, *Miracles* (New York, N.Y.: Macmillan, 1978), p. 143.

[35]Edwin Yamauchi, "Easter—Myth, Hallucination, or History? Part Two," *Christianity Today,* March 29, 1974, p.13.

[36]Ibid., pp. 15ff.

[37]See William Lane Craig, *Knowing the Truth about the Resurrection* (Ann Arbor,

Mich.: Servant Books, 1988), p. 21.

[38]Pinchas Lapide, *The Resurrection of Jesus* (Minneapolis: Augsburg Publishing House, 1983), pp. 98-99.

[39]Gary Habermas and Anthony Flew, *Did Jesus Rise from the Dead?* ed. Terry L. Miethe (San Francisco, Calif.: Harper and Row, 1987), p. 23.

[40]See Lapide, p. 95.

[41]See Craig, pp. 53-55.

[42]On the alleged contradictions between the Gospel's accounts of the resurrection see John Wenham, *Easter Enigma* (Grand Rapids, Mich.: Zondervan, 1984).

[43]C. F. D. Moule, *The Phenomenon of the New Testament* (Naperville, Ill.: Alec R. Allenson, Inc., 1967), p. 13; emphasis his. See pp. 1-20 for his entire argument.

[44]Lapide, p. 46.

[45]Michael Green, *The Empty Cross of Jesus* (Downers Grove, Ill.: InterVarsity Press, 1984), p. 94.

[46]Ibid.

[47]Craig, pp. 109-10.

[48]See Norman Anderson, *Jesus Christ: The Witness of History* (Downers Grove, Ill : InterVarsity Press, 1985) pp. 140-44, Craig, pp. 109-13, and Green, pp. 113-19.

[49]Lapide, p. 126.

[50]It can be argued that Lapide's refusal to recognize Jesus as the Messiah of all is quite inconsistent if he believes in Jesus' literal resurrection. As one letter to the editor in *Time* magazine commented, "Pinchas Lapide's logic escapes me. He believes it is possible that Jesus was resurrected by God. At the same time he does not accept Jesus as the Messiah. Why would God resurrect a liar?" *Time*, June 4, 1979, quoted in Norman Geisler, *False Gods of Our Time* (Eugene, Oreg.: Harvest House, 1985), p. 165. See also Craig, p. 152.

[51]Lapide, p. 92.

[52]Ramm argues that those who deny Jesus' resurrection face more difficulties than those who affirm it. See Ramm, pp. 195-207.

[53]For a much more detailed discussion of this see Douglas Groothuis, *Confronting the New Age* (Downers Grove, Ill.: InterVarsity Press, 1988), pp. 94-98.

[54]Wilbur M. Smith, *Therefore Stand* (Boston: W. A. Wilde Co., 1945), p. 385. See also Gary R. Habermas, "Resurrection Claims in Non-Christian Religions," *Religious Studies*, 25 (June 1989): 167-77.

[55]For more on a Christian view of social involvement see Douglas Groothuis, *Confronting the New Age* (Downers Grove, Ill.: InterVarsity Press, 1986), pp. 47-61.

[56]The fact that Christians or people calling themselves Christians have been hypocritical is no argument against the truth of the biblical Jesus. Jesus himself predicted such people would appear—he knew of one firsthand in Judas—and warned his followers ahead of time. For more on this see Francis J. Beckwith, "The Problem of Hypocrisy," *Christian Research Journal,* Summer 1987, pp. 14-17.

[57]G. K. Chesterton, "The Unfinished Temple," *G. K. Chesterton: The Collected Works,* 28 vol. (San Francisco, Calif.: Ignatius Press, 1987), 4:61; quoted in Gary DeMar and Peter Leithart, *The Reduction of Christianity* (Ft. Worth, Tex.: Dominion Press, 1988), pp. 122-23.

[58]For an explanation of how Jesus used parables in ways that seemingly withheld information from people see Gordon D. Fee and Douglas Stuart, *How to Read the*

Bible for All Its Worth (Grand Rapids, Mich.: Zondervan Publishing House, 1982), pp. 124-25.

[59]See S. Moyter, "Mystery," *Evangelical Dictionary of Theology,* ed. Walter Elwell (Grand Rapids, Mich.: Baker Book House, 1986), pp. 741-42. On the differences between Christianity and the mystery religions of antiquity see R. C. Kroeger and C. C. Kroeger, "Mystery Religions," *Dictionary,* ed. Elwell, pp. 742-44; and Ronald Nash, *Christianity and the Hellenistic World* (Grand Rapids, Mich.: Zondervan, 1984), pp. 115-99.

[60]On the fallacies of esoteric interpretation see Groothuis, *Confronting the New Age,* pp. 87-91.

Appendix:
The New Testament Canon

In a sense the following brief discussion of how the twenty-seven books of the New Testament were recognized as Scripture (as divinely inspired) is superfluous. We have argued in chapter six that the entire New Testament has historical *integrity* and we've shown that the Gospels, Acts and several key writings of Paul have *authenticity* and *veracity* as well. This alone should lead us to trust reports concerning Jesus of Nazareth as reliable. We need not understand every detail of the historical process that led to the inclusion of all the New Testament books into our Bible in order to trust the documents themselves.

But misconceptions linger on this issue, especially in New Age circles. For instance, *The Other Bible* consists of what it calls "ancient esoteric texts" from Gnosticism, the Kabala, and a variety of other non-biblical sources. The introduction deems these non-biblical texts to be inspired works that were not included in the Bible for merely historical or political reasons. But, thanks to *The Other Bible,* "today, free of doctrinal strictures, we can read the 'greater bible' of the Judeo-Christian world."[1] This attitude completely ignores the facts surrounding the formation of the biblical canon and assumes that all the religious books of the ancient world were equal. In light of this a few facts will be highlighted.

We have already noted in chapter six that the church fathers from early on quoted many New Testament books. In many cases, they even put them on the same level as the Old Testament itself. So intoxicated with the New Testament were the early church fathers (through the third century) that nearly the entire New Testament can be reproduced from their writings. J. Harold Greenlee has written that "these quotations are so extensive that the New Testament could virtually be reconstructed from them without the use of the New Testament Manuscripts."[2]

The process of formally recognizing these documents as Scripture inspired by God was not one of *creating* a Bible, but rather of *discovering* what was already functioning as the authoritative rule in the historic church. This cannot be emphasized enough. The idea of a power-hungry, or simply incompetent, bunch of ignorant clerics arbitrarily including and excluding books into the New Testament is a pervasive but historically indefensible notion.

The voting members who induct members into baseball's Hall of Fame do not create the candidate's batting, fielding and pitching statistics. They rather recognize a previous greatness worthy of sporting fame. The inclusion of our four Gospels into the official canons of the fourth century was probably as automatic and uncontroversial as Willie Mays's induction into the Hall of Fame as soon as he was eligible. In fact the Gospels, Acts and the major Epistles of Paul (the sources from which we derive virtually all our knowledge of Jesus' life) were never a matter of dispute.

Although the final official recognition of our New Testament did not occur until the end of the fourth century, all of the books included were several centuries old by then and had long been in circulation. The Muratorian Fragment, referred to in chapter six, dates at the end of the second century and lists twenty-one of the twenty-seven New Testament books as authoritative. Justin Martyr, writing in the early second century, speaks of Christians congregating on Sunday when "the memoirs of the apostles or the writings of the apostles are read, as long as time permits,"[3] thus putting the Gospels on the same level as the Old Testament Scriptures.

Even earlier than this, when Polycarp writes to the Philippian church, he hopes that they are "well versed in the Sacred Scriptures." He continues, "It is declared in these Scriptures, 'Be ye angry, but sin not,' and 'Let not the sun go down upon your wrath.' "[4] The first reference can refer to either Psalm 4:4 from the Old Testament or to its quotation by Paul in Ephesians 4:26 in the New Testament. But although the second quotation is not found in the Old Testament, it is found in Paul's writings. And Polycarp sees both references equally as Sacred Scripture. There are also many other examples from the church fathers that illustrate this point.

We also see a recognition of New Testament writings as Scripture even in the

New Testament itself. In 1 Timothy 5:18 a quotation of Jesus (Lk 10:7) is put side by side with an Old Testament passage (Deut 25:4), and both are referred to as Scripture. Second Peter 3:16 speaks of Paul's writings as Scripture.

Even the early protests of the Gnostics indirectly testified to an authoritative body of written teaching. The previously mentioned Gnostic document, the *Gospel of Truth,* dating from the mid-second century and likely written by Valentinus, shows an acquaintance with the Gospels, the Pauline letters, Hebrews and Revelation and traces of Acts, 1 John, 1 Peter and perhaps other New Testament books as well.[5] John Wenham notes that the writer's language is "permeated by [the New Testament books], because for him the language of these books is the language of the church."[6] W. C. van Unnik shows the significance of this:

> Before the [New Testament] Books could be used in the way they are used in the *Gospel of Truth,* they must have already enjoyed authority for a considerable time. To treat them as a collection was not a discovery of a few months before.[7]

Wenham also comments that "this evidence alone gives us the New Testament in the middle of the first half rather than the second half of the second century."[8] At the very least the *Gospel of Truth* shows us that several New Testament books were handled as authoritative early on even by the heretics, whether or not the entire New Testament was so considered.[9]

Irenaeus agrees when he states that the Gospels are so securely established "that the very heretics themselves bear witness to them, and, starting from these [documents], each one of them endeavors to establish his own peculiar doctrine."[10]

The fact that the church did not officially recognize the canon until the fourth century can be understood in light of several historical contingencies. First, communication and transportation were less rapid than today, "hence, it took much longer for the believers in the West to become fully aware of the evidence for the books first written and circulated in the East, and vice versa."[11] Teleconferences on the canon were not possible. Second, because of widespread persecutions until A.D. 325 (including the destruction of biblical manuscripts), the church lacked the resources and circumstances needed for such universal and definitive decisions.[12] Shortly after, theological peace prevailed with Constantine, the councils of Hippo (A.D. 393) and Carthage (A.D. 397), and our New Testament was officially recognized.[13] Third, it was not necessary to define a precise canon until various other unorthodox or deficient documents vied for attention.[14] The Gnostic challenge was a major prod in that direction.

The official recognition of the New Testament documents was not haphazard or politically charged, akin to the selection of a presidential candidate at the political party's convention. Documents were recognized as authoritative and deemed canonical on the basis of their apostolic authorship or approval, their antiquity, doctrinal content, universality of acceptance (or catholicity), traditional use and inspiration. While the selection process took time and did not lack some debate on certain books, it was not haphazard.[15]

Bruce Metzger's summary of this situation deserves full quotation:

The slowness of determining the final limits of the canon is testimony to the care and vigilance of early Christians in receiving books purporting to be apostolic. But, while the collection of the New Testament into one volume was slow, the belief in a written rule of faith was primitive and apostolic. . . . In the most basic sense neither individuals nor councils created the canon; instead they came to perceive and acknowledge the self-authenticating quality of these writings, which imposed themselves as canonical upon the church.[16]

New Age inclinations to the contrary, the canon of the New Testament is not an ad hoc collection of material created to suppress legitimate documents that present a New Age version of Jesus. No one should reject the biblical presentation of Jesus on the basis that the books of the New Testament were merely a result of political or theological prejudice. That idea simply does not bear historical scrutiny.

Notes

[1]Willis Barnstone, ed., *The Other Bible* (San Francisco: Harper and Row, 1984), p. xvii.

[2]J. Harold Greenlee, *An Introduction to New Testament Textual Criticism* (Grand Rapids, Mich.: Eerdmans, 1964), p. 54; cited in Norman L. Geisler and William E. Nix, *A General Introduction to the Bible* (Chicago, Ill.: Moody Press, 1986), p. 430.

[3]Justin Martyr, *The First Apology of Justin,* ch. 67.

[4]Polycarp, *The Epistle of Polycarp to the Philippians,* ch. 12.

[5]John Wenham, *Christ and the Bible* (Grand Rapids, Mich.: Baker Book House, 1984), p. 154.

[6]Ibid.

[7]*The Jung Codex,* ed. by F. L. Cross (London, 1955), p. 125, cited in Wenham, p. 154.

[8]Wenham, pp. 154-55.

[9]Bruce thinks that Unnik's comments (from which Wenham elaborates) may be a bit overstated but grants that the *Gospel of Truth* alludes to and cites New Testament books "in terms which presuppose that they are authoritative." He also notes that the writer's allegorical method of interpreting the New Testament materials demonstrates his high view of the texts as authoritative and inspired to some degree. See F. F. Bruce, *The Canon of Scripture* (Downers Grove, Ill.: InterVarsity Press, 1988), p. 147.

[10]Irenaeus, *Against Heresies,* 3.11.7.

[11]Geisler and Nix, p. 231.

[12]Ibid., pp. 278-82.

[13]Ibid., p. 231.

[14]Ibid.

[15]See Bruce, *The Canon,* pp. 255-69 for a treatment of the "criteria of canonicity." See also B. B. Warfield, "The Formation of the Canon of the New Testament," in *The Inspiration and Authority of the Bible* (U.S.A.: Presbyterian and Reformed, 1970), pp. 411-16. For a more theological discussion of canonicity see Carl F. H. Henry, *God Revelation and Authority* (Waco, Tex.: Word Books, 1979), 4:403-49.

[16]Bruce Metzger, *The New Testament: Its Background, Growth and Content* (New York: Abingdon Press, 1965), p. 276.

Bibliography

This bibliography is not exhaustive, but it will direct the reader toward some core books on the topics addressed in this book. Since some books fit nicely into several of the categories below, I have tried to note this in the annotation. Those seeking more specifics on references and other sources should consult the footnotes throughout the chapters, which give specific page numbers and list articles as well as books.

General Analysis of the New Age Movement
Chandler, Russell. *Understanding the New Age*. Waco, Tex.: Word, 1988. Extensive, fair, but critical treatment by a thoughtful journalist.
Groothuis, Douglas. *Unmasking the New Age*. Downers Grove, Ill.: InterVarsity Press, 1986. Examines the New Age world-view, its effect on society and offers a biblical critique.
Groothuis, Douglas. *Confronting the New Age*. Downers Grove, Ill.: InterVarsity Press, 1988. Aimed at meeting New Age challenges biblically and logically.
Hoyt, Karen, ed. *The New Age Rage*. Old Tappan, N.J.: Fleming H. Revell Company, 1987. A collection of worthy critical essays.
Miller, Eliot. *A Crash Course on the New Age*. Grand Rapids, Mich.: Baker Book House, 1989. A thoughtful and critical overview.
North, Gary. *Unholy Spirits*. Ft. Worth: Dominion Press, 1986. A large, in-depth, but sometimes idiosyncratic treatment.

Jesus Christ: Biblical Perspectives
Anderson, Norman. *Jesus Christ: The Witness of History*. Downers Grove, Ill.: InterVarsity Press, 1985. Explains the biblical meaning of Jesus and gives reasons to believe it is historically true. Good material on the resurrection also.
Ankerberg, John; Weldon, John; and Kaiser, Walter. *The Case for Jesus the Messiah*. Chattanooga, Tenn.: The John Ankerberg Evangelistic Association, 1988. Presents and explains many Old Testament prophecies for Jesus as the Messiah.
Ankerberg, John, and Weldon, John. *The Facts on the "Last Temptation of Christ."* Eugene, Oreg.: Harvest House, 1988. Revealing booklet on the controversial movie and book.
Athanasius, St. *The Incarnation of the Word of God*. New York: Macmillan, 1946. A classic from the fourth century.

Buell, Jon A., and Hyder, O. Quentin. *Jesus: Ghost, God or Guru?* Grand Rapids, Mich.: Zondervan, 1978. Helpful introductory treatment of the biblical Jesus.

Gallup, George, and O'Connell, George. *Who Do Americans Say That I Am?* Philadelphia, Penn.: Westminster, 1986. Interesting survey material with some comment.

Green, Michael. *The Empty Cross of Jesus.* Downers Grove, Ill.: InterVarsity Press, 1984. A solid treatment of the meaning of the cross and the resurrection.

Harper, Michael. *The Healings of Jesus.* Downers Grove, Ill.: InterVarsity Press, 1986. Explains the meaning, methods, and kinds of Jesus' healing.

Jones, E. Stanley. *The Christ of the Indian Road.* New York: Grosset & Dunlap, 1925. A classic by a missionary on how Jesus relates to a largely Hindu culture.

Kreeft, Peter. *Socrates Meets Jesus.* Downers Grove, Ill.: InterVarsity Press, 1987. The important issues about Jesus are discussed in an engaging and entertaining dialog format.

Lockyer, Herbert. *Everything Jesus Taught.* San Francisco: Harper and Row, 1984. Summary of his teaching.

Mangalwadi, Vishal. *World of the Gurus.* New Delhi, India: Nivedit Good Books Distributors Pvt Ltd., 1977. A look at contemporary Hindu gurus in relation to Jesus. Written by an Indian.

Ramm, Bernard. *An Evangelical Christology.* Nashville, Tenn.: Thomas Nelson Publishers, 1985. Christology from a veteran theologian very conversant with modern theology.

Speer, Robert E. *The Finality of Jesus Christ.* Westwood, N.J.: Fleming H. Revell Company, 1933. A classic statement defending the uniqueness of Jesus.

Sproul, R. C. *Who Is Jesus?* Wheaton, Ill.: Tyndale House, 1988. A concise and informative booklet.

Stott, John R. W. *Christ the Controversialist.* Downers Grove, Ill.: InterVarsity Press, 1972. A balanced, biblical analysis.

Stott, John R. W. *The Cross of Christ.* Downers Grove, Ill.: InterVarsity Press, 1987. A masterful treatment of the atonement.

Warfield, B. B. *The Person and Work of Christ.* Philadelphia: The Presbyterian and Reformed Publishing Company, 1950. A collection of important essays from a leading American theologian from two generations ago.

Wells, David F. *The Person of Christ.* Westchester, Ill.: Crossway Books, 1984. A scholarly, but readable perspective.

Jesus Christ: New Age Perspectives

Campbell, Joseph. *The Power of Myth.* New York: Doubleday, 1988. Although not specifically about Jesus, Campbell often comments on Jesus and Christianity, from a neo-Gnostic point of view.

The Christ. *New Teachings for an Awakening Humanity.* Santa Clara, Calif.: Spiritual Education Endeavors Company, 1986. Purportedly channeled material with the channeler not listed.

Fox, Matthew. *The Coming of the Cosmic Christ.* San Francisco: Harper and Row, 1988. While retaining some orthodox points, Fox's view of Jesus is in many important ways closer to the New Age vision than to the biblical picture.

Hall, Manly P. *The Mystical Christ.* Los Angeles: The Philosophical Research Society, 1951. Developed treatment by an influential New Age writer.

Houston, Jean. *Godseed: The Journey of Christ.* Amity, N.Y.: Amity House, 1988. Meant primarily as a manual for sacred rituals, it also gives a neo-Gnostic portrait of Jesus.

Lewis, H. Spencer. *Mystical Life of Jesus.* San Jose, Calif.: Supreme Grand Lodge of AMORC, 1974. A Rosicrucian perspective appealing to an esoteric tradition.

Lewis, H. Spencer. *The Secret Doctrines of Jesus.* San Jose, Calif.: Supreme Grand Lodge of AMORC, 1981.

MacLaine, Shirley. *Going Within.* New York: Bantam, 1989. Not specifically about Jesus, but mentions some New Age interpretations, including Jesus as an Essene.

Spangler, David. *Reflections on the Christ.* Glasgow, Scotland: Findhorn, 1978. An influential New Age treatment.

Steiner, Rudolf. *Christianity As a Mystical Fact.* New York: Anthroposophic Press, 1972. A reinterpretation of Jesus along neo-Gnostic lines.

Gnosticism

Brown, Harold O. J. *Heresies.* Garden City, N.Y.: Doubleday, 1984. Includes a helpful chapter comparing Gnosticism with orthodoxy.

Dart, John. *The Jesus of Heresy and History.* San Francisco: Harper and Row, 1988. A thoughtful journalist's treatment of the Nag Hammadi find and its meaning. Sympathetic to Gnosticism.

Helmbold, Andrew. *The Nag Hammadi Gnostic Texts and the Bible.* Grand Rapids, Mich.: Baker Book House, 1967. An early Christian analysis.

Irenaeus. *Against Heresies.* In *Ante-Nicene Fathers.* Edited by Alexander Roberts and James Donaldson. Grand Rapids, Mich.: Wm. B. Eerdmans, 1987. The classic orthodox response to Gnosticism. Still quite relevant today.

Jonas, Hans. *The Gnostic Religion.* Boston, Mass.: Beacon Press, 1963. A landmark study by a philosopher in the Existentialist tradition.

Layton, Bentley. *The Gnostic Scriptures.* Garden City, N.Y.: Doubleday & Company, 1987. Layton's introductions and annotations make the Gnostic materials more accessible.

Meyer, Marvin W. *The Secret Teachings of Jesus.* New York: Random House, 1984. A small selection of Nag Hammadi texts with commentary.

Nash, Ronald. *Christianity and the Hellenistic World.* Grand Rapids, Mich.: Zondervan, 1984. Contains several helpful chapters on Gnosticism, defending the originality and authenticity of Christianity in confrontation with Gnosticism.

Pagels, Elaine. *The Gnostic Gospels.* New York: Random House, 1979. A watershed book that opened Gnosticism to the masses. Quite sympathetic to Gnosticism.

Robinson, James M. *The Nag Hammadi Library.* San Francisco: Harper and Row, 1988. The standard reference work with introductory materials but no annotation.

Rudolph, Kurt. *Gnosis.* San Francisco: Harper and Row, 1987. A comprehensive major work by a German scholar.

Summers, Ray. *The Secret Sayings of the Living Jesus.* Waco, Tex.: Word, 1968. An early Christian analysis of the *Gospel of Thomas.*

Wenham, David, ed. *The Jesus Tradition outside the Gospels.* Gospel Perspectives Series, vol 5. England: JSOT Press, 1985. Contains two excellent scholarly articles on the authenticity of biblical Christianity in relation to Gnosticism. The entire "Gospel Perspectives" series presents a scholarly defense of the reliability of the New

Testament against criticism.

Winterhalter, Robert. *The Fifth Gospel.* San Francisco: Harper and Row, 1988. A New Age devotional commentary on the *Gospel of Thomas.*

The Historical Reliability of the New Testament

Archer, Gleason L. *Encyclopedia of Biblical Difficulties.* Grand Rapids, Mich.: Zondervan Publishing House, 1982. Defends the non-contradictory character of the Bible by explaining many difficult passages.

Barnett, Paul. *Is the New Testament History?* Ann Arbor, Mich.: Servant, 1986. A simple but compelling case for the New Testament as reliable history.

Blomberg, Craig. *The Historical Reliability of the Gospels.* Downers Grove, Ill.: Inter-Varsity Press, 1987. An excellent treatment of the trustworthiness of the Gospels in light of modern scholarship.

Bruce, F. F. *The New Testament Documents—Are They Reliable?* 6th ed. Grand Rapids, Mich.: Eerdmans, 1987. A classic defense.

Bruce, F. F. *The Canon of Scripture.* Downers Grove, Ill.: InterVarsity Press, 1988. A clear and scholarly treatment by a seasoned scholar.

Bruce, F. F. *Jesus and Christian Origins outside the New Testament.* Grand Rapids, Mich.: Eerdmans, 1982. Careful treatment of non-biblical sources on Christianity.

Bruce, F. F. *Paul: Apostle of the Heart Set Free.* Grand Rapids, Mich.: Eerdmans, 1979. Shows, among other things, the harmony of Paul with the Gospels.

Dunn, James D. G. *The Evidence for Jesus.* Philadelphia: Westminster, 1985. More liberal than most books in this category, but still provides helpful insights, particularly on Gnosticism.

France, R. T. *The Evidence for Jesus.* Downers Grove, Ill.: InterVarsity Press, 1986. Helpful look at the historical evidence for the biblical Jesus.

Geisler, Norman L., and Nix, William E. *A General Introduction to the Bible.* Chicago: Moody Press, 1986. A comprehensive treatment of biblical reliability and inspiration.

Guthrie, Donald. *New Testament Introduction.* Downers Grove, Ill.: InterVarsity Press, 1970. Especially helpful in dealing with the authorship of New Testament books and the relationship between the Gospels.

Habermas, Gary. *The Verdict of History.* Nashville, Tenn.: Thomas Nelson Publishers, 1988. Excellent resource for material on Jesus and early Christianity culled from non-biblical sources.

Hagerty, Cornelius. *The Authenticity of the Sacred Scriptures.* Houston, Tex.: Lumen Christi Press, 1969. A Roman Catholic defense of biblical authority with many good insights.

Juedes, John P. "George Lamsa: Christian Scholar or Cultic Torchbearer?" *Christian Research Journal* (Fall 1989), pp. 9-14. Lamsa's translation of the Bible is popular in some New Age circles. This article shows the inadequacies of Lamsa's translation, his scholarly deficiencies and the unbiblical beliefs of Lamsa himself.

Moreland, J. P. *Scaling the Secular City.* Grand Rapids, Mich.: Baker Book House, 1987. Contains a very instructive chapter on biblical reliability and another on the historicity of the resurrection of Christ.

Phillips, J. B. *The Ring of Truth.* New York: The Macmillan Company, 1967. A small, often insightful, testimony to the New Testament's truth by a translator of the New

Testament.

Robinson, John A. T. *Can We Trust the New Testament?* London and Oxford: Mowbrays, 1977. He answers yes and gives reasons to date the books quite early, despite a few less than orthodox positions.

Wenham, John. *Christ and the Bible.* Grand Rapids, Mich.: Baker Book House, 1984. Deals with both Christ's view of the Bible and with the reliability of the Bible.

Yamauchi, Edwin. *The Stones and the Scriptures.* Philadelphia: J. B. Lippincott, 1972. Discusses the relevance of archaeology to the Bible.

Biblical Interpretation

Barker, Kenneth. *The NIV Study Bible.* Grand Rapids, Mich.: Zondervan, 1985. An excellent study Bible, by a team of biblical scholars, based on the New International Version.

Fee, Gordon D., and Stuart, Douglas. *How to Read the Bible for All Its Worth.* Grand Rapids, Mich.: Zondervan, 1982. Very important work for reliably interpreting the biblical documents.

Sire, James. *Scripture Twisting.* Downers Grove, Ill.: InterVarsity Press, 1980. Explains twenty ways in which religious groups misinterpret the Bible. Very helpful in spotting faulty interpretations.

The Lost Years of Jesus

Beskow, Per. *Strange Tales about Jesus.* Philadelphia: Fortress Press, 1985. An invaluable aid in evaluating many unconventional views of Jesus. His treatment of the Essene Jesus of Szekely and the Aquarian Christ of Levi are also very helpful. Written by a New Testament scholar as an update on Goodspeed's work (see below).

Bock, Janet. *The Jesus Mystery.* Los Angeles: Aura Books, 1984. Reproduces Notovitch's *The Life of Saint Issa* and defends the lost years idea in the context of promoting the Hindu mysticism of Indian guru Sai Baba.

Goodspeed, Edgar J. *Modern Apocrypha.* Boston: The Beacon Press, 1956. A classic, critical treatment not only of the Notovitch materials, but also the Aquarian Christ and other controversial claims.

Kersten, Holger. *Jesus Lived in India.* Longmead, England: Element Book, Ltd., 1986. Uses and adds to the Notovitch and Levi material in the context of Indian legends.

Notovitch, Nicholas. *The Unknown Life of Jesus Christ.* Translated by J. H. Connelly and L. Landsberg. New York: R. F. Fenno & Company, 1890. Notovitch's book went through several American editions. This incorrectly lists the copyright date as 1890 when, in fact, the first publication in the United States was not until some five years later. See Goodspeed, *Modern Apocrypha,* p. 4.

Prophet, Elizabeth Clare. *The Lost Years of Jesus.* Livingston, Mont.: Summit University Press, 1984. The most thorough defense of the "lost years" thesis. Includes the text of *The Unknown Life of Christ* by Notovitch and other accounts of the "Life of Saint Issa."

Jesus and the Essenes

Bruce, F. F. *Second Thoughts on the Dead Sea Scrolls.* Grand Rapids, Mich.: Eerdmans, 1980. Careful treatment of a sometimes misunderstood phenomenon.

Bruce, F. F. *New Testament History.* Garden City, N. Y.: Doubleday, 1980. Valuable background material to the New Testament environment.

Charlesworth, James H. *Jesus within Judaism.* New York: Doubleday, 1988. Useful information on recent studies on Jesus and Essenism and other ancient writings. Not a conservative treatment.

Cross, Frank Moore. *The Ancient Library of Qumran and Modern Biblical Studies.* Grand Rapids, Mich.: Baker Book House, 1980. A careful treatment by a world-renowned scholar.

Graystone, Geoffrey. *The Dead Sea Scrolls and the Originality of Christ.* New York: Sheed & Ward, 1956. A short and early treatment which, nevertheless, puts many important issues in clear focus.

LaSor, William Sanford. *The Dead Sea Scrolls and the New Testament.* Grand Rapids, Mich.: Eerdmans, 1983. A helpful introduction.

Pfeiffer, Charles F. *The Dead Sea Scrolls and the Bible.* Grand Rapids, Mich.: Baker Book House, 1984. A simple but insightful overview.

Szekely, Edmond Bordeaux. *The Essene Jesus.* San Diego, Calif.: Academy Books, 1977. Distills materials from his supposed manuscript finds.

Szekely, Edmond Bordeaux. *The Essene Gospel of Peace: Book One.* USA: International Biogenic Society, 1981.

Szekely, Edmond Bordeaux. *The Essene Gospel of Peace: Book Two.* San Diego, Calif.: Academy Books, 1977.

Szekely, Edmond Bordeaux. *The Essene Gospel of Peace: Book Three.* San Diego, Calif.: Academy Books, 1977.

Szekely, Edmond Bordeaux. *The Discovery of "The Essene Gospel of Peace."* San Diego, Calif.: Academy Books, 1975. The romantic story of a highly questionable document.

Vermes, G. *The Dead Sea Scrolls in English.* London, England: Penguin Books, 1988. His introductory comments are very helpful in separating fact from fiction on the beliefs of the Essenes as revealed in the scrolls.

Jesus and Channeling

A Course in Miracles. 3 vol. Farmington, N.Y.: Foundation for Inner Peace, 1981. Voluminous material purportedly received from Jesus.

Alexander, Brooks. *Spirit Channeling.* Downers Grove, Ill.: InterVarsity Press, 1988. A concise but brilliant analysis of modern channeling.

Ankerberg, John, and Weldon, John. *The Facts on Spirit Guides.* Eugene, Oreg.: Harvest House, 1988. Helpful booklet on the essential issues involved.

Cayce, Edgar. *Edgar Cayce's Story of Jesus.* Edited by Jeffrey Furst. New York: Berkeley Books, 1976. Material collected and summarized from the Cayce readings.

Cayce, Edgar. *Edgar Cayce on Jesus and His Church.* Edited by Hugh Lynn Cayce. New York: Paperback Library, 1970. Another collection similar to the above.

Downing, Levi. *The Aquarian Gospel of Jesus the Christ.* Marina Del Rey, Calif.: DeVorss & Co, 1981. An influential New Age treatment supposedly transcribed from the Akashic Records.

Klimo, Jon. *Channeling.* Los Angeles: Jeremy P. Tarcher, 1987. A thorough, sympathetic treatment.

Perry, Robert. *An Introduction to "A Course in Miracles."* USA: Miracle Distribution Center, 1989. Introductory booklet.

Ramtha, with Mahr, James Douglas. *Voyage to the New World.* New York: Fawcett Gold Medal, 1985. Material channeled through J. Z. Knight on assorted subjects.

Swihart, Philip. *Reincarnation, Edgar Cayce and the Bible.* Downers Grove, Ill.: InterVarsity Press, 1975. Insightful Christian booklet.

Jesus, the Resurrection and the Cosmic Christ

Albrecht, Mark. *Reincarnation: A New Age Doctrine.* Downers Grove, Ill.: InterVarsity Press, 1987. A careful defense of the biblical doctrine of resurrection over reincarnation.

Craig, William Lane. *Knowing the Truth about the Resurrection.* Ann Arbor, Mich.: Servant Books, 1988. A readable but thorough defense of the resurrection of Jesus which is very knowledgeable of modern scholarship.

Craig, William Lane. *Assessing the New Testament Evidence for the Historicity of the Resurrection of Jesus.* England: The Edwin Mellen Press, 1989. An extremely thorough and scholarly analysis of all the New Testament evidence for the resurrection.

Henry, Carl F. H. *God, Revelation, and Authority,* vol. 3. Waco, Tex.: Word Books, 1979. A large, astute section on Jesus as the Logos makes this especially significant.

Lapide, Pinchas. *The Resurrection of Jesus: A Jewish Perspective.* Minneapolis, Minn.: Augsburg, 1983. A fascinating affirmation of the physical resurrection of Jesus by a non-Christian, Jewish New Testament scholar.

Miethe, Terry L., ed. *Did Jesus Rise from the Dead?* San Francisco: Harper and Row, 1987. The record of a debate on the issue with the case for the resurrection presented by Gary Habermas.

Montgomery, John Warwick, ed. *Myth, Allegory and Gospel.* Minneapolis, Minn.: Bethany Fellowship, Inc., 1974. A collection of essays on the relation of the biblical message to literature. Montgomery's introductory essay is especially provocative on the latent truths embedded in mythologies and literature and how they relate to the Christian message.

Pelikan, Jaroslav. *Jesus through the Centuries.* San Francisco: Harper and Row, 1987. A masterful survey of how Jesus has been seen through the centuries, which discusses the Cosmic Christ as understood by early Christian theologians.

Index